The Great Canal

The Legacy of the
Central California Irrigation District

Alan M. Paterson

Published by Nishihara/Wilkinson Design, Inc.
PO Box 624, Turlock, CA 95381 USA
1.209.668.7627 | www.nishwilkdesign.com

Book design copyright © 2020 by Nishihara/Wilkinson Design, Inc.
All rights reserved.

Cover design by Nishihara/Wilkinson Design, Inc.
Cover photo courtesy of the Milliken Museum

Published in the United States of America

ISBN: 978-0-9990229-1-7
Non-Fiction / Historical
20.03.03

Table of Contents

Introduction   1

1   A Thirsty Land   3

2   No Small Dreams   15

3   Badger Flat and Brereton's Farm   28

4   The Terrible Seventies   37

5   Mr. Miller's Canals   50

6   Milk Can Empire   66

7   The Big District   75

8   The Central Valley Project   102

9   The Birth of CCID   118

10   Under New Management   134

11   Drainage and Ducks   149

12   Water Management for a New Era   168

13   Return to the River   181

Introduction

Canals are common in many parts of the American West; they have become such an unremarkable part of the everyday scene that they usually pass unnoticed. That is no doubt true for the seemingly nondescript earthen canal on the western outskirts of Los Banos crossed every day by thousands of travelers on State Highway 152. But this is no ordinary canal, it was the first big canal in California, built across the treeless, unpopulated plains west of the San Joaquin River by a small army of men and horses in the hot summer of 1871. It was the creation of San Francisco investors, speculators really, who founded the San Joaquin & Kings River Canal & Irrigation Company with sweeping visions of the state's future. A few eventful years later they lost control to far more practical capitalists who were building another kind of empire, an integrated land and livestock company that became one of the state's biggest businesses. Henry Miller and the firm of Miller & Lux expanded the canal and tied it into their other reclamation enterprises to create one the largest and longest surviving privately-owned irrigation systems in California. In time the canal became the foundation for a prosperous community spanning parts of three counties, and in 1951 the Central California Irrigation District was formed to take over the old canal system and give the residents of that community control of their most essential resource. As it nears a century-and-a-half of operation the story of this first big canal is one that is well worth telling.

The canal is not a static landmark, but one that evolved to meet changing conditions, a work of generations. It became—by an exchange of its source of water—a critical link in the federal Central Valley Project, the first of California's great north-south transfer schemes. But while massive dams and long-distance aqueducts capture most of the attention, irrigation is, at its heart, a local affair. The agencies that deliver water to farms are the essential middlemen in the vast water management network. It is up to them to constantly balance supply and demand, and to navigate an increasingly complex regulatory environment. In performing those functions CCID has modernized its canals, participated in regional drainage and water transfer partnerships, and provided millions of dollars in financial assistance to its water users to encourage installation of water-saving technologies. The great canal has truly become a place where the past meets the present, and the future.

As a historian who has spent more than forty years studying the way water is managed in California and as someone who also spent most of his life working at least part time on an irrigated family farm this opportunity to explore the history of the canal system and the irrigation district that operates it has been an especially rewarding experience. Although I grew up not all that far away as measured in miles, I was familiar with the west side of the valley and its very different soils, crops and irrigation practices in only a general way so I had much to learn. The people of the west side have a deep sense of their heritage, and they have shared that knowledge and enthusiasm with me.

This project was sponsored by CCID and had the unstinting support of its staff. General Manager Chris White was deeply interested in local history and often suggested documents or sources for me to explore. CCID's records, including documents from the Miller & Lux era, provided most of the primary documents used to write this book. Tracey Rosin and Gregg Rice made sure that I had access to the district's files, and Maria Sequeira shared her knowledge of the contents of the vault, with its trove of vital records. Marianne Martin, Mary Meza, Janet Ogan and Judy Hudson made sure that I had a pleasant place to work in a crowded office. At the Milliken Museum in Los Banos, Linda Ferdig always responded to my requests for "just one more thing," and Dan Nelson, who had his own extensive expertise with local water issues, provided additional help. Ralph Milliken's notes from interviews with pioneer residents of the Los Banos area and other documents that he collected are a unique and valuable resource. The Gustine Historical Society maintains its own research library, and I enjoyed the assistance of Kim Stadtler and Pat Snoke. Gene Lieb made the files of the *Los Banos Enterprise* available. I am deeply indebted to all those who assisted me in my research, but any errors or misinterpretations are my sole responsibility.

The great canal began with a collection of extraordinary visionaries but it became, decade after decade, the work of the ordinary people who drove the scrapers, pulled the weir boards and planted crops. It is to those who worked with the transits, shovels and plows—past and present—that this book is dedicated.

1

A Thirsty Land

In June 1862 a party of the California State Geological Survey led by
William H. Brewer set out to explore the eastern slope of the Coast Ranges
from the base of Mount Diablo south to Pacheco Pass. They moved in and out
of canyons and climbed brown, almost treeless peaks, camping at the edge of
the plains that sloped away toward the San Joaquin River. The flat lands at the
foot of the Diablo Range held little interest for Brewer and his men. Even
though the previous winter's flood is still remembered as the greatest in
California's history, by early summer the once lush prairie grasses had already
dried, and cattle had retreated to the still-swollen river. Near Del Puerto
Canyon, Brewer reported that, "We take our way across the trackless plain,
sometimes sandy, at others hard, gravelly soil where we can trot a little, but
oftener a clay soil, now dry and cracked by the heat, so that the mules must
pick their way slowly."[1] A few days later at Orestimba Creek "the air grew day
by day hotter and drier ... All the herbage on the hills was dry enough to burn,
and the plain brown and dry as hay."[2]

John Muir's first impression of the plains west of the San Joaquin River
was decidedly different. Crossing Pacheco Pass in April 1868 the great valley
stretched out below him, shimmering like "a sheet of plant gold, hazy and
vanishing in the distance."[3] On reaching the plains he rejoiced in the
abundance of spring:

> Sauntering in any direction, hundreds of these happy sun-plants brushed
> against my feet at every step, and closed over them as if I was wading in
> liquid gold. The air was sweet with fragrance, the larks sang their blessed
> songs ... while myriads of wild bees stirred the lower air with the
> monotonous hum.[4]

---

[1] William H. Brewer, *Up and Down California in 1860-1864: The Journal of William H. Brewer,* edited by Francis P.
Farquhar (Berkeley and Los Angeles: University of California Press, 1966), 279.
[2] Brewer, *Up and Down California,* 284.
[3] John Muir, *The Mountains of California* (New York: The Century Co., 1894), transcription by Library of Congress,
http://www.sierraclub.org/john_muir_exhibit/writings/the_mountains_of_california/chapter_16.aspx, 2.
[4] Muir, *The Mountains of California,* 4.

Muir made his leisurely way north, crossing the San Joaquin River in Stanislaus County at the beginning of May.

Those sharply divergent descriptions of the west side plains were mostly a matter of timing. The wildflower season was short, and the flowers and grasses that greeted Muir would soon wither under the sun and the drying north winds that sweep down the west side in the spring. By June the "winter of dry heat," a season of summer dormancy, descended on the valley in day after cloudless day.[5] Relief arrived in the fall as the heat abated and the first rains began to turn the plains and the slopes of the Diablo Range green again. The west side of the San Joaquin Valley is a rain shadow country, one of the reasons for its aridity. Pacific storms push up against the coastal mountains, squeezing moisture out of the rising air, and leaving only a drier downslope flow on the other side. But the rains do come—sometimes generous, more often not—during the cool season that lasts from late fall to early spring; a season of growth that in earlier times ended with that brief, exuberant burst of wildflowers.

From the top of Pacheco Pass on that April day in 1868 John Muir also saw the Sierra Nevada mountains for the first time. In the hazy distance the mountain range towered above the valley, "miles in height, and so gloriously colored and so radiant, it seemed not clothed with light, but wholly composed of it, like the wall of some celestial city."[6] From the valley floor, the more prosaic William Brewer observed that "The Sierra is ever in sight, the brilliant summits seem ever in the same position" as his party slowly traversed the west side. It is among those brilliant summits that the San Joaquin River has its origin.[7]

From the west flank of the Ritter Range—a group of peaks that include the landmark profile of 13,000-foot Mount Ritter, Banner Peak and the sawtooth Minarets—spring snowmelt collects in subalpine lakes that feed the headwaters of the North Fork of the San Joaquin River. On the other side, in a valley between Mount Ritter and the main crest line of the Sierra, Thousand Island Lake, at almost 10,000 feet in elevation, is the source of the Middle Fork. The South Fork, the largest of the three, begins at Martha Lake, at the base of

---

[5] Muir, *The Mountains of California*, 5.
[6] John Muir, *The Yosemite* (New York: The Century Co., 1912), 5.
[7] Brewer, *Up and Down California*, 283.

massive Mount Goddard, and along its northward course is joined by Evolution, Paiute, Mono and other creeks that drain a line of crest peaks. Mid-elevation tributaries, including Big Creek, Stevenson Creek and Willow Creek. add their flows as the river descends through forests of fir and pine and then oak woodlands and chaparral until it reaches the edge of the mountains near the place where the gold rush settlement of Millerton once stood. Above that point, the river drains an area of a little over 1,600 square miles.

Like the valley, the river has its seasons. In the winter, the San Joaquin is mostly a rain-fed stream, rising and falling with each passing storm, while snow accumulates in its upper reaches. Heavy rains on the lower slopes can produce brief intense floods in the valley but by April the season of storms has passed, and the season of snowmelt has begun. On average, the months of April through July account for about 70 percent of the San Joaquin River's total annual runoff. The Sierra snowpack is often referred to as a natural reservoir, and extension of high flows into the dry summer months had important implications for the irrigation history of the valley. As summer advances, and most of the snow has disappeared from the high mountains, the natural flow in the river gradually drops, usually reaching its lowest point in September.

When it comes to understanding the behavior of the San Joaquin River, averages are notoriously unreliable. That is especially true for the annual runoff, measured during the "water year" that runs from October 1 to September 30. The calculated natural flow of the San Joaquin River averaged 1,778,250 acre-feet for water years 1901 through 2016 (October 1900 through September 2016). Variability in precipitation is higher in California than anywhere else in the country, and just a few storms can make the difference between a wet year and a dry one. Such significant year-to-year variations in precipitation mean that an average year is rare. In almost two-thirds of the 116 years for which data is available for the San Joaquin River, the calculated natural flow has been 25 percent greater than average or 25 percent lower than average, and nearly one-third of the time the variation, higher or lower, has exceeded 50 percent. The highest natural runoff was 3,354,990 acre-feet in 1983, and the lowest was 327,437 acre-feet in 2015.[8]

---

[8] Full natural flow data from California Data Exchange Center (California Department of Water Resources, hereafter cited as "DWR"), Sensor No 65, analysis by the author; DWR, *California's Most Significant Droughts: Comparing Historical and Recent Conditions*, February 2015, 8-11.

From Millerton, which is now submerged beneath the reservoir that bears its name, the San Joaquin flows into the valley in a generally southwesterly direction, hemmed in by bluffs on either side that gradually recede in height until they disappear into the valley floor. As it approaches the valley trough the river makes an abrupt right-angled bend to the northwest. Here the natural banks were low and lined with willows and cottonwoods, and sometimes oaks. When the river was high, it spread out into overflow channels or "sloughs" that branched and merged across a broad swath of lowlands, eventually draining back into the river to the north. In this vast seasonal wetland, clumps of willows marked the path of the meandering sloughs, and cattails and tules filled the low spots where water remained the longest. The slightly higher grasslands between the sloughs were inundated for briefer periods of high water, producing a luxuriant growth of forage. At the western edge of this riparian zone was a broad belt of alkali soil that ran from west of Dos Palos almost forty miles north until it intersected the San Joaquin, the result of accumulated salts deposited by Diablo Range creeks. As summer advanced and the snowmelt was largely exhausted, the river returned to its main channel and the wetlands slowly dried, waiting, like the rest of the valley, for the next cycle of storms.

South of the San Joaquin River was Tulare Lake, named from the extensive tule marshes that surrounded it. The largest freshwater lake in the west, its shallow profile meant that even small changes in depth produced large variations in its surface area, which at its maximum was almost eight hundred square miles. It was fed by the Kings, Kaweah and Tule rivers, and in wetter periods the overflow from the Kern River reached the lake through sloughs that connected it to the smaller Kern and Buena Vista lakes. The Tulare Lake drainage basin is separated from the San Joaquin River by the low, almost imperceptible ridge formed by the junction of the Kings River alluvial fan and the deposits of the Los Gatos Creek fan to the west. That barrier is breached only by Fresno Slough, which joins the San Joaquin River at its great bend. When the elevation of Tulare Lake was below 207 feet above sea level, the slough was a backwater of the San Joaquin, and rose and fell along with the river. When the lake overflowed, it spilled northward through tiny Summit Lake to the network of channels that led to Fresno Slough and the San Joaquin River. The Kings River split into several channels when it reached the valley floor, and when it was in flood, the northernmost of those channels could also discharge into the San Joaquin through Fresno Slough even if Tulare Lake was not overflowing.[9]

Topographical engineer Lt. George H. Derby explored Tulare Lake and Fresno Slough, which he called the Sanjon de San Jose, in May 1850. He described the slough as being 240 yards in width near its mouth, with a sluggish current toward the San Joaquin. Unable to penetrate the marshes south of the river, Derby concluded that, "The whole country for forty miles in extent in a southerly direction by ten in width, between the San Joaquin river and the Tache [Tulare] lake is, during the rainy season and the succeeding months until the middle of July, a vast swamp everywhere intersected by sloughs, which are deep, miry and dangerous."[10] Several wet years filled the lake by 1853, but then it fell until the epic flood of 1862 that brought it to its highest recorded elevation, 216 feet above sea level. It spilled into the San Joaquin until 1863. Heavy runoff in 1867-1868 brought the lake close to its 1862 level, but in the following years it shrank steadily, reaching its then-lowest recorded elevation of 192 feet in 1883. The receding shoreline revealed the stumps of large willow trees, evidence that the lake had once been at least that low for an extended period of time. By the 1880s, irrigation diversions were beginning to reduce inflow to the lake, and it would eventually disappear in all but the wettest years.[11]

From its junction with Fresno Slough, the San Joaquin River flows north and west toward the sea, becoming the hydraulic backbone of its namesake valley. Its east side tributary rivers—the Fresno, Chowchilla, Merced, Tuolumne and Stanislaus—collectively added more than twice the natural flow of the mainstem San Joaquin. The little creeks that originate in the rain-starved Diablo Range can become suddenly torrential following heavy rains, but their contribution to basin outflow is insignificant. Not far below the Stanislaus River confluence, the San Joaquin enters the low-lying region known as the Delta, where it meets the tides from San Francisco Bay. The river divided into several channels as it passed through what was once a vast tule swamp and

[9] Carl Ewald Grunsky, *Irrigation Near Bakersfield, California*, U.S. Geological Survey Water-Supply and Irrigation Papers, No. 17 (Washington, DC: 1898), 15-16; ECORP Consulting, Inc., *Tulare Lake Basin Hydrology and Hydrography: A Summary of the Movement of Water and Aquatic Species* (prepared for us Environmental Protection Agency, Document No. 909R07002), April 12, 2007, 2-8; William Hammond Hall, State Engineer, *Topographical and Irrigation Map of the Great Central Valley of California* (California State Engineering Department, 1886), Sheets 3 and 4.
[10] George H. Derby, "Report to Maj. E.R.S. Canby, July 10, 1850," *Quarterly of California Historical Society* 11 (September 1932), 261.
[11] ECorp Consulting, Inc., *Tulare Lake Basin Hydrology*, 4; Grunsky, *Irrigation Near Bakersfield*, 16-17.

maze of intersecting sloughs. Flowing westward through the marsh it eventually met the much larger Sacramento River and finally lost its identity as a river when it entered Suisun Bay. From its headwaters to that point it measures over three hundred miles, making it the second longest river entirely within the state of California.

This, then, is the landscape that shapes the story of irrigation in a place that extended from the dry eastern slopes of the Diablo Range across treeless plains to the river that was the thread of life in an arid environment. It was a land of long vistas and subtle, sometimes stark, beauty. Describing the almost limitless San Joaquin Valley plains, one observer wrote that:

> [T]hey grow upon the imagination; they exalt and then fill it; they expand upon the mental vision, and in the end leave one with an idea of immensity, of an extension illimitable, exceeding even that that comes to one on the bosom of the old Ocean. Then they grow in beauty as they grow in proportions. In infinite variety of contour and of color develops itself in what was at first monotony. The plains are fascinating with a fascination of their own, as luring as that of the ocean or the mountains; and the traveler who has first been wearied with a tiresome uniformity, and oppressed with the steady down-pour of summer heat, dazzled by the glare from the white skeletons of grasses or of more gleaming stubble, comes to find that an infinite variety and beauty lurk in the landscape; that to the hot noon, a cool eventide succeeds; that there are compensations even for the glare that tries and tires the unaccustomed eyes; and he ends by taking unto himself the soul and heart of the plain's life, and finding a very exultation in its largeness and freedom.[12]

When Americans arrived on the west side, they found a landscape that was immense, empty and harsh but they also saw a landscape of opportunity.

The plains west of the San Joaquin River were a natural grazing land, populated at the beginning of the Gold Rush by tule elk, bands of pronghorn antelope and rangy, nearly wild Spanish cattle, strays from the great coastal herds that had been the mainstay of the early California economy. The elk soon fell to market hunters, and herds of cattle arrived from southern California and

---

[12] *Irrigation in California: The San Joaquin and Tulare Plains* (Sacramento: Record Steam Book and Job Printing House, 1873), 3.

the east to feed the rapidly growing population. William Brewer saw "tens of thousands of cattle" on the plains in 1862.[13] At Orestimba canyon, vaqueros drove hundreds of them past his camp on the way to what Brewer called a "rodeo" where the owners of neighboring ranches separated their stock. There were sheep, too; Rancho San Luis de Gonzaga at the foot of Pacheco Pass owned 18,000, and rented out pasture for even greater numbers.[14]

Little is known about the early days of the west side livestock industry. The population was sparse and widely scattered, located along the river or Diablo Range creeks. Only a few, like the Crow family in the Orestimba Creek area and the Pachecos, would stay very long. In 1858 the Butterfield Overland Stage from San Francisco to St. Louis crossed Pacheco Pass and changed horses at the Pacheco's San Luis Ranch, and at Lone Willow (Mud Slough), Temple's Ranch near the river, Firebaugh's Ferry and Fresno City, which was a hopeful but ultimately short-lived effort to establish a town at the head of navigation on Fresno Slough. Passengers would have seen little more than open country and cattle.[15]

At about the time that the Butterfield stage made its inaugural run, the firm that became synonymous with the development of the west side was founded in the partnership of Henry Miller and Charles Lux. Henry Miller was born Heinrich Kreiser in Brackenheim, Germany in 1827. Raised in the butcher's trade, he arrived in New York in 1847. The wider opportunities of Gold Rush California beckoned, and when he was able to procure a non-transferable ticket in the name of Henry Miller, he adopted that name and kept it. After a difficult passage through Panama, Miller reached San Francisco in September 1850 and went to work for wages as a butcher, but by the following year he had his own shop at the corner of Jackson Street and Cooper Alley. Miller's business, relocated to south of Market Street at Fifth and Howard, expanded and he was soon purchasing cattle, pasturing them on rented land and then selling them when the price was right. In 1854 he ventured into the San Joaquin Valley for the first time to buy a herd of three hundred cattle that had been driven from Salt Lake City. At a price of $33,000 they were far more expensive than the cattle arriving in San Francisco from southern California,

---

[13] Brewer, *Up and Down California*, 283.
[14] Brewer, *Up and Down California*, 285-286, 288.
[15] *New York Times*, October 14, 1858.

but Miller correctly guessed that he could make a profit on better quality stock. The deal was emblematic of the means by which Henry Miller quickly became a leading figure in San Francisco's meat market.[16]

Miller's legend has long overshadowed his partner, Charles Lux. Lux, too, was a German immigrant by way of New York, and he, too, arrived in San Francisco in 1850. Setting up a butcher shop at Sacramento and Kearny streets, his personable nature and social skills increased his trade and allowed him to make the acquaintance of leading men in the city. It was said at his death that, "He made his capital through the capital of his own capabilities. He was a man who saw expedients and means where others saw none; ... a man who seemed to have access to all doors of success, and to whom the gates of opportunity sprang wide open."[17] The acquisition of Rancho Buri Buri offers an example of the way Charles Lux built his fortune. In 1853 land broker and banker John Parrott arranged for Lux (and his partner at the time, Alfred Edmondson) to join banker D.O. Mills and Ansel Easton in buying parts of the Mexican land grant of almost 15,000 acres lying just south of San Francisco. Lux initially bought one-tenth of the rancho, which he used to hold cattle close to the San Francisco slaughterhouses, and where he later built the country home he called Baden. Buri Buri was a valuable asset, and Miller & Lux eventually expanded their holdings on the property, but of even greater value to the partnership was the informal network of financiers, lawyers and land dealers who were part of the social and business circles accessible to the genial Charles Lux; men who could indeed open "the gates of opportunity."[18]

As a one-time venture, the two men jointly bought and sold a large herd of Texas cattle in 1857, but a similar purchase the following year was the beginning of a full partnership. The brusque, plain-spoken Miller, more at home with cattle than with San Francisco society, and the urbane Lux complemented each other's personalities, but they shared a surprisingly similar heritage and ambition. Together they set out to dominate the meat

---

[16] Hubert Howe Bancroft, *Chronicles of the Builders of the Commonwealth: Historical Character Study, Vol. 3* (San Francisco, The History Company, 1892), 373-376; David Igler, *Industrial Cowboys: Miller & Lux and the Transformation of the Far West, 1850-1920* (Berkeley and Los Angeles: University of California Press, 2001), 19.

[17] *Daily Alta California*, March 17, 1887.

[18] Igler, *Industrial Cowboys*, 40, 44, 46-49; Frank M. Stanger, "A California Rancho under Three Flags: A History of Rancho Buri Buri in San Mateo County," *California Historical Society Quarterly* 17, No. 3 (September 1938), 252-257.

markets of San Francisco and the coast; to accomplish that they had to control the supply of cattle, and cattle required land.[19]

Miller and Lux began with rancho land. Including Buri Buri, the partnership acquired all or part of sixteen land grants, by one estimate over 200,000 acres. Legal title to grants made under Spanish or Mexican rule had to be confirmed by the California Land Claims Commission, and its decisions were subject to further and sometimes extended litigation. The process all too often had the effect of leaving the original owners bankrupt and the land in the hands of Americans who had the legal and financial resources to defeat rival claimants and take full title to the property. It was an opportunity for well-connected men to acquire large blocks of land, and it was especially useful for Miller & Lux because the ranchos were often located in the most favorable places for stock raising. That was certainly true in the region around Gilroy. Henry Miller bought the 1,700-acre Bloomfield Farm in 1863 and eventually made his home there. It was strategically located west of Pacheco Pass, and stock could be moved to Gilroy from the San Joaquin Valley and on to Buri Buri and the slaughterhouses. Over time, Miller and the partnership acquired major parts of nine adjacent or nearby ranchos stretching into the Pajaro Valley, including Las Animas, Salsipuedes and San Justo.[20]

In the San Joaquin Valley, Miller took a particular interest in the Rancho Sanjon de Santa Rita, a 48,000-acre tract along the west bank of the San Joaquin River that was crossed by the sloughs—sanjon—that gave it its name. By the late 1850s the property was in the hands of several American ranchers, but their titles would not be secure until the confirmation process was completed. The grant was confirmed in late 1862, and the following year Miller & Lux bought 8,835 acres and 7,500 head of cattle from Thomas Hildreth, as well as his HH brand, for $10,000. By 1866 the firm owned all of the Sanjon de Santa Rita, and in 1868 purchased much of the Orestimba rancho along the river to the north.[21]

The severe drought of 1864 confirmed Henry Miller's assessment of the value of land along the San Joaquin River. William Brewer crossed the valley in June of that year and at San Luis de Gonzaga found that pastures that had

[19] Bancroft, *Chronicles of the Builders of the Commonwealth*, 376-377.
[20] Igler, *Industrial Cowboys*, 36, 49-53; Paul W. Gates, "Public Land Disposal in California," *Agricultural History* 49 (January 1975), 172.
[21] Bancroft, *Chronicles of the Builders of the Commonwealth*, 378; Igler, *Industrial Cowboys*, 53-56.

been green on his previous visit were now barren. On the road to Firebaugh's Ferry he and his men rode for miles without grass, "but in other places there was a limited growth of wire grass or alkali grass, but not enough to make it green. Yet cattle live here—we passed numbers during the day, and countless carcasses of dead animals."[22] Near Fresno Slough, they found "green plains, green with fine rushes, called wire grass, and some alkali grass. The ground is wetter and cattle can live on the rushes and grass. We now came on thousands of them that have retreated to this feed and have gnawed it almost into the earth."[23] Taking advantage of the situation, Miller & Lux was able to buy cheap cattle from drought-stricken ranchers, and move them to the Santa Rita.[24]

The acquisition of land grants was only one part of the scramble for California land; the public domain was a much bigger prize. Land could be purchased in several ways. By 1862 the federal government had given California over 8.8 million acres, the sale of which by the state was intended to fund schools and colleges and other public purposes. Warrants that could be exchanged for land were bought and sold, often at depreciated prices. And not only California land warrants were available; warrants issued to states with little public land of their own or granted to military veterans also flooded the California market. Where restrictions on how much land a single buyer could claim had been enacted, dummy entrymen, recruited from a company's employees or even from the saloons, were employed to make the initial filing and then transfer their rights to the actual purchaser. It was a system that rewarded men with money and inside knowledge. Among the most prominent of the land barons was William S. Chapman, who at one time was the largest landowner in California and perhaps the United States. Chapman also served as an agent for Miller & Lux, and through his connections provided the partners with a supply of warrants and advice on locating and claiming the land they wanted.[25]

The federal government also transferred to the state inundated swamp and overflow lands. There is a well-travelled tale of how Henry Miller mounted a boat on a wagon so that he could lay claim to immense acreages of alleged swamplands by testifying that he had crossed those tracts in a boat. In fact,

---

[22] Brewer, *Up and Down California*, 510.
[23] Brewer, *Up and Down California*, 510.
[24] Igler, *Industrial Cowboys*, 56.
[25] Gates, "Public Land Disposal in California" provides a basic review of land acquisition; Igler, *Industrial Cowboys*, 67.

there was nothing so haphazard or colorful about how Miller & Lux went about acquiring thousands of acres of wetlands. For example, in 1869 the partners had Merced County surveyor William G. Collier map all the land along the San Joaquin River, particularly the swamplands. On land that was usually subject only to seasonal overflow, the definition of "swampland" could be problematic, and Collier told Miller that "It is a sort of three card monte [,] now you see it and now you don't arrangement."[26] Miller & Lux undoubtedly took full advantage of those ambiguities in claiming swamp and overflow land.

Until the late 1860s the broad, empty landscape of the San Joaquin Valley was valued only as pasture. That changed with the rapid emergence of wheat as California's first agricultural bonanza. The wheat boom was driven not by local demand but by world markets, where the state's hard, white grain was in demand. Floods, droughts and the disruption of shipping by the Civil War delayed large shipments until 1867 but the profits of that year were enough to start a rush onto the plains.

California wheat farming was industrialized agriculture on a remarkable scale. Fields of hundreds or even thousands of acres were common, worked with mechanized efficiency. The process began after the fall rains had softened the soil. A line of gang plows—riding plows with four to eight shares—turned the soil to a depth of perhaps three inches, followed by the seeders and harrows. And then the wheat was left to grow through the winter, the success of the crop dependent on getting enough rain at the right times. As heat returned to the valley in the late spring, the harvest began. Headers moved across the fields, cutting only the tops of the wheat, which ran up conveyors into header wagons driving alongside that would carry the crop to the threshers. When the threshers departed and the hundred-pound sacks of grain had begun their long journey, the plains were silent again, visited only by cattle feeding on the stubble. Most wheat farmers grew no other crops; their livelihood depended entirely on weather and distant markets.

On the land along the Diablo Range, farmers spread first into San Joaquin and Stanislaus counties, where rain was usually a little more reliable than it was further south, and steamboat landings were available at Grayson and Hills Ferry. By 1868 pioneer farmers like Nathaniel Bunker, a former Nevada legislator, were moving to the west side of Merced County. Near Los Banos,

---

[26] Igler, *Industrial Cowboys*, 66-67.

the Samuel Smith family arrived in 1868 in time to get a crop in the ground. There were no fences, and they had to guard their first hundred acres of wheat day and night to keep the Miller & Lux cattle from eating it. That first year, only three families planted grain in the Los Banos area and a thresher came down from Cottonwood for the harvest.[27]

The Smiths harvested a good crop in their first year, a poor one the next year and nothing at all the year after that. For farmers who gambled on rainfall—the skyfarmers—crop failure, or near failure, would become a common occurrence in that part of the valley. But by 1871 there were men who planned to change the odds.

[27] Igler, *Industrial Cowboys*, 62; Ralph L. Milliken, interview notes, [O.E.] Smith, 9; John Outcalt, *History of Merced County California with a Biographical Review of The Leading Men and Women of the County Who Have Been Identified with Its Growth and Development from the Early Days to the Present* (Los Angeles: Historic Record Co., 1925), 494-495, 502.

2

No Small Dreams

John Bensley made his first fortune as a trader in Mexico selling mules to General Winfield Scott's army during the Mexican-American War. In New York when the gold excitement began, he and nine partners bought the bark *Eliza* and sent her to California loaded with provisions they thought might prove profitable. Bensley himself arrived in 1849, operated a freight business and then set up a store in Sacramento with supplies from the *Eliza*. Other enterprises followed: river steamers and gas works, linseed oil and electric lights. He was part of the company that delivered the first piped water to San Francisco, and was one of the founders of the Pacific Rolling Mills, the first iron and steel works on the west coast. And in 1866 John Bensley turned his attention to the San Joaquin Valley.[28]

On March 7, 1866 Bensley, Orrin Simmons and Erwin Davis incorporated the San Joaquin & Kings River Canal Company. Of the partners, Simmons probably had the greatest interest in irrigation and was the first to recognize the potential of a canal along the west side. Born in Vermont, he began his business career in Chile and San Salvador before opening a wholesale and retail hardware store in San Francisco, and his ranch across the bay in Berkeley became the site of the University of California. He acquired land along the west bank of the San Joaquin River at its junction with Fresno Slough where he posted a notice in November 1863 claiming the right to divert water for the purposes of irrigation, mining and navigation through a canal that would run to Suisun Bay. Simmons deeded that land—the future site of Mendota Dam— to the new company. He was also involved in other irrigation enterprises, including the Clear Lake Water Company, incorporated on the same day as the San Joaquin & Kings River company and also in association with Bensley and Davis.[29] Just a month earlier Simmons had petitioned the legislature for

---

[28] Bancroft, *Chronicles of the Builders of the Commonwealth*, 206-216; *Daily Alta California*, June 21, 1889.
[29] *Daily Alta California*, March 8, 1866; Bancroft, *Chronicles of the Builders of the Commonwealth*, 212-213; J.M. Guinn, *History of the State of California and Biographical Record of Oakland and Environs, Volume 2* (Los Angeles: Historic

assistance in "certain projects for opening and constructing canals."[30] Less is known about Erwin Davis. He was a banker and a speculator in mining properties, and in 1861 he was part of a short-lived effort to resurrect a controversial reclamation scheme that included a barge canal from Tulare Lake to the San Joaquin River.[31]

Bensley's canal company did not publicize its plans, although the land that it acquired from Simmons was a logical point of diversion for a canal running along the west side of the valley, and the company's name suggested a connection of some kind to the Kings River. Although the project was launched at a time when the public domain was rapidly passing into private hands, the founders of the canal company were not land speculators. Instead, it appears that they placed a bet on the value of a water supply in a region that seemed ripe for agricultural development, and by being first on the ground they undoubtedly hoped to profit from control of that water supply.

The company got off to a slow start. Bensley was unable to obtain financing in San Francisco or New York, and in 1870 his offer to sell Miller & Lux one-third of the canal company did not interest the partners. Beginning in 1868 he arranged for some token construction work to keep his water rights in good standing, and long-time Los Banos resident James McDermott remembered scraping out "a little canal about a hundred feet long with high banks" near the dam site for that purpose. Orrin Simmons visited the settlers near Los Banos Creek to promote the canal, but with no tangible evidence of progress they just thought he was crazy.[32]

Everything changed in 1871. A prolonged drought gripped the valley, and its effects made Miller & Lux appreciate the value of a more predictable system of irrigation to supplement the natural overflow that watered their riparian

Record Co., 1907), 523-524; W.C. Hammatt, "Report to the San Joaquin River Water Storage District on Facts Pertaining to the Water Rights and Diversions by the San Joaquin & Kings River Canal & Irrigation Co.," October 24, 1924, 4

[30] *The Journal of the Assembly During the Sixteenth Session of the Legislature of the State of California, 1865-6* (Sacramento: C.M. Clayes, State Printer, 1866), 336

[31] G.L. Rogers, "A History of the Canal System of the Central California Irrigation District Prior to 1940," November 15, 1970, 3; Donald J. Pisani, *From the Family Farm to Agribusiness: The Irrigation Crusade in California and the West, 1850-1931* (Berkeley and Los Angeles, University of California Press, 1984), 80-89; *Visalia Weekly Delta*, December 8, 1860; Affidavit of James Thomas Boyd, Exhibit B to *Reports of the Joint Committees on Swamp and Overflow Lands and Land Monopoly, Presented at the Twentieth Session of the Legislature of California*, (Sacramento: G.H. Springer, State Printer, 1874), 55-57.

[32] Bancroft, *Chronicles of the Builders of the Commonwealth*, 212-213; Pisani, *From the Family Farm to Agribusiness*, 106; Igler, *Industrial Cowboys*, 73; Milliken, interview notes, James McDermott, October 7, 1924, 1; Milliken, interview notes, Oscar Smith, August 15, 1937, 12.

lands. Setting aside whatever skepticism they may have had about the company's plans, the partners signed a contract with the San Joaquin & Kings River Canal Company on May 18, 1871. The canal company agreed to complete the first sixty miles of the canal beginning at Fresno Slough by January 1, 1872, and to the railroad line near present-day Tracy by April 1872, subject only to delays that might be caused by landowners along the route. The company also committed itself to building a canal at least forty feet wide connecting Cole Slough or Murphy's Slough on the Kings River to Fresno Slough "within a reasonable time."[33]

Under the terms of the agreement, Miller & Lux granted Bensley's company a right-of-way across their land for the canal and its branches, and the right to use any sloughs between the canal and the river. They also promised to pay a $20,000 cash subsidy when sixty miles of the canal had been completed, provided that the canal was capable of irrigating at least 50,000 acres of their land; if not, the subsidy would be reduced in proportion to the acreage it was actually able to irrigate. When the canal was completed from the Kings River to Suisun Bay, and carried enough water to irrigate "in all seasons of the year" 50,000 acres of Miller & Lux land and enough water to carry boats with a seventy-five-ton cargo capacity for nine months each year, Miller & Lux would pay an additional $10,000 subsidy. On the other hand, if the canal did not reach the vicinity of Garzas Creek, Miller & Lux were granted the right build their own canals to irrigate 5,000 acres in that area. The cattle company agreed to pay $1.25 per acre for each crop actually irrigated from the canal, but water for cattle and for domestic use would be free of charge. Miller & Lux realized that the diversion of water into the canal could reduce the seasonal overflow they depended on, and if that happened the canal company was required to release from the canal, between April 1 and June 15, enough water to replace the lost overflow.[34]

The agreement made it clear that the canal would be used for transportation as well as irrigation. Conceptually at least the union of the two purposes made sense because irrigation was expected to yield large crops of wheat that had to be shipped to port cities. In 1871 the railroad was being

[33] Igler, *Industrial Cowboys*, 71-73; agreement, San Joaquin & Kings River Canal Company and Miller & Lux, May 18, 1871, 1-2.
[34] agreement, San Joaquin & Kings River Canal Company and Miller & Lux, May 18, 1871.

extended down the east side of the valley, but the west side still depended on river steamers. Unfortunately, the flow of the San Joaquin River was usually falling just as wheat arrived at the river landings near the head of navigation. Canal boats were expected to solve that problem and open up trade from the remote valley interior but the idea was probably doomed from the outset. In an 1867 study of a similar canal plan on the west side of the Sacramento Valley, engineer W.H. Bryan determined that the two functions could not be combined at any reasonable cost because an irrigation canal demanded a stronger flow than navigation could tolerate.[35]

The 1871 contract recognized a fundamental reality: Bensley needed the cooperation of Miller & Lux. In the five years since the launch of the canal scheme, the cattle company had cemented its control of land along the canal route through Fresno and Merced counties. In exchange for their indispensable right-of-way, and cash subsidies tied to the achievement of goals that the partners probably believed were hopelessly optimistic, Miller & Lux would be able to significantly increase their irrigated acreage at a reasonable cost and with little risk. At the same time the agreement almost certainly made it possible for the canal company to get the financial backing it needed. Joining Bensley and Simmons as trustees were well-known San Francisco capitalists Alvinza Hayward, Charles Webb Howard and A.H. Rose as well as Charles Lux. As the *Daily Alta California* noted, these were men "whose wealth is sufficient to secure success in this undertaking."[36]

Muddying the waters was the simultaneous appearance of another canal company. On Saturday, May 13, 1871, the *Pacific Rural Press* reported that San Francisco capitalists "who are largely interested in lands on the west side of the San Joaquin river, have arranged the preliminaries for a canal from Tulare lake along the west side of the valley, close to the foothills of the Coast Range mountains, designed for the double purpose of irrigation and navigation." On the same day, the articles of incorporation of the San Joaquin Canal & Irrigation Company were filed in San Francisco. The purpose of the new company was the construction of canals and reservoirs for navigation, irrigation, mining and manufacturing. Eight canals were identified. The

---

[35] *Report of the Engineer of the Sacramento Valley Irrigation and Navigation Canal* (Sacramento: D.W. Gelwicks, State Printer, 1874), 3-4.
[36] *Daily Alta California*, June 3, 1871.

longest would extend from Buena Vista Lake at the far southwestern corner of the valley along the length of west side to Antioch, on Suisun Bay. A canal from Millerton on the San Joaquin River and another from the Kings River near the edge of the valley would join at Summit Lake on the divide between the San Joaquin and Tulare Lake basins, and then flow west to supplement the main canal from Buena Vista Lake. Other ditches would tap the Kern, San Joaquin, Merced, Tuolumne and Stanislaus rivers. It was a spectacular vision, and among its well-known trustees were land barons William S. Chapman and Issac Friedlander, banker John Parrott, smelter owner T.H. Selby and former Senator Milton S. Latham.[37]

Historians have tended to confuse the two companies, sometimes associating Bensley's reinvigorated project with the even more ambitious plans of the new San Joaquin company. Although their backers had often been allied with one another in other enterprises and they had the same general purpose, the companies appeared to be separate and distinct entities. The San Joaquin Canal & Irrigation Company was valley-wide in scope, but conspicuously absent from its plans was the canal described in Bensley's agreement with Miller & Lux. Still, the timing could hardly have been a coincidence given that the incorporators were all part of the same business and social network; it may be that the second company was simply meant to supplement and extend Bensley's older one. The organizational muddle was apparently resolved in early September when articles of incorporation were filed for the San Joaquin & Kings River Canal & Irrigation Company with a projected capital of $10 million. It was the designated successor to Bensley's company, but its trustees now included backers of the San Joaquin Canal & Irrigation Company, which effectively ceased operation. With construction already underway and their agreement with Bensley intact, Miller & Lux subscribed 8,500 shares in the new company.[38]

The San Joaquin & Kings River Canal & Irrigation Company was the creation of a group of wealthy San Franciscans, and their story is part of its history. They were a colorful lot. Prominent among them was Isaac Friedlander, the grain king. He made and lost and made again fortunes in the

---

[37] *Pacific Rural Press,* May 13, 1871; *Daily Alta California,* May 16, 1871
[38] Pisani, *From the Family Farm to Agribusiness,* 107; Igler, *Industrial Cowboys,* 73-74; *Daily Alta California,* September 3, 1871.

flour business, and more than anyone else he had established the wheat trade between San Francisco and Liverpool that revolutionized California agriculture. Months before the crop was ready to harvest, Friedlander was chartering hundreds of ships from around the globe and then re-leasing them, at a profit to himself, to California traders and exporters. It was a risky business that depended on a detailed knowledge of shipping and grain markets and a close watch on the progress of each growing season and the likely size of the crop. He bought and sold wheat as well, and came to dominate the traffic in grain. Some of his profits were invested in land, often in association with William S. Chapman, and he accumulated 145,000 acres in Merced and Fresno counties alone. Friedlander and Chapman were land speculators, hoping to profit on the rising value of cheaply acquired public lands. Because irrigation encouraged settlement and increased land prices, they backed canal projects. At the same time that they joined the investors in the west side canal, which would serve an area where they owned relatively little land, they were also promoting the development of irrigation colonies in the Fresno area.[39]

Other trustees of the new canal company were less directly interested in the appreciation of San Joaquin Valley land. J. Mora Moss was a banker who had profited from early railroad investments. In 1852 he had put together an imaginative scheme to cut ice from Alaskan glaciers for sale in San Francisco, and in 1867 joined an unsuccessful attempt to take control of the Alaskan fur trade when the United States acquired the territory from Russia. Charles Webb Howard was best known as the president of the Spring Valley Water Company, the competitor and then successor to Bensley's San Francisco municipal water business. Alvinza Hayward made a fortune in gold mines in Amador and Calaveras counties and increased it on Nevada's Comstock Lode, and A.H. Rose also got his start in Amador County mining. Nicholas Luning was a banker.[40]

[39] Rodman W. Paul, "The Wheat Trade between California and the United Kingdom," *Mississippi Valley Historical Review* 45, no. 3 (December 1958), 400-403; Gates, "Public Land Disposal in California," 174; Khaled Bloom, "Pioneer Land Speculation in California's San Joaquin Valley," *Agricultural History* 57, no. 3 (July 1983), 303, 305-306; *History of Fresno County, California with Illustrations Descriptive of its Scenery, Farms, Residences, Public Buildings, … with Biographical Sketches* (San Francisco: Wallace W. Elliott & Co., 1882), 111-118.
[40] David Lavender, *Nothing Seemed Impossible : William C. Ralston and Early San Francisco* (Palo Alto: American West Publishing Co, 1975), 224, 351; *Amador Ledger*, Feb. 19, 1904; Justus H. Rogers, *Colusa County: Its History Traced from a State of Nature through the Early Period of Settlement and Development, to the Present Day with a Description of its Resources, Statistical Tables, Etc. Also Biographical Sketches of Pioneers and Prominent Residents* (Orland, California, 1891), 405.

The name of the reorganized canal company's most important supporter was not found in the list of its trustees. William Chapman Ralston was the blazing star at the center of San Francisco's financial universe. Genial, magnetic and often extravagant, Ralston combined the impulses of the speculator and the builder. He founded the Bank of California in 1864 and took the position of "cashier" while the respected banker D.O. Mills was installed as president, and he almost immediately made the bank the predominant force on the Comstock Lode. With the wealth of the Comstock's silver mines behind him, Ralston became the consummate investor, financing every kind of industry. It was Ralston who provided Friedlander with the credit he needed to charter ships, and he had been associated with all of the other trustees in their mining, transportation, reclamation and industrial works. Ralston and his allies saw in California and the West the wonderful prospect of an imperial future. And they saw themselves as the builders of that future, and by right its natural beneficiaries.

By early June 1871 work on the canal was beginning. Thirty farmers and their teams were said to have started from Ellis station in San Joaquin County—the place where the canal was expected to meet the railroad—to join the work force near the head of the canal. The canal company was paying $3.50 in cash and fifty cents in scrip per day, and offering room and board for $4.00 a month. At the beginning of July, one hundred teams were on the job and three hundred more were expected within two weeks. Most of the labor was being provided by farmers from Merced and Fresno counties, who, like their counterparts from Ellis, were suffering the effects of drought and crop failure. A summer in the construction camp could help them meet their expenses and pay for next season's seed, and as future irrigators they had an interest in the rapid progress of the canal. In that dry year, grazing conditions were so poor that four hundred tons each of hay and barley had to be sent from the coast. Hay for the horses was being sold at $50 per ton and barley at two-and-a-half cents per pound. Men and teams continued to arrive. In mid-August, the work was fifteen miles from the head of the canal. Three hundred-and-fifty teams and four hundred men were excavating and shaping two-thirds of a mile per day, and the numbers employed were expected to double by the middle of September. There was confidence that the ditch could be ready along its entire length by the following spring, and there were reports that land values along the route had already doubled.[41]

While clouds of dust marked the progress of construction on the remote valley plains in the summer of 1871, Ralston sought the advice and assistance of a consulting engineer. The man he chose was Robert Maitland Brereton. A professionally-trained British engineer, Brereton had gone to India in 1857 to work on building a railroad across the subcontinent from Bombay to Calcutta. He helped survey the route, and then as an inspector sometimes clashed with the contractors building the line over their shoddy construction of bridges and masonry structures. In 1868, he was made chief engineer of the Calcutta section of the railroad and in 1870 completed it, and opened the route from coast to coast, some eighteen months ahead of schedule. His accomplishment was hailed as a triumph by his fellow engineers and government officials, but instead of offering its congratulations the railway company promptly fired him. Returning to a cool reception in London, Brereton found that his stubborn insistence on quality work had annoyed too many powerful contractors and suppliers. After fourteen years in India, he now turned his attention westward.[42]

Robert Brereton arrived in America in the spring of 1871 with an interest in its railroads and with letters of introduction that gave him access not only to well-known engineers but to the upper levels of American business and political life. He met railroad barons Cornelius Vanderbilt and Thomas Scott, financier Jay Cook and President Ulysses S. Grant, and in Wyoming General Phil Sheridan hosted a buffalo hunt. Reaching San Francisco, he naturally sought out Ralston. Brereton had continued his travels to Victoria, British Columbia when Ralston sent word that he wanted to see him. At a conference on August 10, Brereton was asked to examine the canal work and give his opinion "on the irrigation prospects of this project, and on the merits of the canal as it is located."[43] Four days later, accompanied by Charles Webb Howard, he examined the west side as far as Hills Ferry and the next day

---

[41] *Sacramento Daily Union*, June 12, 1871; *Daily Alta California*, July 2, 1871; *Daily Alta California*, August 1871.
[42] Robert Maitland Brereton, *Reminiscences of an Old English Civil Engineer, 1858-1908* (Portland: The Irwin-Hodson Co., 1908), 7-17.
[43] Robert M. Brereton, *Reminiscences of Irrigation-Enterprise in California, Suggestions for Oregon, Idaho and Washington in Regard to the Present System of Appropriation and Utilization of Public Waters Under Existing Laws of the State of Oregon, and to the More Complete Ownership and Control Thereof by the State* (Portland: The Irwin-Hodson Co., 1903), 54.

arrived at Firebaugh's Ferry, where he met the canal company's chief engineer, M.L. Stangroom. In a report addressed to "Friedlander, Ralston, Chapman, and others" on August 19, Brereton noted that the uniform slope of the west side and the quality of its soil made it ideal for irrigation and for crops of wheat, corn, cotton, sugar beets, tobacco and hemp. Even the low summer flow of the river above Firebaugh's Ferry would be sufficient, he believed, to supply a one hundred-mile canal irrigating fodder crops, which required much more water than wheat. Brereton had no specific experience in irrigation engineering, but he had been a careful observer of the irrigation systems being built in India, and he based his conclusions on that example, including his vigorous support for using main and branch canals as transportation arteries.[44] In regard to the canal itself, he was far less sanguine: I have been unable to obtain any data, or accurate information, regarding the present actual or even the estimated cost of this project, as the chief engineer, on taking charge of the works, found the canal, already started, and no plans, [cross-]sections or estimates have been furnished to him by the projectors, and I conclude that the works were started without any; and am afraid that no complete and comprehensive plan of the entire project has been made, consequently, in the absence of plans, sections and estimates, with no actual location of the canal beyond the point in progress, and with no definite plan on record for the distribution of the water to guide me, it is quite impossible for me to examine the costs, details, and prospects of this present project in any definite or satisfactory manner.[45]

Brereton estimated that the canal as it was being constructed would be able to irrigate "36,000 acres of such crops as grasses that are cut four or five times annually; or 100,000 acres of grain and cotton," but the potential irrigated acreage served could be increased by almost 50 percent if it was deepened two feet. Deepened or not, the grade and the velocity of the flow "would be too great for navigation." He concluded that "this canal is very useful for a local purpose, but is not available for the length proposed, viz: from the Fresno Slough to Antioch, and could not irrigate more than one-third of the area contemplated."[46] A better option, he believed, would be a canal from Tulare Lake and the Kings River.

---

[44] Brereton, *Irrigation-Enterprise in California*, 54-55.
[45] Brereton, *Irrigation-Enterprise in California*, 57-58.
[46] Brereton, *Irrigation-Enterprise in California*, 59.

Brereton was no more impressed with the financial prospects of the canal: I find that on the first 50 miles of this canal, which is about the length that this canal will be available for such crops as rice, sugar beet, and 4 to 5 crops of grass, Messrs. Miller & Lux own nearly all the land, and could therefore take all the water. I am told that these parties own over 300,000 acres lying along and below this canal, and if they thought proper to place, say 50,000 acres of this under the above cultivation, they would require all your water.[47]

At the time he wrote his report, Brereton had apparently not yet seen the contract the canal company had made with Miller & Lux that made the irrigation of 50,000 acres of the cattle company's land one of the criteria for the payment of a subsidy. Brereton suggested water rates of $3 per acre for wheat and grass and $5 per acre for more valuable crops like rice, sugar beets and cotton, warning that "otherwise the company would be making the rapid fortunes of other parties without receiving for their enterprise a fair quid pro quo."[48] Again, he seemed unaware that Miller & Lux had already fixed their price at $1.25 per acre. In sum, Brereton's report revealed an amazing absence of forethought, both in the design of the canal and in plans for its profitable operation.

Brereton's bluntly cautionary report did nothing to deter the ambitious and confident Ralston. On September 2, 1871—a date coincident with the incorporation of the San Joaquin & Kings River Canal & Irrigation Company—Brereton was appointed consulting engineer at a salary of $1,000 in gold per month, and he henceforth became a tireless advocate for the canal. His appointment gave him the authority to pursue whatever "preliminary explorations and surveys as may in your judgment be necessary."[49] Those explorations and his second report, dated October 6, 1871, were perfectly aligned with the scope of his sponsors' vision and with his own belief that Tulare Lake would provide a better supply for the entire west side. Brereton had embarked on a reconnaissance of the San Joaquin Valley from the foot of the Tehachapi Mountains to the Delta, and in the space of a single month had developed a comprehensive irrigation plan. It envisioned storage reservoirs on

---

[47] Brereton, *Irrigation-Enterprise in California*, 58.
[48] Brereton, *Irrigation-Enterprise in California*, 58.
[49] Brereton, *Irrigation-Enterprise in California*, 17

Sierra streams and a network of canals from the Kern and Kings rivers plus hundreds of miles of levees to channel rivers and reclaim swamplands. A canal from Tulare Lake would intersect the foot of the Diablo Range somewhere near Los Banos Creek and irrigate land above the canal already being built and further north. From a dam on the San Joaquin River where it passed through a narrow gorge at Table Mountain, five miles above Millerton, canals would run north as far as Snelling on the Merced River and south to the Kings River. He did not explore the east side streams beyond the Merced River.[50] The enormity of the works meant that they would have to be built gradually, as the increase in the region's population justified the expense, but he projected "a splendid moral and financial reward" for the irrigation of such vast acreages.[51] Although differing in detail from the scheme outlined by the promoters of the San Joaquin Canal & Irrigation Company just a few months earlier, Brereton's report seemed to confirm that it was an achievable dream; an outcome that undoubtedly pleased Ralston, Friedlander, Chapman and their associates.

Meanwhile the work went on. A small army of men and their horses and mules moved methodically across the vast treeless plains; a tableaux of heat, dust and sweat. Behind them stretched the freshly shaped embankments of California's first great irrigation canal. For the most part, their implements were simple. Plows and wooden slip scrapers with iron edges and even wheelbarrows did most of the work; the famous Fresno scraper would not be invented until 1883. The legion of small scrapers created a canal that had a bottom width of about thirty feet and over fifty feet on top, with sides rising up to seven feet above the elevation of the bottom.[52]

Camps were set up every two miles along the canal route, and two or three of them were in use at any one time. They became the most populated places in a largely empty landscape. In those makeshift communities the men rested, fed and watered their animals and perhaps visited the saloon on wheels that followed them. Supplying the construction force continued to be a challenge. In the spring, the supplies needed to support life and work in a remote corner of the San Joaquin Valley had come by river to the nearest usable landing but

---

[50] Brereton, *Irrigation-Enterprise in California*, 59-73.
[51] Brereton, *Irrigation-Enterprise in California*, 72.
[52] Carl Ewald Grunsky, *Irrigation Near Merced, California*, U.S. Geological Survey Water Supply and Irrigation Papers, No. 19 (Washington, D.C.: Government Printing Office, 1899), 22; *Pacific Rural Press*, October 7, 1871; *Sacramento Daily Union*, November 2, 1871.

after the river fell in early summer they mostly had to be hauled over Pacheco Pass from Gilroy. Besides food and replacements for all the harnesses and tools worn out or broken by steady work, men and horses needed water. Well borers had to stay ahead of the progress of construction but it was slow work, and when it became difficult to find water fast enough, the entire operation was moved to the Los Banos area where pioneer farmer S.A. Smith advised the company that the water table was closer to the surface. They later worked back into the gap when wells were finally available. The canal company's headquarters was also moved from the Helm ranch near the head of the canal to the Smith place, which served as a depot for wagon-loads arriving from the other side of the mountains.[53]

By mid-September progress of as much as three-quarters of a mile per day was being reported, but the farmers who had come to help dig the canal were leaving to prepare for the fall planting season.[54] Despite two successive crop failures, there was a sense of optimism. The *California Farmer* noted that "such is the faith in great results from this Canal, that lands are sold, farms laid out, and confidence felt that a large area with great crops will be gained upon large tracts of land never before plowed or planted."[55] It was still widely assumed that the canal would reach Antioch by spring, making irrigation of the whole west side seem like a real possibility in time for next spring's wheat crop. In fact, those hopes were becoming increasingly unrealistic. It was unlikely that the present pace of construction could be maintained through the rainy season, and near Grayson in Stanislaus County the survey stakes for the canal were only a mile from the river, leaving a width of five miles above the canal without access to irrigation even if the project was completed as planned.[56]

Thirty miles of the canal had been completed by the beginning of October and two hundred men were at work, and the following month it reached Los Banos Creek, not quite forty miles from its head. Northward progress stopped there, and the construction force was moved back to the river to work on the diversion dam. Materials for the structure had begun arriving months earlier and were stockpiled until the river reached its lowest flow. Construction began

---

[53] Milliken, interview notes, S.A. Smith, December 12-13, 1917, 4-5; Milliken, interview notes, James McDermott, October 7, 1924, 2.

[54] *Sacramento Daily Union*, September 12, 1871.

[55] *California Farmer and Journal of Useful Sciences*, October 5, 1871.

[56] *Sacramento Daily Union*, November 18, 1871.

in early October, and there were soon sixty carpenters on the job. The dam had two sections, anchored by a small island. To the east of the island, a 350-foot brush dam—stacks of brush held in place by sandbags, sixty feet thick at its base and forty feet on top—kept the river six to eight feet above its natural low-water level. In the narrower channel west of the island there was a fifty-foot wide wooden control structure referred to as a "falling dam," which was said to resemble those used in India, testimony, perhaps, to Brereton's influence. Positioned between timber sidewalls, the dam rested on two rows of sheet pilings held in place by pilings driven thirty to forty feet into the riverbed. Wooden gates hinged on the bottom were attached to that foundation. In periods of high flow, the gates were lowered to allow water to pass, and as the river fell, the gates were pulled up to raise the water level behind them, and were held in place by a hook-and-rod arrangement. About 150 feet above the dam was the intake to the canal, which used similar gates.[57]

The dam was obviously an impediment to river navigation, even though it was supposedly designed to allow the passage of steamboats. One early account by an assistant state engineer stated that "The sluiceway on the west side of the island is arranged to permit the passage of steamers and barges during the season when the river is navigable, the vessels being drawn up the steep incline of its apron by means of a capstan."[58] If so, it would have been a strenuous and unwieldy process. Later accounts suggest that with the falling section of the dam lowered, steamboats could pass through the churning water of the chute when the river was high enough but it was said that some captains preferred to take their chances crossing the overflow of the brush dam.[59]

Although the rain-swollen river made completion of the dam more difficult, by January 1872 construction was finished. The great canal was ready for its first test.

---

[57] *Pacific Rural Press*, October 7, 1871; *Sacramento Daily Union*, November 18, 1871; *History of Merced County, California: With Illustrations Descriptive of Its Scenery, Farms, Residences, Public Buildings ... including Biographical Sketches* (San Francisco: Wallace W. Elliott & Co., 1881), 172; *Irrigation in California*, 16-17; *Report of the Examining Commission on Rivers and Harbors to the Governor of California* (Sacramento: J.D. Young, Supt. of State Printing, 1890), 86; Grunsky, *Irrigation Near Merced*, 18-19.

[58] James D. Schuyler, "Report on Works and Practices of Irrigation: San Joaquin and Kings River Canal, and Chowchilla Canal," December 20, 1879, Appendix D to *Report of the State Engineer to the Legislature of the State of California—Session of 1880* (Sacramento: J.D. Young, Superintendent of State Printing, 1880), 163.

[59] *Report of the Examining Commission on Rivers and Harbors*, 86; Grunsky, *Irrigation Near Merced*, 18-19.

3

Badger Flat and Brereton's Farm

After two years of drought, rain returned to California in November 1871, and December brought a welcome drenching. The plains turned green again, and farmers became more and more optimistic about prospects for the coming harvest. Mud washed into the new canal from its freshly constructed banks, and teams had to be sent in to repair the damage.[60]

The weather turned dry in the spring and the sun and strong winds began to take their toll on the maturing grain. Water was turned into the canal in mid-April but the canal company, which had set up its headquarters, barn and bunkhouse at Central Point, had not finished all the structures needed to control the flow of water through the system. Where weirs were not yet in place, sandbag dams were substituted and local farmers spent several days hauling willow wood from Salt Slough to build a make-shift weir where the canal emptied into Los Banos Creek in order to hold back water so they could irrigate. Three thousand acres took water that first season, two-thirds belonging to Miller & Lux. The results were dramatic. Where water reached it in time, the wheat and barley recovered; where it did not—on land above the canal or where farmers were slow to build their ditches—the grain dried up, with small yields where it was even worth harvesting at all. Most of the farmers in the Badger Flat area east of Los Banos Creek were also planting patches of alfalfa, and John Fowler put in more than forty acres. Alfalfa planted in March in expectation of irrigation was already a foot high by early May. The irrigation era had arrived.[61]

Officials of the canal company were as optimistic as the farmers. In February 1872 company president John Bensley signed a revised contract with Miller & Lux. The new document acknowledged that the company had been reorganized and that it had not been able to meet its original goal of reaching

---

[60] *Irrigation in California*, 17; *Sacramento Daily Union*, January 31, 1872.
[61] *Pacific Rural Press*, May 25, 1872; *Pacific Rural Press*, June 1, 1872; *Daily Alta California*, June 24, 1872; *Daily Alta California*, June 24, 1872, Milliken, interview notes, Joe Webb, September 1, 1938, 2; Milliken, interview notes, O.E. Smith, April 18, 1929, 2.

Antioch in a single year. As a subsidy for the section of canal already constructed, Miller & Lux gave two promissory notes, dated August 1, 1872 and August 1, 1873, each for the sum of $6,666.67. Another note in the same amount would be issued if the canal company extended the canal eighteen miles, to a total length of fifty-eight miles, and provided sufficient water to irrigate 50,000 acres of Miller & Lux land. The agreement specified that the extension would have a grade of six inches per mile, a tacit admission that the original grade of one foot per mile was unnecessarily steep, and if extended at the same slope would push the canal to lower elevations closer to the river and reduce the area it could irrigate. Alternatively, the company could build a separate canal from Tulare Lake or some other source that would irrigate the same acreage of the cattle company's land that the extension was expected to cover. The other provisions of the 1871 agreement remained in place. Construction had paused, but the canal's backers, as well as farmers on the west side, were confident that it would soon resume.[62]

The new canal alluded to in the agreement with Miller & Lux was already being planned. Robert Brereton had, of course, quickly concluded that the canal under construction in 1871 could not achieve its promoters' great expectations. He was known to be engaged in a survey of a route from Tulare Lake, and in January 1872, the company had four engineering parties in the field. A few months later a plan to build a navigable irrigation canal from Summit Lake (about thirty miles south of the headworks of the just completed canal) to Antioch was unveiled, and it was expected that Summit Lake could be easily connected to Tulare Lake, which Brereton thought of as a vast reservoir. The new plan was, in all likelihood, simply a more detailed version of the west side elements of the comprehensive irrigation scheme that Brereton had described in his October 1871 report to Ralston. While there were hopeful reports of pending contracts for the first stretch running northwest from Summit Lake, no work was ever done. Instead by the following year speculation turned to extending the original canal from Los Banos Creek northward to meet the river upstream from Antioch. The prospective terminus was described variously as Moore's Landing on the Old River branch of the

---

[62] indenture, Henry Miller and Charles Lux and San Joaquin & Kings River Canal & Irrigation Company, February 7, 1872.

San Joaquin north of Ellis Station or further upstream at a point near San Joaquin City, close to the mouth of the Stanislaus River. Both sites were accessible to river steamers most of the year.[63]

Meanwhile on the existing forty-mile canal "The sight of a mast sweeping along the plain," was, in the words of one canal enthusiast, striking evidence of "the grand fact that canal navigation has opened in California."[64] Navigation had always been an integral part of the canal company's plans, and it wasted little time in providing a practical demonstration. Four boats were built for the company's own use, each sixty-three feet long and nine and a half feet wide, double-ended with square prows, since they were too long to turn in the canal. In theory, they had a capacity of sixty-four tons at a four-foot draft, but in practice they only carried three tons. The boats were pulled by two mules hitched in tandem on one side of the canal, the 150-foot tow rope attached to a mast or staff. The crew consisted of two-men: one with the mules and one steering the slow-moving craft. Israel Dollarhide remembered working on the boats when a trip from one end of the canal to the other could take two or three days and the mules strained to pull a loaded boat upstream against a strong current.[65]

Irrigation canals require control structures, commonly called weirs today and "stop-gates" then, to keep water levels high enough upstream from the weir to maintain flow through the outlet gates that deliver water to farmers. Putting boats in the canal required heavier and more expensive timber structures than would otherwise have been necessary, and five of the six early weirs were equipped with drawbridges. Those structures cost from $3,000 to $5,000 apiece, which was several times what a simpler installation would have cost. When a boat approached a weir it had to stop, pull the boards that held back the water and let the level equalize before passing through and replacing the boards. Dollarhide recalled that, "Sometimes people would be irrigating and would have the water backed up so they could get the water out in their ditches. When the canal boat came along and let the water out of the weir they would have to wait until the section filled up again before they could go on

[63] *Pacific Rural Press*, November 25, 1871; *Daily Alta California*, January 30, 1872; *Daily Alta California*, May 13, 1872; *Daily Alta California*, June 24, 1872; *Daily Alta California*, June 30, 1873.
[64] *Irrigation in California*, 18.
[65] *Irrigation in California*, 18; Milliken, interview notes, Israel Dollarhide, November 19, 1928, 5-7.

irrigating."[66] Ordinary wagon bridges had to be high enough to allow the boats to pass, but even so the boat crew had to carry the tow rope under the bridge and lower the staff. Only one boat was used at a time, and then for only a short period in the summer and fall, hauling supplies to the company's maintenance camps, and sometimes carrying gravel quarried from Los Banos Creek upstream as far as the headworks. A store under a canvas awning was built on one of the boats for the convenience of canal employees. Experience soon proved that without an even more expensive system of locks, irrigation was incompatible with navigation, and the experiment was abandoned in the mid-1870s.[67]

Among the hard lessons that the canal company learned during its first year in operation was that erosion was one of its greatest enemies. The adobe soil in the first thirty miles of the canal proved admirably impervious to seepage, but when it dried it crumbled and was easily washed away at the water's edge. Blame was immediately placed on the wind. "The fierce winds which sweep over these plains from north to south throughout the summer season raise a strong ripple on the waters of the canal, actually curling the waves over into small 'white-caps," wrote one observer, who called those waves "a source of substantial inconvenience in washing away the adobe banks of the work."[68] The wind no doubt contributed to the problem but the real culprit was the swift flow caused by the canal's one-foot-per-mile gradient, and banks on the outer side of curves were most susceptible to damage. Experience in the first season suggested that the slope of the canal banks was too steep to withstand wind and swift water. The original cross-section had a bed width of twenty-eight feet and two-to-one slopes carrying a four-foot depth of water. In 1873, the sides were regraded to slopes as gentle as five-to-one and the depth was increased to five-and-a-half feet with a surface width of sixty-eight feet. The worst stretches were lined with bundles of willow brush, delivered by canal boats. Later, willows were planted in some sections in an effort to anchor the soil, and banks were seeded with salt grass. By 1880, material was being added

<hr>

[66] Milliken, interview notes, Israel Dollarhide, 6.
[67] Milliken, interview notes, Israel Dollarhide, 5-7; Milliken, interview notes, O.E. Smith, 25-26; Schuyler, "Report on Works and Practices of Irrigation," 164.
[68] *Irrigation in California*, 17.

to the outside of eroded banks in the hope that the flowing water would eventually give the inner slope a natural, and more stable, shape.[69]

The distribution of water to farms began at the outlet gates in the side of the canal. By 1880 there were twenty-one ditches connected to the main canal between the dam and Los Banos Creek; thirteen serving the big Miller & Lux Dos Palos Farm, and the remainder supplying Badger Flat and Miller & Lux's Canal Farm. The original outlet gate design was described as "a massive structure, provided with a heavy gate of four-inch planks raised by a screw" from a floor that was level with the bottom of the canal.[70] Although the unusually heavy construction of the weirs could be excused by the necessities of canal navigation, the "ponderous" design of the outlet gates suggests a preference for a certain standard of construction; one that had no precedent in contemporary California experience and was soon abandoned in favor of simpler, less expensive structures. The replacement gates had removable boards that were pulled out to control the flow into each distribution ditch. The ditches themselves were built, maintained and operated by their users, although Brereton thought it was a mistake not to keep them under company control. On the three-mile-long Badger Flat ditch, which cost $1,000 to build and $200 a year to maintain, irrigators set up a formal organization with officers and by-laws and issued one share of stock for each irrigated acre.[71]

Irrigation was a new science on the west side. There were a few examples in other parts of the valley and with some trial and error the inexperienced farmers quickly learned the rudiments of laying out and managing farm ditches. As to the manner in which they irrigated the following example from the second year of irrigation may be typical of the earliest practices. J.W.A. Wright of Turlock visited the Badger Flat area in May 1873 and reported on the experience in two long letters to the *Pacific Rural Press.* It had been another dry year, and he passed already parched grain fields that would produce a scant yield and some that would not even be worth cutting for hay, but as he neared the irrigated section the view changed dramatically. Los Banos Creek carried the wastewater from the canal in a stream sixty feet wide and two or three feet

---

[69] Schuyler, "Report on Works and Practices of Irrigation," 162, 164-165; Grunsky, *Irrigation Near Merced*, 22.
[70] Schuyler, "Report on Works and Practices of Irrigation," 164.
[71] Schuyler, "Report on Works and Practices of Irrigation," 164, 175; Brereton, *Irrigation-Enterprise in California*, 58.

deep. Instead of hard and dusty surfaces he encountered roads that "all at once became soft and boggy in places, and as many ditches of running water have not yet been bridged, it was difficult to make our way in a light spring wagon. The finest wheat and barley stood in green waving walls on each side of us."[72]

Wright carefully examined a quarter-section owned by George W. Cotton about a mile east of Los Banos Creek and eight miles from the river. From an outlet gate near the end of the canal, water was carried in a ditch along the creek until it reached an "old and shallow slough" running in a northeasterly direction that served as a distribution channel for Cotton and his neighbors, and would later be turned into an excavated canal. The slough ran through Cotton's land, and he had a distributing ditch on each side, parallel to the slough, that he made with only his plow and a V-scraper. A single pass with a plow formed a low ridge around the entire tract, and two plow furrows ran in straight lines from the main ditches at intervals of about forty steps to make check levees and shallow distributing ditches. Water from the main ditches was let into those channels, which were cut or overflowed to spread water across the crop. Cotton and H.S. Gest farmed the land on shares that year, and the two men were able to irrigate 150 acres in seven days, often working at night when other irrigators were not using the water. The land was not leveled and Wright found that "in some places the water will not stand more than two inches deep, in others it will have a depth of two or three feet. But, after the supply has been shut off, it all disappears by absorption in three or four days."[73]

Wright noted that even though they had access to canal water, many farmers had delayed irrigation until the wheat had begun to show signs of stress, hoping that late rains would spare them further trouble and expense. Wheat was the only important cash crop in the early days but other irrigated crops were being grown on a smaller scale:

> The ten acres on Mr. Cotton's ranch not sown in grain, besides furnishing room for his buildings and for a good-sized yard, garden, orchard and barnyard, are also occupied by a 'patch' for corn, potatoes, alfalfa and melons, or whatever else he chooses to grow there. Through this there are

---

[72] *Pacific Rural Press*, September 6, 1873; also see Wayne Pimentel, *Dogtown and Ditches: Life on the Westside* (Los Banos, California, Loose Change Press, 1987), 48-51.
[73] *Pacific Rural Press*, September 6, 1873; Milliken, Joe Webb interview notes, September 2, 1938, 2-3.

two small ditches, about three feet wide and six inches deep, in which a constant stream of water is allowed to flow whenever needed; and from these the adjoining land can be flooded, if necessary.[74]

Nearby, one member of the Fowler family had fenced a ten-acre alfalfa field and was grazing 150 head of cows, sheep, horses and goats on it. Everywhere he looked, Wright saw the benefits of irrigation. He also noticed the effect that irrigation had on wells. Even though the acreage and duration of irrigation was still relatively limited, the abundance of water seeping into the ground caused simple dug wells to collapse, and Wright saw families drinking canal water because they had lost their domestic wells. Bored wells that were properly lined were reportedly undamaged by the rising water table.

Even though irrigation at Badger Flat was an immediate success, the canal company set up its own model farm as a demonstration project. Ralston instructed Brereton to "illustrate what irrigation would do" as a way to attract additional investors.[75] The site of what Brereton called "this object-teaching" was six thousand acres between the canal and Dos Palos Slough northwest of Firebaugh's Ferry leased in late 1872 from Miller & Lux, a place later known as the Dos Palos Ranch. During the first year of the five-year lease, the entire property would be seeded to grain, but thereafter alfalfa was to be planted on 1,500 acres annually, so that when the land reverted to Miller & Lux it would be covered with that irrigated forage crop. Brereton laid out an elaborate irrigation system that had main and secondary ditches, the latter equipped with small distribution boxes that directed water into diagonal plow furrows running in two directions that divided the land into diamond-shaped sections measuring 120-by-150 feet. Some years later, engineer C.E. Grunsky noted that, "The experiment, involving the introduction of methods that may be successful in India, where labor is abundant and cheap, proved a complete failure, and seems to have brought the entire canal project into temporary bad repute."[76] How much damage Brereton's "object-teaching" did to the reputation of the canal company or to irrigation in general is debatable, but his plan was badly mistaken and was abandoned at a cost of $50,000 to the canal company. In its place, a simpler system of check levees following six-inch

---

[74] *Pacific Rural Press*, September 13, 1873.
[75] Brereton, *Irrigation-Enterprise in California*, 7.
[76] Grunsky, *Irrigation Near Merced*, 1899, 20.

contour lines was installed, and that practice of making fewer and larger levees enclosing greater areas of ground (referred to as "checks") with more or less the same level also replaced the pioneer methods that J.W.A. Wright found at Badger Flat and eventually spread across the west side.[77]

Miller & Lux became, by virtue of its vast holdings, the largest irrigator. At first it rented out large tracts of land and built Farmers Camp to serve its tenants before developing its own Canal Farm. By October 1873 it had seven thousand acres fenced and in crops and was fencing another six thousand acres in addition to the six thousand acres leased to the canal company. Superintendent J.H.A. Mills tried a variety of new crops, including fifty acres of cotton. It was not irrigated and only ten acres matured but it was enough to demonstrate that cotton could grow on the west side. Mills also grew just enough tobacco to prove its potential. Although it dabbled in new or exotic crops, and its renters probably planted wheat, Miller & Lux made irrigation part of its livestock business by growing alfalfa and barley or other feed grains. Miller & Lux had initially given Bensley's canal only lukewarm support, but once they began irrigating the job was done with the company's customary attention to detail. A few years after irrigation began, visitors to Miller & Lux farms saw checks precisely laid out by engineers and tended by a half-dozen Italian irrigators.[78]

Wheat was the most important crop, accounting for over half of the fifteen thousand acres irrigated in 1873. In the first few years irrigation was used only to mature a wheat crop that was otherwise planted and grown with natural moisture. Too often farmers waited until the drying effects of sun and wind were already evident before turning to the canal and as a result they sometimes lost a portion of their potential yield. Habits soon changed. By the late 1870s, farmers began irrigating in October to prepare the soil for planting, and on deep soils that retained moisture it was sometimes the only irrigation that was needed if spring rains were plentiful. Winter grain irrigation continued until January or even February, depending on the weather. In the spring months, grain on the heavier adobe soils, which absorbed relatively little water at each irrigation, had to be irrigated every three or four weeks, while other places

[77] *Sacramento Daily Union*, December 10, 1872; Grunsky, *Irrigation Near Merced*, 19-20; Schuyler, "Report on Works and Practices of Irrigation," 167-168; Paul Bailey, "Irrigation Under the San Joaquin and Kings River Canal and Irrigation Company," c. 1908, 7-8.
[78] *Pacific Rural Press*, October 18, 1873; *Pacific Rural Press*, August 17, 1877; Pinentel, *Dogtown and Ditches*, 50.

required only one or two waterings to bring the crop to maturity. Alfalfa irrigation began in the spring and during the hot months it was the only major crop that relied on the canal. The greatest irrigation demand therefore came in the spring and the lowest in the summer; a schedule that coincided with the pattern of seasonal runoff on the San Joaquin River.[79]

The great canal of the San Joaquin & Kings River Canal & Irrigation Company was a work of impressive magnitude and a landmark in the history of California water development. It quickly made irrigation a proven success on the west side but with progress halted at Los Banos Creek that success was still incomplete.

---

[79] *Daily Alta California*, November 9, 1874; Schuyler, "Report on Works and Practices of Irrigation," 166-167.

4

The Terrible Seventies

The great canal was an expensive undertaking. The canal company itself claimed that the original section cost $9,000 per mile to build, and the 1879 report by assistant state engineer James D. Schuyler put the "enormous cost" of the works at over one million dollars, including repairs and improvements to the canal and the "difficult and costly" maintenance of the headworks, especially the brush dam that rotted and settled. Ralston, Bensley and the other San Francisco financiers were wealthy men, but they had a multitude of other interests and neither the appetite nor the ability to indefinitely increase their gamble on irrigation in the distant San Joaquin Valley. Yet that gamble had to be increased if it was to have any hope of success. For the enterprise to succeed the northward extension of the canal, a new canal from Summit Lake or both had to be built, and that depended on new sources of funding.[80]

On January 12, 1872 the editors of the *Sacramento Daily Union* were shown a map of the Central Valley watersheds "on which are drawn the projected lines of canals, designed to catch, convey and distribute the waters of the mountains and the large streams of the State over the entire central regions of California, for irrigation and navigation purposes." That imaginative rendering was the work of Robert Maitland Brereton and the paper explained that the intention was to "invite capital from Europe to take hold of the irrigating enterprise."[81] In fact, it was part of Ralston's plan; a plan that could pay for the extension of his San Joaquin & Kings River project, and embrace even wider, but still vague, irrigation schemes elsewhere in the valley. The financier presented his ideas informally to Governor Newton Booth, evidently in the hope of an endorsement that could be used to sway European investors. The governor, who had come into office only the month before, dismissed Ralston's scheme as impractical and labeled Brereton an "adventurer." Ralston

---

[80] San Joaquin & Kings River Canal & Irrigation Company (hereafter cited as SJ&KRC&I Co.), *Prospectus: Agricultural Lands and Waters in the San Joaquin and Tulare Valleys* (San Francisco: A. L. Bancroft, 1873), 6; Schuyler, "Report on Works and Practices of Irrigation," 163.
[81] *Sacramento Daily Union*, January 13, 1872.

was obviously stunned; the financial elite had usually enjoyed the close cooperation of state government. He replied immediately, defending Brereton's qualifications as well as "the influence he can bring to bear in Europe, where he is known and appreciated." The value of irrigation had been established, Ralston wrote, and the plans Brereton had drawn up would extend its benefits to the Central Valley. He concluded "If the scheme is Utopian, then I fear my views of the resources and capabilities of this state are Utopian also."[82] There may have been no better expression of Ralston's faith in the rapid development of California.

Since irrigation was thought to be such an important public benefit, the canal capitalists felt justified in asking for public support. Their petition in the form of a "memorial" was presented to the California legislature on January 23, 1872 which, if approved by that body, would request that Congress make special federal land grants for the San Joaquin & Kings River Canal & Irrigation Company and the California Irrigation Company, a corporation said to have plans for irrigation on the west side of the Sacramento Valley. Such assistance was necessary, it said, because "it will be indispensable to the success of the operations of these companies that foreign capital, in large amounts, shall be enlisted, which, in our opinion, can hardly be brought about unless the aid of Government shall be given, at least to the extent herein asked." What the memorial asked for was the grant of the even-numbered sections of the public domain for five miles on each side of the canals constructed by the two companies, and if the specified land had already passed into private ownership they could choose an equivalent acreage anywhere in the same federal land district.[83] There were ample precedents for the use of land grants to finance infrastructure projects, especially railroads, but the request for such a large transfer of public land to private interests came at a time of mounting and often fierce criticism of land monopoly in California. The *Sacramento Daily Union* reflected that sense of popular outrage over "these land sharks and water sharks" when it opined that "to take land or money from the rest of the people to round out and complete their speculations, is one of the most audacious

---

[82] W.C. Ralston to Newton Booth, January 18, 1872 in Brereton, *Irrigation-Enterprise in California*, 14-15.
[83] *Sacramento Daily Union*, January 24, 1872.

propositions of this most audacious age in public plunder."[84] For the time being at least, the path to government assistance was blocked.

Meanwhile, Brereton was preparing for a trip to Europe to raise money for the canal company. Besides seeking capital, he hoped to encourage immigration and settlement on the newly irrigated lands, particularly from the English middle class. In February 1872 he privately approached Miller & Lux with an offer to act as their agent for the sale and settlement of their land in exchange for a hefty salary, a home in the valley, the use of ten thousand acres of irrigated land for five years, and 10 percent of the profits from land sales. Brereton met with Henry Miller in early April but the conference apparently went badly because thereafter Brereton corresponded only with Charles Lux, and Miller became more openly critical of the English engineer.[85]

Before Brereton's departure for London in May, Ralston wrote a letter of endorsement that prophesied "large revenues" to the canal company and underscored the fact that "We have not the means to accomplish so grand an undertaking as this." Other leading figures including former Governor H.H. Haight and the local agent for the Rothschilds signed a similar letter.[86] Brereton wooed British investors, and published a tract entitled *Project for English Middle and Yeoman Class Colonies for California* in furtherance of his immigration plans.[87] It was all to no avail. Too much money had too recently been lost on shady mining stocks and other speculative American investments. Ironically, one of the canal company's original incorporators, Erwin Davis, may have contributed to the problem. After going bankrupt in California, Davis relocated to London and engaged in a manipulation of mining stocks so blatant that it was finally halted by the Utah courts.[88] As one British banker informed Ralston, "John Bull was suffering from a too credulous a belief in Pyramids of Silver and the like, not to mention the Erie Railway and would not

---

[84] *Sacramento Daily Union*, January 29, 1872.

[85] Igler, *Industrial Cowboys*, 75, 78, 209 (Note 78); on recruitment from the English middle classes, see Ralston to Booth, January 18, 1872 and the text of the memorial printed in the *Sacramento Daily Union*, January 24, 1872.

[86] W. Ralston to R.M. Brereton, May 9, 1872 and Agard Foulkes & Co. and others to R.M. Brereton, May 9, 1872, both in Brereton, *Irrigation-Enterprise in California*, 18-20.

[87] The pamphlet has no date. The entry in *Catalogue of the Library of the Institution of Civil Engineers, A-G* (London: The Institution of Civil Engineers, 1895), 173 gives suggests 1875 but in the context of other statements 1872 appears to be the more likely date.

[88] Clark Spence, *British Investments and the American Mining Frontier, 1861-1901* (Cornell University Press, 1958; reprint 1993), 26.

look at anything American—so that the San Joaquin Valley has not had a fair chance."[89] It was not all a matter of bad timing; Brereton had tried to sell canal company stock at seven or eight dollars per share, but the would-be purchasers soon discovered that it could be had for half that much in San Francisco.[90]

With the failure of Brereton's European mission, Ralston once again turned his attention to the pursuit of government assistance, and dispatched Brereton to Washington in late 1872 in support of the effort to win a federal subsidy. Senator Cornelius Cole of California introduced a bill on January 17, 1873 that would grant the canal company two sections of land for each mile of a canal stretching three hundred miles from Buena Vista Lake to Oakland, an additional one hundred acres per mile to pay for reservoirs and a right-of-way through federal lands extending three hundred feet on each side of the main canal and one hundred feet on each side of branch or feeder canals. In all, the grant could total up to 256,000 acres (400 square miles). Extension of the canal for navigation west of Antioch had never been publicly discussed, and it is hard to escape the suspicion that the dramatic increase in the scope of the project was primarily for the purpose of inflating the size of the land grant. Other provisions of the bill would give the canal company the right to use the waters of Buena Vista and Tulare lakes, and the San Joaquin and Kern rivers. The canal would be subject to state taxation, and the state would regulate irrigation rates and navigation tolls.[91]

Brereton had undoubtedly had a hand in drafting the subsidy bill, and now he worked to line up support for it. He met with the head of the Corps of Engineers, General A.A. Humphreys, and with national politicians like James G. Blaine and James Garfield. With the assistance of Samuel Ward, the famous "King of the Lobby," he hosted dinner parties for members of Congress and other influential men. Despite those efforts, the subsidy bill faced stiff opposition. In California, Governor Booth led the anti-monopoly and anti-subsidy forces, and the bill was denounced by every major California newspaper except the *San Francisco Chronicle*. On Capitol Hill, a backlash

[89] C.J.F. Stuart to William Ralston, August 15, 1872, in Pisani, *From the Family Farm to Agribusiness*, 112.

[90] Pisani, *From the Family Farm to Agribusiness*, 110, 112.

[91] Pisani, *From the Family Farm to Agribusiness*, 112; W. Turrentine Jackson, Rand F. Herbert and Stephen R. Wee, *Engineers and Irrigation: Report of the Board of Commissioners on Irrigation of the San Joaquin, Tulare and Sacramento Valleys of the State of California, 1873, Engineer Historical Studies, No. 5* (Fort Belvoir: VA, Office of History, U.S. Army Corps of Engineers Office of History, 1990), 14.

against railroad subsidies carried over to the proposed canal subsidy. Senator Cole warned Ralston in early February that the bill's prospects were fading. Late in the month, California's other senator, Eugene Casserly, offered an amended bill that substituted the proceeds from the sale of the designated lands for the direct land grant in Cole's original bill, reduced the reservoir subsidy and set the maximum irrigation rate at $1.25 per acre, but Casserly acknowledged that no action would be taken on the matter until there had been further investigation.[92]

In mid-February, with the subsidy bill stalled, Ralston's allies launched an effort to fund just such an investigation, one that they hoped would improve their chances for eventual federal aid. A bill introduced by Senator William M. Stewart of Nevada, a long-time associate of Ralston's who was sometimes referred to as "California's third senator," would authorize a five-man Board of Irrigation Commissioners to survey the San Joaquin and Tulare basins and report to Congress and the president on the best system of irrigation for the region. At the urging of Sacramento Valley representatives, the bill was quickly amended to include the entire Central Valley. Although critics understood that its purpose was to build support for the canal company, the idea of an expert investigation was sufficiently benign to win easy passage on March 3, 1873, the final day of the legislative session. Brereton hailed it as the first national legislation dealing with irrigation.[93]

The Board of Commissioners was to consist of two Army engineers and one member of the U.S. Coast Survey appointed by the president, to be assisted by the chief of the California Geological Survey and "one other civilian distinguished by his knowledge of the subject." The federal officers named to the board were Lieutenant Colonel B.S. Alexander, Major George Mendell and George Davidson of the Coast Survey. Josiah D. Whitney, the head of the state geological survey, was planning to retire from his underfunded office and declined to serve. The board offered the other spot to Robert Brereton. He was the logical choice because he probably knew more about large-scale irrigation plans than any other California engineer at the time, but he wisely declined since his work for the canal company—he was identified as its business

---

[92] Pisani, *From the Family Farm to Agribusiness*, 112-113; Jackson, et.al., *Engineers and Irrigation*, 15-17; Brereton, *Old English Civil Engineer*, 26-27.
[93] Pisani, *From the Family Farm to Agribusiness*, 113; Jackson, et.al., *Engineers and Irrigation*, 17-18; *Sacramento Daily Union*, February 15, 1873; Brereton, *Old English Civil Engineer*, 25.

manager as well as consulting engineer in 1873—would have been a clear conflict of interest and could have undermined the credibility of the commission. Brereton did, however, give the commission access to his maps and the data he had collected, and he accompanied them on their travels in the San Joaquin Valley.[94]

The now three-man board began work in May with most field surveys completed by August. In its report dated February 20, 1874, the commission asserted that "it is the duty of government, both State and national, to encourage irrigation" and it advocated government studies of streamflow and topography in support of a system of comprehensive irrigation planning that would avoid haphazard and inefficient development. It was a groundbreaking vision of systematic, scientific irrigation under broad public supervision, but with such limited time and resources the commission could make only the most general recommendations for specific canals. On the west side of the San Joaquin Valley it largely adopted the plans of the San Joaquin & Kings River company for the extension of the existing canal to Old River at Moore's Landing, and for the canal from the Tulare Lake basin via Summit Lake to Antioch, including plans for canal navigation. The commission proposed an equally ambitious canal for the west side of the Sacramento Valley running from Red Bluff to Fairfield.[95]

Like Brereton's plans, and like all the other grand plans of the time, the commission simply presented lines on a map representing routes for canals based on the most cursory of surveys. They did not have any dependable information about how much water there was to divert into those canals, and in the case of Tulare Lake in particular the availability of water was easily overestimated. To their credit, Alexander, Mendell and Davidson recognized that better hydrographic knowledge was a necessary foundation for a comprehensive irrigation program. The federal engineers did not, however, endorse a subsidy for canal construction.

---

[94] "Act of Congress to Provide a Board of Commissioners to Report a System of Irrigation for the San Joaquin, Tulare, and Sacramento Valleys, in California, March 3, 1873" in Brereton, *Irrigation-Enterprise in California*, 10; Jackson, et.al., *Engineers and Irrigation*, 23-24.

[95] Jackson, et.al., *Engineers and Irrigation*, 24-31; Pisani, *From the Family Farm to Agribusiness*, 113-117; B.S. Alexander, George H. Mendell, George Davidson, *Report of the Board of Commissioners on Irrigation of the San Joaquin, Tulare and Sacramento Valleys of the State of California*, (Washington, D.C., Government Printing Office, 1874), 28-29, 33. The quotation is on page 78.

While Brereton labored in Washington in early 1873, the canal company made further efforts to raise money at home. At a January 1873 meeting of its board, a resolution proposed by Isaac Friedlander was adopted that would "invite the people of California to come forward and participate in this great enterprise." To that end it offered for public sale three-quarters of the company's capital stock of 100,000 shares at $100 per share, and to insure that the opportunity was broadly distributed, no one could buy more than 500 shares.[96] Based on the prices quoted during Brereton's recent visit to London, it seems doubtful that the shares were worth anything close to their par value. Later that same year, the canal company offered 30,000 shares at the cost of the actual work done to date with the intent to make an additional assessment against each share of not over $3.00 to pay for extension of the canal to Orestimba Creek through lands already settled "where the demand for water is great and assured."[97]

By that time the company was operating at a substantial loss; in 1873 it made only $10,000 from the sale of water but spent $109,000. A quarter of the water payments came from Miller & Lux, but fully half of the expenses were paid out to the cattle company for the rent of land, presumably for Brereton's demonstration farm. Investors were understandably reluctant to join such an unsuccessful enterprise.[98]

The early 1870s witnessed the rise in California of the Patrons of Husbandry, better known as the Grange. The Grange, and the farmers clubs that preceded it, were vocal critics of monopoly and the unfair advantage enjoyed by the men who, in their view, controlled the state's commerce and resources; men who had amassed millions of acres of land and who manipulated the price of wheat. The San Joaquin & Kings River Canal & Irrigation Company came in for special scorn because among its directors were the state's leading land barons and the Granger's arch-enemy, the wheat king, Isaac Friedlander. They believed that the company, and its companion

---

[96] *Sacramento Daily Union*, January 25, 1873
[97] SJ&KRC&I Co., *Prospectus*, 6
[98] M. Catherine Miller, *Flooding the Courtrooms: Law and Water in the Far West* (Lincoln: University of Nebraska Press, 1993), 42

schemes, now threatened to turn an important part of California's irrigated future into another monopoly.[99]

Against that background, in July 1873 there was alarm over a bill to force farmers to finance the extension of the canal. As described in newspaper articles, the plan would require all landowners that could be served by the canal to pay an annual assessment that would become a lien on the land, and for five years to pay one-sixteenth of the value of their crops whether they irrigated or not, and make other payments in addition to the company's regular rates.[100] A correspondent calling himself "San Joaquin Farmer" from Grayson in Stanislaus County condemned this "contract for subsidy," and said of it, "of all the schemes which the various monopolies of California have on various occasions imposed and attempted to impose upon the people, with the object to oppress the masses in order to enrich the few, this scheme is the most infamous." In a rhetorical flourish frequently quoted by historians, the outraged farmer continued:

> Why, sirs, you would own us, we would be but your serfs, beholden to your mercy for the bread we would put in our childrens mouths. You would, with a high hand, backed by legal authority, rob a large community of their homesteads and of their birthright, and with the combined wealth of these spoils would make yourselves millionaires. What do you take us for? Fools outright? Slaves from some foreign lands, used to despotism, and ready and willing to bow our necks for the yoke of the burden you would place upon us?[101]

Farmers were urged to let Congress hear their protests, but Congress had not been in session since March, and in any event there seems to be no evidence that this implausible subsidy scheme was anything more than a rumor. It was reported that the company was seeking a definite commitment from farmers along its route that they would buy water at the price of $1.25 per acre for the delivery of about one acre-foot of water, but the terms of that commitment were not specified. The trumped-up excitement was short-lived but it served

---

[99] Pisani, *From the Family Farm to Agribusiness*, 132-133; Rodman W. Paul, "The Great California Grain War: The Grangers Challenge the Wheat King," *Pacific Historical Review* 27, no. 4 (November 1958), 331-349.
[100] Pisani, *From the Family Farm to Agribusiness*, 133-134.
[101] *Sacramento Daily Union*, July 19, 1873.

as a dramatic reminder of the degree to which the Grangers distrusted the canal company and its efforts to win government support.[102]

Frustrated by the fervent opposition to their plans, the canal company's trustees, including Charles Lux, sent a memorial to Governor Booth in December 1873 offering to sell the canal to the state. They pointed out that their work had been welcomed when it began during the 1871 drought:

> During the past year, and after the expenditure of a large amount of money on the undertaking, there has been much discussion by the press and the people, indicating a public sentiment in opposition to the ownership of such property by individuals and corporations.

> Your Excellency has also expressed, in official documents and otherwise, the opinion that such enterprises ought not to be under the control of private corporations, but that all the inland waters in the State ought to be controlled by the State alone for the purpose of irrigation.[103]

Claiming that they did not wish to "occupy an attitude in opposition to the public welfare," the trustees proposed the passage of a law to provide for a sale by condemnation, the value of the company's rights, contracts and property to be determined by a commission appointed by the governor or the legislature. In making this request they admitted that they "undertook this important enterprise as a private speculation, but they understood at the same time that it would be a great public good in increasing so largely the taxable property of the State." They also claimed that 80 percent of the stock had been subscribed by men who owned no land on the west side.[104] The memorial portrayed the company as the victim of changing public sentiments, but it was, in effect, an admission that its speculation had gone badly. If the state accepted its offer Ralston and his friends might at least recover some of their investment. Governor Booth ignored the company's proposal; as an ally of the Grangers he had long been critical of the canal company and had no reason to want to rescue its wealthy backers from a money-losing project at state expense. The trustees probably expected as much.

Perhaps to show that they still had confidence in their enterprise, in March 1874 the canal company advertised for bids on the construction of the

---

[102] *Sacramento Daily Union*, July 2, 1873; *Daily Alta California*, July 5, 1873.
[103] *Daily Alta California*, December 19, 1873.
[104] *Daily Alta California*, December 19, 1873.

extension to Orestimba Creek on plans drawn up by chief engineer R.M. Brereton. Bidders were advised that the canal would be thirty feet wide on the bottom with an average depth of cut of three-and-a-half feet. Excavation was estimated at 30,000 cubic yards per mile. Bids were due on April 16 and construction of the thirty-mile segment had to be completed by August 15.[105]

On May 15, 1874 a party of over thirty capitalists, dignitaries and reporters left San Francisco for a tour of the company's project. Organized by Brereton, the group included Governor Leland Stanford, Army engineer B.S. Alexander and canal investors Ralston, Bensley, Friedlander and Chapman as well as Charles Lux. They came at a time of year when wheat was at its full growth and the contrast between irrigated fields and the rapidly browning acres surrounding them was most apparent. The visitors remarked on the "solid character" of the wooden structures in the canal as they travelled along it. At the company's farm, they saw four thousand acres of wheat "grown where the alkali was thick on the ground as if a package of saleratus had burst." On a mile-and-a-half section of finished but dry canal, they were given a demonstration of canal construction using the recently invented Slosser's excavator. The two-horse machine was a combination chisel-shaped plow, scoop and elevator that conveyed the dirt from the top of the chisel into a specially-designed dump wagon. It is not clear where this section of canal was located; it may have been on the route to Orestimba Creek.[106] Despite the call for bids, no work was done on the extension in the summer of 1874. Opposition from the Grangers was cited for the reason for the company's decision to suspend work, but there is no way to tell whether that was true or if it simply lacked the money. And if Brereton had hoped that the excursion to the west side would inspire new investment, he was disappointed in that as well.[107]

From his first reports to Ralston, Brereton had emphasized that the value of water was inseparable from the value of land, and the company suffered because it could not benefit from the increase in the value of irrigated land. In another effort to raise funds abroad, Brereton now proposed that landowners pledge 100,000 acres to the canal project. In exchange they would receive one

---

[105] *Daily Alta California*, March 28, 1874.
[106] *San Francisco Post*, May 18, 1874 in Brereton, *Irrigation-Enterprise in California*, 52-54; see also *Daily Alta California*, May 18, 1874.
[107] *Daily Alta California*, October 5, 1874.

share of stock with a par value of $25 for each acre, which was Brereton's estimate of the cost of an irrigation system. At Ralston's suggestion, Brereton returned to London in 1874-1875 and managed to get his "friends" there to form a syndicate to provide $2,500,000 using the 100,000 acres of land as security. The deal fell apart, Brereton recalled, when the landowners "backed out of this proposition," and he again returned empty-handed. Brereton's memoirs provide only sketchy details of this final effort to finance the extension of the canal, and among the most intriguing questions was that of the identity of the landowners who had supposedly joined the scheme in the first place.[108]

The San Joaquin & Kings River canal was only one of William C. Ralston's speculations, many of which, like the canal, were visionary but unprofitable. For years, Ralston had freely mingled his own affairs with those of the Bank of California, and in 1875 he, and thus the bank, were seriously overextended. The effects of the national depression that began with the Panic of 1873 were being felt in California, the price of silver was falling and money had become tight. Ralston began to quietly sell some of his properties in an increasingly desperate attempt to raise cash, all the while maintaining his customary appearance of absolute confidence. Time ran out on August 26, 1875. Prices on the San Francisco stock exchange fell as Ralston's erstwhile friend and partner William Sharon dumped his stock in the Ophir mine, and that afternoon, as rumors swept the city, there was a run on the bank by a growing crowd of nervous depositors. Its reserves soon exhausted, the Bank of California was forced to close its doors. The following day the bank's trustees learned that Ralston's debts amounted to more than $9.5 million, half of it owed to the bank, while his assets were valued at $4.5 million. His immediate resignation was demanded. Leaving the bank, Ralston walked to North Beach, where he often swam in the bay. That day it was reported that he moved through the water with easy strength, but then was seen to struggle; a rescue boat found him floating face down. Some thought it was suicide, but evidence pointed to a stroke.

---

[108] Brereton, *Old English Civil Engineer*, 66. In *Irrigation-Enterprise in California* Brereton placed the syndicate in 1872 but that source lacks the level of detail in his later writing and does not appear to fit other accounts of his activities in 1872.

The collapse of the Bank of California and Ralston's death contributed to a decade of economic and political upheaval that has been called "the terrible seventies." The canal company, already in dire straits, found its position increasingly untenable. As early as 1874 it had clashed with Miller & Lux over the interpretation of its contract with the cattlemen. The contract required the canal company to make available sufficient water for the irrigation of 16,667 acres in 1872 "whenever required" by Miller & Lux, increasing to 33,334 acres in 1873 and reaching a maximum of 50,000 acres in 1874. The canal company argued that Miller & Lux should pay for the water to which it was entitled rather than only for the much smaller acreage that it actually chose to irrigate. The question was tested in court and the canal company lost. In 1876 it attempted to double the rate paid by Miller & Lux, and an infuriated Henry Miller threatened to take no water at all at the higher rate. The following year the canal company escalated the fight by cutting off all of Miller & Lux's water, and it is said that Miller then used an ax to smash outlet gates in the canal to get water to his land. In a similar vein, Oscar Smith remembered that when water was not getting to Canal Farm, Miller had a sandbag dam put in the canal and stationed a man with a rifle on top of it. In both stories, the canal company pursued criminal charges against Henry Miller.[109]

The canal company and Miller & Lux clearly had opposing agendas; the company needed to increase the price of its water and Miller & Lux wanted water at the lowest possible cost to support its livestock business, and wanted to insure its control of vital water resources. For Miller & Lux the best way to resolve that conflict was to take control of the company. Miller & Lux started to increase its holding of canal company stock in 1876, and the following year Henry Miller reminded his partner that "By having control of the water we could make all the grass needed in a dry season."[110] The financial turmoil that followed the collapse of Ralston's empire made it easier for Miller & Lux to accumulate large blocks of canal company stock at low prices. As it struggled to recover, the Bank of California called in its loans to Ralston's associates,

---

[109] Miller, *Flooding the Courtrooms*, 43; Igler, *Industrial Cowboys*, 84; John Outcalt, *History of Merced County California with a Biographical Review of The Leading Men and Women of the County Who Have Been Identified with Its Growth and Development from the Early Days to the Present* (Los Angeles: Historic Record Co., 1925), 221; Milliken, interview notes, Oscar E. Smith, 4-5. James McDermott remembered a canal superintendent named Kaufman "who fought Miller so hard. He was all for the Canal Company and down on Miller." Milliken, interview notes, James McDermott, October 7, 1924, 1.
[110] Henry Miller to Charles Lux, August 8, 1877, in Igler, *Industrial Cowboys*, 84.

driving some of them to bankruptcy. Friedlander fell and so did Chapman and Bensley. Robert Brereton, who moved on to a mining job in Eureka, Nevada in 1876, was forced to sell his 4,250 shares, which had cost him $34,000, to Miller & Lux for a mere $1,000. In December 1877 it was reported that Miller & Lux had taken control of the canal company, although a list of stock owned by the partners did not show majority ownership until October 1878. They kept accumulating stock until they owned virtually all of it.[111]

In his letter to Governor Booth in January 1872, William C. Ralston said that the canal's backers had made their investment "not rashly or at haphazard, but upon the most mature consideration and examination. They are not in the habit of embarking in wild, impracticable schemes."[112] In fact the investors had the instincts of gold rush gamblers and the canal proved to be an unwise bet. As an engineering concept, the idea was sound enough, even if canal navigation was never really feasible. The real problem was the connection that the company made between land and water, or rather the lack of that connection. The irrigation projects that did succeed, public and private, combined land and water, so that the costs of canal building were recouped from the increased value of the irrigated land. That is something the canal company could not do because it had no land. Brereton recognized the problem immediately yet he was mesmerized by Ralston's expansive vision and labored to make it a reality, reaping only disappointment for his efforts. Certainly the virulent opposition of the Grangers could not have been anticipated, but in the end Bensley's dream simply proved to be unrealistic. Miller & Lux, on the other hand, understood what the combination of land and water meant. The water could "make grass;" grass that was the foundation on an integrated system of raising and marketing livestock that would allow the partners to master the regional meat market. While skeptical of the canal company's grand ambitions, Miller & Lux recognized the canal's usefulness and put themselves in a position to benefit from it, and then to own it. By 1878 land and water had been reunited, and a new era of irrigation expansion was about to begin.

---

[111] Igler, *Industrial Cowboys*, 84-85; Brereton, *Old English Civil Engineer*, 25-26; *Daily Alta California*, December 10, 1877.
[112] W.C. Ralston to Newton Booth, January 18, 1872 in Brereton, *Irrigation-Enterprise in California*, 15.

5

Mr. Miller's Canals

The Grangers turned the San Joaquin & Kings River Canal & Irrigation Company into a hated symbol of monopoly and thwarted its expansion, but farmers still wanted a canal. In April 1875 a meeting called by the West Side Grange endorsed the creation of a public irrigation district to build the Tulare Lake to Antioch canal that Robert Brereton had laid out and that the federal irrigation commission had endorsed. A bill authorizing the West Side Irrigation District was introduced in December, and the *Daily Alta California* predicted that Brereton would oppose it because it would "upend" his company's plans. However by that time Brereton was preparing to leave California and after Ralston's fall the canal company was in no position to mount a legislative campaign. The same could not be said of Miller & Lux. The irrigation district's canal would be financed by $4 million in bonds that would have to be repaid by taxes on property in the district, including thousands of acres of Miller & Lux pastures. The bill also gave the district the power of eminent domain to condemn land and existing canals, and that too was a threat to the cattle company's interests. Miller & Lux lobbyists could not prevent the west side irrigation bill from becoming law in April 1876, but they were able to secure passage of a supplemental bill that delayed the bond election until May 1877 and required a new engineering survey.[113]

The survey was placed in the hands of William Hammond Hall, later to become California's first State Engineer, with Army engineer B.S. Alexander serving as a consultant. Their report confirmed that the canal was feasible but advised against making it navigable in order to reduce the cost. Condemnation of the San Joaquin & Kings River canal was another necessary, and potentially expensive, part of the plan. Hall professed confidence in Tulare Lake as the source of supply, but he pointed out that too little was known about the streams flowing into the lake and therefore upstream reservoirs might be

---

[113] *Pacific Rural Press*, May 1, 1875; *Daily Alta California*, December 12, 1875; Pisani, *From the Family Farm to Agribusiness*, 140-142; Igler, *Industrial Cowboys*, 86-87.

required to replenish the lake and keep it high enough to feed the west side canal. By the time Hall made his report in March 1877 one of the state's most severe droughts had made irrigation seem more necessary than ever on the west side.[114]

Even with an urgent demand for water, controversy erupted over the imbalance of costs and benefits within the massive district, especially to the north in Contra Costa County where the canal would irrigate relatively few acres but the larger population would pay a greater share of district taxes than the sparsely settled counties to the south that stood to gain the most from the canal. That disparity was reflected in the results of the May 1, 1877 election. District supporters won an easy victory, losing only in Contra Costa County and in Firebaugh, where Miller & Lux was dominant. In Los Banos the vote was sixty to thirty-two in favor of the district, and sixty-two to one in the Cottonwoods precinct. The governor joined the Grangers for a victory celebration in Grayson, but the sense of triumph was short-lived. Miller & Lux promptly sought and got an injunction against the district based on the alleged unconstitutionality of the 1876 legislation, but even without the injunction it was clear that the plan had to go back to the legislature to remove Contra Costa County from the district and to eliminate navigation as one of the project's purposes. In 1878 the legislature removed the cattle company's land and the San Joaquin & Kings River canal from the irrigation district. Although $2 million in bonds were now authorized to build an irrigation-only canal, the shrunken district was no longer financially viable.[115]

While the drama of the West Side Irrigation District election was playing out, the canal company began to show signs of renewed life. As early as January 1877 it was reported that it was finally ready to begin work on the extension of the canal to Orestimba Creek, with the intention of having it ready to deliver water that fall. The announcement turned out to be premature, but by October carpenters were at work on a dam and flume to carry the canal across Los Banos Creek. It could hardly be a coincidence that the revival of construction coincided with Miller & Lux's control of the company, and there was really no question that the extension was a Miller & Lux project. A year later, in October 1878, the canal had been completed to Orestimba Creek, over 28 miles from

---

[114] Pisani, *From the Family Farm to Agribusiness*, 142-144.

[115] Pisani, *From the Family Farm to Agribusiness*, 144-147; *Pacific Rural Press*, November 16, 1878.

its former terminus. Learning from mistakes made in the original design, the extension had a grade of only six inches per mile, and the bed of the old canal was raised one foot in elevation, beginning about two miles south of Los Banos Creek. The new section cost $150,000, which was a substantial reduction in the cost per mile compared to the earlier work. Simpler structures contributed to the economy of construction; the eleven weirs on the extension cost only about $1,000 piece compared to as much as $5,000 for the heavy, drawbridge-equipped weirs designed for the passage of canal boats. By the end of 1878, farmers near Hills Ferry were flooding their fields in preparation for wheat planting. About 8,000 acres were irrigated in the first year, primarily along the section between Garzas Creek and Orestimba Creek where there were eighteen private ditches by late 1879. Between April 1880 and December 1881, the canal was pushed a few miles further north to serve the Crows Landing area.[116]

For Miller & Lux the extension accomplished two things. First, by building the section promised in the 1872 contract with the canal company, it made water available to more of the partners' land. Second, and perhaps equally important, it effectively preempted demand for an irrigation district. In April 1877, just a few weeks before the West Side Irrigation District election, Henry Miller attended an irrigation meeting in Grayson and reported to Charles Lux that "every one seems to think a Canal is the only salvation."[117] For farmers from the Cottonwoods to Crows Landing, Miller & Lux promptly provided that salvation, and in the process reduced the number of potential customers and supporters of an irrigation district. Wheat growers who might have once railed against the canal company now had water at a reasonable price, and without the taxes and other obligations that would have accompanied a public district.

Additional demand on the Orestimba extension required enlarging the capacity of the canal from the river to Los Banos Creek, and that was accomplished by construction of the Parallel Canal, a separate canal alongside the original Main Canal and emptying back into it. Work on the project began as soon as the Main Canal reached Orestimba Creek in October 1878, beginning about eleven miles from the dam and four miles northwest of

---

[116] *Daily Alta California*, January 22, 1877; *Pacific Rural Press*, March 3, 1877; Schuyler, "Report on Works and Practices of Irrigation," 163-164; 170; Grunsky, *Irrigation Near Merced*, 23; *Pacific Rural Press*, November 9, 1878; *Pacific Rural Press*, December 28, 1878; W.C. Hammatt, "Report to the San Joaquin River Water Storage District," 2.
[117] Henry Miller to Charles Lux, April 11, 1877, in Igler, *Industrial Cowboys*, 87.

Firebaugh at the eastern edge of the Dos Palos Ranch. The original "loop canal" ran seven miles and allowed water to be held at a higher elevation for diversion into the Dos Palos Ranch distribution ditches without interfering with flow in the Main Canal. It was gradually extended northward and in March 1885 reached Los Banos Creek. The Parallel Canal was thirty-five feet wide on the bottom and carried a four-foot depth of water on the same one foot per mile grade as the Main Canal. At the same time, the Main Canal itself required further corrective work. The side slopes had been reduced soon after construction in an effort to control erosion, but reeds and other plant growth took root in the shallow water of the gently sloping banks and spread to deeper water to the point that it was increasingly difficult to maintain flow in the canal. To combat the weed infestation the company resorted to dragging a heavy chain along the bottom, pulled by a horse on each bank. In the late 1880s the canal was thoroughly cleaned and reshaped with nearly vertical banks, a forty-five foot bottom and a six foot depth. Silt and the mass of roots of the remaining canal-side vegetation held the banks in place, and the steep banks limited further weed growth in the canal.[118]

The creeks that flowed out of the Diablo Range and crossed the line of the canal were another perennial engineering problem. Those streams were usually dry in the summer but heavy rains could quickly turn them into destructive torrents. When the canal was built no provision was made for flows from the small creeks that it intercepted, but that soon proved to be a mistake when floods washed out sections of the canal. Reports of the construction of a dam and flume at Los Banos Creek containing 100,000 board feet of lumber in 1877 suggest that an attempt was made to build a structure that could withstand and control occasional floods. Within a few years, however, a different approach had been adopted. Weirs were installed in the canal on each side of the creek and a gravel embankment was placed across the creek to carry the canal. The weirs protected the canal and let high water wash out the embankments, which could then be rebuilt at minimum expense.[119]

---

[118] Hammatt, "Report to the San Joaquin River Water Storage District," 2; Schuyler, "Report on Works and Practices of Irrigation,"164; Frank Soule, "Irrigation from the San Joaquin River" in *Report of Irrigation Investigations in California*, U.S. Department of Agriculture, Office of Experiment Stations, Bulletin No. 100, (Washington, D.C.: Government Printing Office, 1901), 249; Grunsky, *Irrigation Near Merced*, 23.
[119] Grunsky, *Irrigation Near Merced*, 23.

The steep grade of the first section of canal kept its route at a lower elevation and left otherwise irrigable land above it literally high and dry. With the success of irrigation on the west side, Henry Miller decided to build a new canal on a much flatter grade to put additional acreage "under the ditch." The question was how far to push the canal toward the edge of the Diablo Range, and on that subject there was a difference of opinion among the local Miller & Lux superintendents. "Poso" Smith favored the highest possible route, while Dos Palos superintendent D.A. Leonard thought the new canal should run closer to the old one. A high line canal could take in so much land that there might not be enough water to irrigate it, so Miller opted for a lower canal on a grade of four inches per mile. When the first surveyor assigned to the job proved to be too cautious in his location, Miller ordered another survey by a company surveyor named McCray who moved the canal further west and added thousands of acres to the prospective service area. The new line apparently suited Miller but Poso Smith was still dissatisfied and briefly delayed sending the excavators from his division to the construction camp.[120]

Work began in August 1896 and what became known as the Outside Canal was completed from its head on the Main Canal a few miles below the dam to Los Banos Creek in November 1897, where it ended until it was extended to Quinto Creek beginning in 1901. In 1904 Miller & Lux assured the purchasers of the Sturgeon Ranch that the canal would be extended to Garzas Creek, which was accomplished in 1907. The Sullivan Extension of the Outside Canal north of Garzas Creek was undertaken later by local landowners. The distance between the new canal and the Main Canal varied depending on the terrain but averaged about one mile.[121]

Alfalfa fields had been planted in anticipation of the Outside Canal, and in spring 1898 canal superintendent W.M. Wiley put a small head of water in the canal to irrigate them even though not all the structures had been completed. Two weeks later a farmer half a mile from the new canal near Los Banos found that his well had collapsed and swallowed his windmill and water tank, the victim of an unexpectedly high rate of seepage. As Wiley later recalled, the next incident occurred further north and a half mile west of the main canal:

---

[120] Milliken, interview notes, James Huston, January 5, 1926.
[121] Hammatt, "Report to the San Joaquin River Water Storage District ," 3; author unknown, "Notes on Conference, May 20, 1936, at Modesto," May 20, 1936; *Pacific Rural Press,* January 9, 1904): 23; Grunsky, *Irrigation Near Merced,* 23.

[A] man was coming to Volta Warehouse with his first load of grain on two wagons and six horses. Suddenly his team stopped with a short jerk. Looking back the hind end of his trailer seemed to have lost a wheel on the right side. Going back to see what had happened he found that the wheel had broken through the top of the road which was only a heavy gravel cover, had sunken down into the ground nearly to the hub and the water was running out of the hole and down into the small ditch along the road. This was about five miles from the canal.[122]

Even on the other side of the Main Canal, wells overflowed and water reached the Simon Newman Company warehouse at Ingomar causing its foundation to sink. Silt eventually sealed the Outside Canal, and after it had been extended to the north, Wiley put the muddy overflow from San Luis Creek into the canal to hasten that process.

Diversion into the Outside Canal required that water behind the dam be held at a higher elevation so the original dam was replaced in 1898 by a timber dam nearly four hundred feet long with flashboards to control the water level. A fifty-foot section was built as a falling dam for the passage of river traffic, identical in concept to the gate on the first dam. Although reports suggested that boats had passed through, or over, the original dam, river traffic had been effectively barred since 1871, and steamboats only ventured upriver as far as the Miller & Lux Salt Slough warehouse and to Firebaugh during the brief periods when the water was high enough. By 1900 even those visits were rare. Apparently at the urging of Fresno merchants, the federal Rivers and Harbors bill passed in February 1911 authorized a new study of navigation on the San Joaquin River. That spring the 105-foot steamer *J.R. McDonald* headed up the river with a barge in tow to demonstrate the feasibility of navigation to Skaggs Bridge near Fresno. It was a wet year and warm weather rapidly melted the snowpack, sending the river over its banks in places and over the top of the Miller & Lux dam. When the boat reached Firebaugh, canal company superintendent J.F. Clyne took its measurements and went ahead to open the gate at the dam. Hundreds of people watched as the steamer easily passed

---

[122] W.M. Wiley to Ralph L. Milliken, April 5, 1956. The quotation is on page 3.

through the dam and the following day reached Skaggs Bridge. The trip was possible only because the river was in flood and was not repeated.[123]

On a map prepared in 1886, State Engineer William Hammond Hall showed the areas then being irrigated in the San Joaquin Valley. On the San Joaquin & Kings River system there was an extensive section along the river north of Firebaugh that merged with the Miller & Lux Dos Palos Ranch and extended three or four miles from the canal. Other large areas were found in the vicinity of Canal Farm and Badger Flat and from Quinto Creek and Hills Ferry to the end of the canal at Crows Landing.[124]

On the Miller & Lux lands along the river, another irrigation system was evolving. Levees were constructed and gates were installed to manage flow through the sloughs that spread the spring runoff across the company's pastures. By the end of the century there were three such systems along the San Joaquin River. At Poso Slough about eight miles north of Firebaugh a twenty-four-foot wide gate admitted water into a section of slough also known as the Dos Palos Canal. A few miles further downstream Temple Slough had a sixteen-foot culvert-type gate that, like the structure at Poso Slough. also served as a road bridge. Santa Rita Slough did not have a gate but was connected to a ditch that irrigated a few hundred acres at the Santa Rita Ranch. Water running into the sloughs was used in a system of swamp irrigation. Designed to cover a large acreage with minimal scraping, water was directed into natural swales where low embankments had been built to slow and control its progress. The water was kept slowly flowing because if it stagnated in the heat it could kill the grasses it was meant to grow. It was a simple but effective system for growing wild grass on large acreages for grazing or hay production during the spring floods.[125]

Sometimes those floods did not come. Facing a severe drought in 1898, Miller & Lux was forced to drive 10,000 head of cattle north to the Sacramento-

---

[123] Victor M. Cone, *Irrigation in the San Joaquin Valley, California*, U.S. Department of Agriculture, Office of Experiment Stations, Bulletin No. 239 (Washington, D.C.: Government Printing Office, 1911), 40; Report of H.H. Wadsworth in "San Joaquin River, Cal., Up to Herndon," House Document No. 332, 65th Congress, 1st Session, 1917, 24-26; *San Francisco Call*, June 12, June 14, June 15 and June 18, 1911.

[124] California State Engineering Department, *Topographical and Irrigation Map of the San Joaquin Valley*, 1886, Sheets 2 and 3;

[125] Grunsky, *Irrigation Near Merced*, 24; Paul Bailey, "Irrigation Under the San Joaquin and Kings River Canal and Irrigation Company," c. 1908, 4-6.

San Joaquin Delta, where the company leased 30,000 acres of unreclaimed swampland. Some of those animals were lost when rain in the spring of 1899 filled the rivers and flooded the Delta pastures before the herds could be moved back to the west side. Referring to the land between Firebaugh and Newman, Henry Miller observed in 1899 that "Last summer it was all stock and no feed, while this year is all feed and no stock."[126]

The drought came at a time when Miller & Lux was embarking on a program of canal construction. The Colony Main Canal had been built in the early 1890s to the site of the Dos Palos colony, followed by the Outside Canal in 1896-1897. Those canals were part of the San Joaquin & Kings River system, which by 1908 was divided into eight operating sections. Each section had a house for the "section man" in charge of that division of the canal and the houses were connected by a company-owned telephone system. It took about twenty-five men to operate the canal and deliver water to irrigators.[127]

The details concerning many other canals have been largely lost and by the 1930s even Miller & Lux attorneys were forced to rely on the memories of long-time employees to reconstruct the history of the company's irrigation activities. Based on those recollections, it appears that the Central Canal was dug from the Main Canal near Firebaugh about 1900 when the Central Ranch was put under the plow, and to the west the Parsons Ditch was put in at about the same time. The Laguna Canal was built in 1910, enlarging an earlier ditch to Holland Farm. Further north, at least parts of the Riverside and Lucerne canals were in operation by 1903 and they were soon extended. Construction of the Poso Canal seems to have started about 1900 from the Main Canal but details of its construction and its connection to other canals are missing. When a new concrete intake gate for Temple Slough was built in 1911 it included a flume across the top to carry the Poso Canal and allow it to connect to the Riverside-Lucerne system. Meanwhile, a new diversion from Mendota dam—the Helm Canal—had been started in 1906. In 1907 the Helm Canal was connected to the Main Canal at a point downstream from the head of the Outside Canal, in effect increasing the flow in the Main Canal to replace water being diverted to the Outside Canal. In 1917 the Helm Canal was opened to

---

[126] *Pacific Rural Press*, April 23, 1898; *Pacific Rural Press*, July 30, 1898; *Pacific Rural Press*, May 13, 1899; *Pacific Rural Press*, August 26, 1899.
[127] Paul Bailey, "The Canal System of the San Joaquin & Kings River Canal & Irrigation Company." c. 1908, 5.

Firebaugh and connected to the Poso Canal, so that the Poso system of canals serving exclusively Miller & Lux land was linked directly to Mendota Dam. The Helm Canal was soon extended to replace the Main Canal as a source of supply for Parsons Ditch and the Laguna Canal. During the same period, Temple Slough was deepened to serve the Arroyo Canal and a separate network of Miller & Lux canals north and west of the Poso and Dos Palos service areas.[128]

The pace of canal building in the early years of the twentieth century was relentless. In a novel set on a semi-fictional cattle empire on the west side, former Miller & Lux superintendent H.A. Van Coenen Torchiana wrote that, "Making the desert bloom like a rose may sound poetical, but in reality it was a grim business, done in a grim way by grim men."[129] It was a business that tested the endurance of men and animals:

> The sun rose—a ball of fire in the cloudless skies. Soon it beat down mercilessly on sweating men and beasts, and gradually the temperature rose to 110° in the shade—with no shade anywhere.
>
> He could already hear the shouting of the men as they took their teams out to work; they were hitching up—two mules to a sled-scraper, four mules to a fresno-scraper, eight horses to the heavy, breaking plow, twenty horses to an excavator, and then the real work started.
>
> The soil offered a rebellious resistance, never having been broken before; dirt rose in clouds. Now and then a single-tree snapped under the strain of an animal, or a lap ring would suddenly lengthen out or part in the middle, and the men would curse.[130]

That was the hard reality of canal building in the early twentieth century.

Canal construction was also an expensive business. Building a ditch with a thirty-foot bottom capable of carrying water three feet deep cost over $1,000 per mile including board for the men and feed for the horses. After they were built the canals had to be cleaned at about ten-year intervals to remove the accumulated weeds and silt at a cost of about $500 per mile. In 1908 a typical cleaning crew consisted of three New Era wagon loaders as the primary

---

[128] Hammatt, "Report to the San Joaquin River Water Storage District ," 3-4; "Notes on Conference," May 20, 1936; author unknown, "Memorandum of Discussion with Henry Bader, May 21, 1936, at Los Banos," May 21, 1936.

[129] H.A. Van Coenen Torchiana, *California Gringos* (San Francisco: Calif: P. Elder, 1930), 23.

[130] Torchiana, *California Gringos*, 25.

excavators followed by thirty four-horse Fresno scrapers. During the winter Miller & Lux could put up to two hundred men to work on maintenance and repair of the canal system.[131]

According to W.C. Hammatt, the chief engineer for Miller & Lux and the San Joaquin & Kings River Canal & Irrigation Company from 1907 to 1912, the Miller & Lux lands at that time were "operated exclusively as a cattle ranch." The company irrigated thousands of acres of pasture and grew crops of alfalfa and feed grains that supported the livestock enterprise. The development of the canal system after 1900 was accompanied by a gradual expansion of the crop area along the river, while grazing shifted to the poorer alkali soils of the grasslands. The San Luis Canal, which had its head on the Main Canal south of Los Banos, was originally conceived as part of the San Joaquin & Kings River system, but was then extended north to supply the grasslands. The Agatha Canal, built in 1916 from an extension of the Helm Canal, and the Santa Fe Canal served the same purpose. Although a separate corporate entity with other customers, the San Joaquin & Kings River system was closely integrated with the other Miller & Lux canals and with the livestock and farming operations. Surplus water was carried in the Main Canal and discharged for the use of the cattle company through spillways into Los Banos, San Luis and Garzas creeks and through the Camp 13 spillway into Camp 13 Slough. Five spillways (or "outlet canals") in the Outside Canal could transfer water for release through the Main Canal spillways, and irrigation gates in the Outside Canal supplied grazing land between the two canals.[132]

Large quantities of surplus water from the canal and the river were used in an effort to reclaim thousands of acres of nearly worthless "sagebrush alkali." Water was reported to be backed up to the Santa Fe Grade to a depth of two feet in 1894, and "After standing on the land for a few weeks the water is drawn off, carrying with it large quantities of the alkali permeating the soil. Much of the alkali in the soil, too, is forced by the water down to the underlying hardpan and carried off through underground courses."[133] By 1911 it was estimated that 15,000 acres of wild grassland was flooded from the canal and 50,000 acres

[131] Bailey, "The Canal System of the San Joaquin & Kings River Canal & Irrigation Company," 3-4, 9.
[132] W.C. Hammatt to Miller & Lux, Inc., January 2, 1943; W.C. Hammatt, map, "Miller & Lux Grass Land Irrigation as of March 1, 1913," December 31, 1942.
[133] *Pacific Rural Press*, April 21, 1894): 314.

from the river, most of it contributing to alkali removal. The flooding occurred during about two months each year in the spring and early summer when water was available in excess of other irrigation requirements.[134]

The firm of Miller & Lux had escaped the financial carnage that followed Ralston's failure because it had not tied its fortunes to the Bank of California and because even in hard times there was a demand for the company's meat. The partners continued the rapid expansion of their holdings during the 1870s and 1880s, acquiring rangeland in eastern Oregon and northwestern Nevada. In the midst of what appeared to be boundless growth, Charles Lux died on March 15, 1887 at the age of sixty-four. It was soon revealed that the partners had signed an agreement three years earlier stipulating that in case of the death of either of them, the surviving partner would have up to seven years to liquidate the business. Henry Miller was building an empire, and he had no intention of stopping. Lux's widow and a group of "German heirs" took Miller to court to compel him to abide by the terms of the partnership agreement. Settlements were reached, only to be subjected to new legal challenges, and in a long, complicated and contentious process the partnership was turned into a corporation and Henry Miller was eventually able to buy out the Lux heirs. By 1900 Miller & Lux was among the nation's biggest businesses, marshaling the hinterland resources of three states to funnel cattle from Winnemucca, Nevada to a network of San Joaquin Valley ranches from Buena Vista to Orestimba and on to the company's slaughterhouses. And it was not only cattle, but sheep and hogs, too; in 1887, for example, the company herded 140,000 sheep to Firebaugh for shearing. It was an industrial colossus designed to command markets and environments, and nowhere was that more apparent than on the west side of the San Joaquin Valley.[135]

To supply a steady stream of cattle for market, Miller & Lux had to reduce, so far as possible, the risks posed by the natural environments where it operated. Irrigation—the antidote to dry seasons and dry years—was vital to the success of its business. Equally important was the mitigation of legal and political risks by means of litigation, lobbying and alliances. At the intersection of the natural and legal environments was the question of water rights. The

---

[134] Cone, *Irrigation in the San Joaquin Valley*, 40-41; Paul Bailey, "Irrigation Under the San Joaquin and Kings River Canal and Irrigation Company," 4-6.

[135] Igler, *Industrial Cowboys* is an excellent introduction to Miller & Lux as a western business enterprise; *Pacific Rural Press*, April 9, 1887.

control of the water resources that it depended on was so vital that the establishment and protection of water rights became one of the company's greatest and most enduring challenges.

The first and most famous contest was waged on the Kern River. The southernmost of the valley's rivers, the Kern flowed west from the mountains and broke into shifting channels leading to Kern and Buena Vista lakes. Miller & Lux acquired tens of thousands of acres along Buena Vista Slough, which ran north, when there was enough water, from Buena Vista Lake to Tulare Lake. James Ben Ali Haggin, William B. Carr and Lloyd Tevis claimed a much larger tract of land further up the river and began building canals that threatened to cut off water to Miller & Lux's lower lands. California law recognized both riparian rights—the right of property owners along a stream to use the water of the stream—and appropriative rights, a concept born in Gold Rush mining camps that established the right to divert water to lands away from the stream under a "first in time, first in right" priority system. Miller & Lux claimed that their rights as riparian owners on Buena Vista Slough were superior to Haggin's right to appropriate water for his canals. In 1886 the California Supreme Court decided the case of *Lux vs. Haggin* in favor of Miller & Lux and established the primacy of riparian rights. *Lux vs. Haggin* became a landmark in California water law, and for a company that owned over a hundred miles of San Joaquin River frontage it was an immensely valuable decision.[136]

As powerful as the riparian doctrine was, it was not impregnable. A rival diversion that went unchallenged for five years could ripen into a prescriptive right to the detriment of a riparian property owner. For that reason, Miller & Lux was quick to oppose any new project, no matter how small. Plans to develop hydroelectric power, however, presented the company with a conundrum; power projects had to store water to continue operation through the dry season and storing water infringed on downstream riparian rights, but by releasing stored water through their generators later in the year the power companies made more water available for irrigation when it was needed most.[137]

---

[136] The story of *Lux vs. Haggin* and the arguments made by both sides are described in depth in Pisani, *From the Family Farm to Agribusiness*, 191-249 and in Igler, *Industrial Cowboys*, 97-111.
[137] Miller, *Flooding the Courtrooms*, 20-21.

The first powerhouse on the San Joaquin River opened in 1895 but it was a run-of-the-river plant without a storage reservoir and had no effect on riparian rights. The proposed development of a large reservoir on Big Creek was a different matter. Rather than run the risks of litigation, and to avoid presenting itself as an unreasonable opponent of economic development, Miller & Lux chose to negotiate with the power company headed by Los Angeles electric railway magnate Henry E. Huntington. The resulting contract dated August 17, 1906 recognized Miller & Lux's right to all the flow of the San Joaquin River, and acknowledged the value of reservoir releases to the cattle company. The power company agreed to divert water to storage only when the flow in the river at Lone Willow Slough (several miles above Mendota Dam) exceeded 3,000 cubic feet per second, and during the months of November through March storage in excess of specified levels had to be released at the request of Miller & Lux. A similar agreement with the San Joaquin Light & Power Company in 1909 paved the way for construction of a hydroelectric project on the North Fork of the San Joaquin, and later supplemental agreements covered expansion of the Big Creek and North Fork systems.[138]

The contracts with the power companies were a straightforward assertion of riparian rights, but it was more difficult for Miller & Lux to simultaneously defend both the primacy of riparian rights and the appropriative rights of its San Joaquin & Kings River subsidiary. The extent of the canal company's rights was not immediately clear. Bensley's notices of appropriation in June 1871 (one for diversions from the San Joaquin and another for water from the Kings River flowing in Fresno Slough) did not specify an amount of water, and actual diversions included water delivered to Miller & Lux under the cattle company's riparian right. A contract between Miller & Lux and the San Joaquin & Kings River Canal & Irrigation Company in May 1899 recited that Miller & Lux held riparian rights and had permitted the canal company to appropriate 800 second-feet plus an additional 350 second-feet for the Outside Canal. The parties also agreed that Miller & Lux had the right to use any surplus water in the canal free of charge for the irrigation of its pastures. At the same time, James J. Stevinson, a downstream riparian and owner of the East Side Canal, claimed that the canal company's diversions were interfering with his riparian

[138] Miller, *Flooding the Courtrooms*, 21-24; "Agreement between Miller & Lux ... and John S. Eastwood and others," August 17, 1906; agreement, Miller & Lux and others with San Joaquin Light & Power Company, June 14, 1909.

right, and similar issues surfaced in litigation with Jefferson James, a riparian owner on Fresno Slough. In 1905 Stevinson won an injunction limiting the San Joaquin & Kings River appropriative right to only 760 second-feet, setting in motion a quarter-century of litigation. However, long before the Stevinson case was finally settled, the canal company's right was generally recognized to be 1,360 second-feet, consisting of an original right of 760 second-feet plus the full 600 second foot appropriation for the Outside Canal made in 1896.[139]

In the early twentieth century the competition for water in California was increasing, and so were the political and regulatory pressures on Miller & Lux. The reform movement known as Progressivism arrived in California with full force when Hiram Johnson was elected governor in 1910, ushering in a period of intense legislative activity. California's system of water rights had already been harshly criticized for producing such a thicket of litigation that irrigation development had been hobbled and ordinary water users had to fear for the security of their rights. After 1910 efforts were renewed to remake the state's water law and insure management of the resource in the public interest.

As part of the reform agenda, a Conservation Commission headed by former Governor George Pardee was appointed to investigate forestry, water use, reclamation and mining, and to lay the groundwork for new laws. Predictably it called for the reform of water rights. Under the heading "Misuse of Riparian Rights," the commission stated that:

> Neither should the riparian proprietor be permitted to put all his riparian water to an entirely inferior or unnecessary use, to the exclusion of many others who, by appropriation, could put some of it to a far superior use. One large riparian proprietor for instance in the San Joaquin Valley, floods his almost limitless cattle pastures with unnecessarily enormous quantities of water, and does not permit even the excess to be used on the irrigable lands of others, where its use would be of great value to those others and therefore to the State.[140]

---

[139] Miller, *Flooding the Courtrooms*, 68-89; agreement, SJ&KRC&I Co. and Miller & Lux, May 18, 1899; Vincent J. McGovern, "The Water Rights of the San Joaquin Canal Company," May 24, 1953, 3-4; agreement, Miller & Lux, SJ&KRC&I Co., Gravelly Ford Canal Co., San Luis Canal Co., and Panoche Canal Co., June 5, 1915; *Miller & Lux, et.al. vs. James, et.al.*, February 26, 1919, 179 Pacific Reporter, 178; Cone, *Irrigation in the San Joaquin Valley*, 40.
[140] *Report of the Conservation Commission of the State of California* (Sacramento: Superintendent of State Printing, 1912), 28-29.

Accompanied by photographs captioned "Land flooded by waste water, near Los Banos, California" and "Land swamped by waste water from canals in and about Los Banos, Merced County," there could be little doubt as to which riparian proprietor the commission was referring, although Miller & Lux would undoubtedly have countered that the flooding was part of its effort to reclaim alkali land.[141]

An act creating a state water commission with broad authority over the granting of new appropriative rights and containing language that could limit riparian rights passed the legislature in 1913. Miller & Lux and other opponents to the new law forced a referendum the next year but it survived and went into effect in December 1914, creating a distinction between pre-1914 appropriative rights that were not subject to the water commission and post-1914 rights that were.[142]

Hiram Johnson's gubernatorial campaign was centered on opposition to the politically powerful Southern Pacific Railroad, which led in 1911 to the creation of a state Railroad Commission. Among the commission's duties was the regulation of canal companies. The advent of the Railroad Commission and looming water rights reform prompted a reorganization of the Miller & Lux canals and the formation of a new subsidiary, the San Luis Canal Company, in September 1913. It was a mutual water company, which meant that one share of stock was attached to each acre of land, giving the landowners control of their water supply, although in this case the only landowner was Miller & Lux. More importantly, mutual water companies were outside the jurisdiction of the new Railroad Commission. The new company also promptly filed its own notice of appropriation for 1,100 second-feet, a move that was intended to reinforce the water rights of the Miller & Lux system as a whole before the Water Commission Act could take effect. The new company's water would flow through the Helm Canal to the San Luis Canal and into the Santa Fe Lateral Canal, and through other Miller & Lux canals including the Poso, Central and Midway canals. The San Luis Canal Company would pay Miller & Lux to enlarge existing canals or build new ones to deliver the water the mutual company had appropriated. It was, at the time, only a paper

---

[141] *Report of the Conservation Commission,* 27-29.
[142] Pisani, *From the Family Farm to Agribusiness,* 352-371.

company, but it was one of the measures that Miller & Lux employed to protect its rights in the face of mounting legal and political challenges.[143]

Asked in 1912 what the west side needed most, a farmer replied "What we need is for Henry Miller to live ten years more in order that he can build a third canal to run along the foothills. This would open up thousands of acres of the best land we have, which today can only be used for grazing purposes, on account of the lack of water."[144] There would be no third canal; Henry Miller died in San Francisco on October 14, 1916. It had been years since he had been able to visit his ranches in the San Joaquin Valley, but he remained a legendary presence there. His passing, however, was barely noted. The *Pacific Rural Press* surveyed his accomplishments but also felt compelled to acknowledge the widespread criticism of "the concentration of such large land holdings in the hands of a single individual," yet wondered too "whether the land which he controlled would have been better used, or used at all, had he not appeared on the scene."[145] Certainly no one had a greater influence on the development of the west side than Henry Miller, and his legacy would be part of the history of the land, and the water that made it valuable, for decades to come.

---

[143] Miller, *Flooding the Courtrooms*, 114-115; agreement, San Luis Canal Company and Miller & Lux in San Luis Canal Co., "Minutes of the Board of Directors," November 16, 1913.
[144] *Pacific Rural Press*, January 27, 1912.
[145] *Pacific Rural Press*, October 21, 1916.

6

Milk Can Empire

Irrigation was vital to the agricultural development of the west side, but the region was still largely isolated from the markets for its products. Except for wheat that was shipped on river steamers, the grass, alfalfa and feed grains produced with water from the San Joaquin & Kings River canal went into the bellies of cattle that could be herded out of the valley. But the second half of the nineteenth century was the railroad age in America, and the west side needed the kind of connections that only a railroad could provide.

In California the dominant railroad was the Southern Pacific, which had grown from the western arm of the first transcontinental railroad to become a powerful and often reviled transportation monopoly that novelist Frank Norris famously labeled *The Octopus*. In 1870-1871 the railroad was extended down the east side of the San Joaquin Valley. After it reached Los Angeles in 1876, it laid tracks to the Colorado River crossings at Yuma and Needles in an effort to pre-empt those routes and keep competitors out of California. Meanwhile, the Atchison, Topeka & Santa Fe was aggressively pushing westward and when it reached the Pacific coast through Mexico in 1881, it gained the leverage it needed to win a lease of the Needles to Mojave route, and from there it entered Los Angeles in May 1887. The arrival of the Santa Fe touched off a rate war with the Southern Pacific that brought the price of a ticket from Kansas City to Los Angeles down to as little as one dollar and launched a spectacular real estate boom in southern California.

The competition between the Southern Pacific and Santa Fe soon extended to the San Joaquin Valley. Apart from a short-lived proposal for a narrow-gauge line from Antioch to Bakersfield in 1884, plans for a railroad down the west side had languished. That changed in September 1887 when a group of investors led by I.R. Wilbur and A.C. Paulsell incorporated the San Francisco & San Joaquin Valley Railway, and announced plans to build a line from Antioch down the west side, skirting Tulare Lake on its east side and continuing across Tejon Pass to connect to the Santa Fe at Mojave. As John

Bensley had learned, anyone contemplating a route through the west side needed the cooperation of Miller & Lux. The cattle company could benefit from a direct railroad connection to its Nevada range and from the valley to its slaughterhouses in San Francisco, and it willingly granted rights-of-way over its lands. By December 1887, the new railroad had grading crews at work on Miller & Lux land from Dutch Corners, southwest of Hill's Ferry, to White's Bridge on Fresno Slough; the embankment they constructed came to be known as the Santa Fe Grade.[146]

All of that activity forced the Southern Pacific to defend its San Joaquin Valley monopoly by starting work immediately on the extension of its line south from Tracy along the west side, with surveyors, graders and construction crews in the field in November 1887. Again, Miller & Lux made land available for the line. While I.R. Wilbur tried to raise enough money to begin laying track, the Southern Pacific pushed ahead, and for good measure started a new branch down the east side of the valley.[147] The result of this uneven rivalry was soon apparent. The *Los Angeles Herald* observed that "The Wilbur road people must feel very sore at seeing themselves headed off in this fashion, as the Southern Pacific has gridironed the San Joaquin in such a manner that a new line will find it rather hard work to obtain a good stretch of territory."[148] The Southern Pacific had won, and in the process the west side got a railroad.

When the railroad came down the valley, the focus of economic and community life shifted. That happened first at Newman. German-born Simon Newman had arrived in Hill's Ferry in 1869, bought a store and then expanded into farming and stock raising, especially after the San Joaquin & Kings River canal reached the Hill's Ferry area. In time he became a grain merchant and banker, and in later years was involved in businesses as diverse as a pickle and vinegar works in Hayward and the North Alaska Salmon Company. Newman understood that the railroad meant new business opportunities so he gave a tract of land to the Pacific Improvement Company, a subsidiary of the Southern Pacific, to be developed as a town site bearing his name. In April 1888 lots were auctioned and a special train from San Francisco carried prospective buyers. Within months, Simon Newman had a two-story store in the new town

---

[146] *Pacific Rural Press*, February 23, 1884): 11; *Daily Alta California*, September 11, 1887; *Los Angeles Herald*, December 17, 1887.
[147] *Daily Alta California*, November 5, 1887; *Los Angeles Herald*, November 16, 1887.
[148] *Los Angeles Herald*, August 14, 1888.

as businesses and residents abandoned the old river town of Hill's Ferry for life along the railroad. The story was the same in Los Banos. The old Los Banos settlement was well west of the tracks so when the railroad reached the Los Banos area in late 1889 Henry Miller had a new Los Banos surveyed and soon built an impressive brick hotel as well as a store and a bank.[149]

The Southern Pacific laid out stations and towns at intervals along its route but not all succeeded. The Volta Improvement Company recorded a subdivision map in March 1890, only to have their hopes wither when Miller & Lux threw its weight behind the relocated Los Banos.[150] In 1904 a visitor to the Quinto Ranch, which stretched into Santa Clara County, told of departing from the station at Ingomar:

> I consulted my little guide book of the San Joaquin valley and read as follows: "Ingomar. The town is small, but in a rich and thickly populated country."
>
> As we crossed the canal, Harry said, "Just a mile and three-quarters to Ingomar from here."
>
> "Where is the town?" I asked, for I couldn't see any.
>
> "Town!" said Harry, as he turned his face to see whether or not I was in earnest, "Why, they ain't no town, there's only Bradley's store and house and the grain warehouse." And sure enough these and salt grass was all I found.[151]

Further up the line, Linora was another place that never progressed beyond a minor railroad stop.

The tracks were extended south of Los Banos in late 1890, followed in April 1891 by an agreement between Miller & Lux and brothers Bernard and Howard Marks for the development of the Dos Palos Colony. Bernard Marks was an experienced colonizer. He and William S. Chapman had founded the Central Colony just south of the new city of Fresno in 1875, where they sold twenty-acre irrigated farms and planted the grapes that helped launch the raisin industry. At Dos Palos, Marks acquired six sections of some of the first land to be irrigated by the San Joaquin & Kings River canal for $40 per acre

---

[149] Newman Centennial Association, *Chronicle of the Century: Newman, 1888-1988* (1988), 16; *Daily Alta California*, April 12, 1888; *Pacific Rural Press*, November 24, 1888; Outcalt, *History of Merced County*, 369-370; Pimentel, *Dogtown & Ditches*, 26-27, 65.

[150] Outcalt, *History of Merced County*, 369.

[151] *Pacific Rural Press*, July 23, 1904.

with the intention of reselling it as small farms at $60 an acre. For Henry Miller, it was a chance to raise cash to satisfy the claims of the Lux heirs. Settlers were recruited from the Midwest, but when the first ones arrived in Dos Palos in the summer and fall of 1891 they found alkali soil and no usable well water for their homes. Marks hurried back from the Midwest to face the angry buyers who had been lured to California by images of orchards and the promise of productive "white ash" soils. Taking the problem to Henry Miller, Marks was able to arrange an exchange of the original colony tract for pasture land to the north that had never been plowed. The settlers' houses and barns would be moved at Miller & Lux's expense, and Marks would pay the company to build new ditches. The following year more than thirty buildings were moved. Miller also assisted the displaced settlers by providing cows and horses from the Santa Rita ranch; rent for cows was their weaned calves, and the horses could be returned or purchased in installments.[152]

In its new location the colony prospered. By 1898 it was six miles square with a new townsite called Colony Center that boasted a cooperative store and no saloons. About 180 families had come to the colony, mostly from Iowa, Nebraska, Michigan and New York. In typical booster style, Bernard Marks advertised Dos Palos as "the most prosperous population in all California," with superlative advantages in irrigation, fruit, poultry, pork and vegetables. "At this colony," he claimed," you do not risk a dollar in money, a day in time, nor a season in crop." Evidence to support that vision came from the testimony of successful colonists. In one year the sixteen-acre farm of Fred Hadley produced sixty tons of alfalfa hay, two tons of corn, thirty sacks of potatoes on the first crop, plus twelve head of cattle on a three-acre alfalfa field for a total value in excess of $1,500. The story of Mr. Hadley's farm and others like it was clearly told for promotional purposes but it nevertheless provided evidence that the Dos Palos Colony had become an oasis of small diversified farms in the midst of Miller & Lux's vast holdings.[153]

Even more important than the new or relocated towns, the railroad made possible the next phase in the development of irrigated agriculture, the rapid

---

[152] *Daily Alta California*, December 12, 1890; Pisani, *From the Family Farm to Agribusiness*, 122-123; Manuscript by Frank Marks furnished to Ralph L. Milliken, February 15, 1954; "Reminiscences of Chance Waggoner" in Ralph L. Milliken, "Notes for History of Dos Palos."
[153] *Pacific Rural Press*, November 19, 1898; The quotation is found in an advertisement titled "Dos Palos Colony, Most Prosperous Population in California," *Pacific Rural Press*, May 13, 1899; *Pacific Rural Press*, January 7, 1899.

growth of the dairy industry that transformed the economy of the territory served by the San Joaquin & Kings River canal. Among the pioneer dairymen was Swiss immigrant Peter Giavannoni who was working at a dairy in San Jose when C.C. Crow and his father asked him to set up a commercial dairy on their Crows Landing farm. It was, at the time, a novel enterprise for the San Joaquin Valley, where the limited dairy production was consumed locally and cows were milked only when their calves were by their sides. The partnership of Giavannoni and Crow was established in 1890 along with the Orestimba Cheese Ranch, and starting with just a few cows they had over three hundred in 1893. In 1892, Giavannoni and his brothers built a dairy of their own on 160 acres in the Cottonwood area where they installed the first cream separating machine in the region. It had long been assumed that the valley's hot climate would make large-scale dairying impossible, but improvements in refrigeration and processing machinery began to change that perception. The first creamery on the west side, the New Era, went into operation south of Newman in August 1895 and proved that good quality butter could be produced in the valley.[154]

Irrigated alfalfa, a crop grown under the canal since 1872, was the foundation of the burgeoning dairy industry in the San Joaquin Valley. The severe drought of 1898 had provided a critical test. Although Miller & Lux had been forced to move thousands of cattle to the Delta in search of pasture, the San Joaquin & Kings River canal had not dramatically curtailed deliveries. As one correspondent reported in 1899:

> The experience of last year is urging forward all effort to get in as large an area of alfalfa as possible this spring. Four cuttings last summer and fall from land seeded in the spring gave farmers hay to sell when everybody wanted it and the return was large. All the year shipments of cattle and hay from Los Banos continued and did much to help the State through the most depressing season it has ever experienced.[155]

Coastal pastures dried out, forcing some dairymen there to sell their herds to valley farmers. The industry was now shifting inland and expanding rapidly.[156]

---

[154] Outcalt, *History of Merced County,* 479-482; *Pacific Rural Press,* June 11, 1898; *Transactions of the California State Agricultural Society for the Year 1904* (Sacramento: W.W. Shannon, Superintendent State Printing, 1905), 130-131.
[155] *Pacific Rural Press,* March 4, 1899.
[156] *Pacific Rural Press,* November 11, 1899.

In the spring of 1899, the creameries at Newman and Los Banos were "distributing money in considerable quantities among the hundreds of owners of small herds which furnish the material for manufacture. All through the vicinities of these creameries there is activity, extension of herds, improvements of homes, increased area of alfalfa and progressive enterprise and development."[157] Thousands of acres were ready to be seeded to alfalfa, some under the recently opened Outside Canal. By 1903, 15,000 pounds of butterfat per month were shipped by rail from Los Banos and Dos Palos to processing plants in San Francisco and Oakland. The previous year, Miller & Lux had reportedly sold more than a hundred farms averaging twenty acres in size in the Dos Palos colony, with most of the acreage going into dairies.[158]

The town of Gustine was itself a product of the dairy boom. Located on Miller & Lux land about five miles south of Newman, it began in 1890 as a railroad siding for the shipment of cattle. Its name honored Henry Miller's daughter Sara Alice, or "Gussie," who had died in a childhood riding accident. In 1906 Henry Miller donated land to the New Era creamery, which wanted to relocate to the railroad at Gustine where it was also better able to dispose of its wastewater. The townsite was laid out by Miller & Lux later that year, and lots were auctioned in 1907. It was a Miller & Lux town; the company owned a general merchandise store, butcher shop, lumberyard and bank, and ran the water and sewer system. By 1909, the new town also had a hotel and a newspaper. In 1912 it was estimated that Gustine was surrounded by 18,000 acres of alfalfa and 12,000 cows on farms ranging from thirty to six hundred acres. The ratio of one and a half acres per cow seems to have been common.[159]

Many of the dairies were leased to tenants, and by one estimate three-quarters of the dairymen were Portuguese or Swiss. Farm practices differed, but all relied on alfalfa—fed green or grazed, and stored as hay or silage. Seventy percent of the land irrigated from the San Joaquin & Kings River system was devoted to alfalfa, although some of that was grown by Miller & Lux for beef cattle at places like the 1,240-acre Grove Farm near Gustine.

[157] *Pacific Rural Press*, March 4, 1899.
[158] *Pacific Rural Press*, November 11, 1899; *Pacific Rural Press*, February 21, 1903.
[159] *Pacific Dairy Review* 10 (July 12, 1906): 11; Outcalt, *History of Merced County*, 372; "Gustine History," Gustine Historical Society, http://www.gustinehistoricalsociety.org/Gustinehistory.html; *Pacific Rural Press*, November 16, 1912; J.W. Nelson, et.al., *Reconnoissance Soil Survey of the Lower San Joaquin Valley*, U.S. Department of Agriculture, Bureau of Soils (Washington, D.C.: Government Printing Office, 1918), 28.

Foxtail, an otherwise difficult weed, was also used as feed. Near Gustine, P.W. Daly insisted that cows actually preferred foxtail silage to alfalfa, so "the first or the 'foxtail crop' of alfalfa becomes, by the use of the silo, the best instead of the worst of the alfalfa cuttings."[160]

At first the west side creameries received whole milk and processed it on the premises, but by 1912 the New Era Creamery, with a new brick building and now leased to the Dairy Delivery Company of San Francisco, was the only one still producing butter and there was just one cheese factory. Instead cream was separated at the dairy and was delivered to receiving stations along the railroad for pasteurization and shipment to plants in the Bay Area, shifting more of the responsibility for sanitary handling to the farmer. Sweet cream, described as "a fine article for city consumption," brought a higher price than churning cream used for butter manufacturing, and encouraged even greater dairy development. At Gustine in 1912 there were seven creamery companies competing for the supply of cream, picked up from the farm each morning or sometimes twice a day in hot weather.[161]

The ten-gallon milk can was emblematic of the dairy age on the west side. It was used to haul milk or separated cream from farms to processing plants in the railroad towns, and pasteurized cream in those cans was loaded onto express freight cars bound for the Bay Area. In 1908 daily shipments of 150 cans of cream were made from Los Banos, and over 200 cans per day left Gustine in 1912, a more than ten-fold increase from just four years earlier with a total value of $1,000,000 to local farmers. Land suitable for alfalfa was in demand; the Sullivan Tract just west of Gustine was described as "an ideal dairy section" when it was subdivided into farms of twenty to forty acres or more in 1915. Five years later, W.E. Bunker sold forty-five acres of land in alfalfa for the remarkable price of $1,000 per acre.[162]

By 1917 dairy processing began to return to the valley to take advantage of the unused skim milk left behind by the sweet cream trade. In that year plants producing casein (used in making glues and varnishes) and sugar of milk (a

---

[160] *Pacific Rural Press*, January 27, 1912; *Pacific Rural Press*, July 23, 1904; The quotation is from *Pacific Rural Press*, November 16, 1912.

[161] *Pacific Rural Press*, January 27, 1912; *Pacific Rural Press*, November 2, 1912; *Pacific Rural Press*, November 16, 1912.

[162] *Pacific Rural Press*, July 25, 1908; *Pacific Rural Press*, November 16, 1912; *Gustine Standard*, January 8, 1915; *Pacific Rural Press*, October 16, 1920.

by-product of the casein process used in medicines) were built in Gustine and Crows Landing, with another in 1922. Also in 1922, the National Ice Cream Company built a plant in Newman. The Carnation Milk Products Company opened a $250,000 condensed milk plant in Gustine in 1920, producing a product that was barely known twenty years earlier.[163]

In the early decades of the twentieth century, alfalfa covered about three-quarters of the roughly 100,000 acres irrigated by the canal company, however in a notable departure from the forage and grain economy, Miller & Lux began to introduce new crops. In 1915 the company had 1,000 acres of rice at the Holland Ranch near Dos Palos, where it grew successfully on alkali soils in rotation with barley. At the same time, cotton became a commercial crop, as shown by a report that five tractors were plowing ground for cotton at Oxalis, along the canal between Dos Palos and Firebaugh. Orchards, which were often associated with irrigation development, remained a rarity on the west side. Miller & Lux had fruit trees at some their main ranch headquarters for their own use, and had planted olive trees near Central Point in the 1880s and sent olive oil to Merced County's first State Fair exhibit in 1889. Farmers grew English walnuts on a few acres near Gustine, and the massive size of some of the trees suggested that the soil was well suited to tree crops; the canopy of one specimen on the Brughelli farm measured eighty feet in diameter and there were other large trees on the F.E. Bunker ranch next door. By the 1920s the Gustine Orchard Company was growing walnuts, almonds, grapes and figs on 131 acres.[164]

In the summer of 1920 a passenger riding a train down the Southern Pacific's west side line witnessed the results of a fifty-year transformation of the region. The dry and empty plains that greeted William Brewer had been replaced by fields of alfalfa extending for miles along the tracks, punctuated by farmhouses, barns and silos. The towns had an air of progress about them; a sense of a quickened pace of life. Visible too were the well-managed irrigated

[163] *Pacific Rural Press*, July 7, 1917; *Hearings Before the Committee on Finance, United States Senate on the Proposed Tariff Act of 1921* (Washington, D.C., Government Printing Office, 1922), 2803-2804; *Pacific Rural Press*, March 18, 1922; "News of Milk Plants ...," *The Creamery and Milk Plant Monthly* 9 (March 1920): 39; *Pacific Rural Press*, March 11, 1922.

[164] "San Joaquin & Kings River Canal & Irrigation Co. vs. Madera Irrigation District, Plaintiff's Opening Brief, Part 1—The Facts" (undated), 44-45; "Rice--Its Status in the San Joaquin Valley," *San Joaquin Light & Power Magazine* 3, no. 8 (1915): 409, 413-417; *Pacific Rural Press*, March 30, 1918; *Pacific Rural Press,* April 15, 1922; *Pacific Rural Press,* January 7, 1893; *Pacific Rural Press,* October 12, 1889.

farms and pastures of the world's largest and most diversified livestock and meat company. The once competing visions of Henry Miller and William C. Ralston had been realized, and the modern west side had been born. Maturity, however, was not the end of the story. The fortunes of the farmers and the canal company were intertwined, and in the coming decades that relationship would be repeatedly tested.

7

The Big District

Following the defeat of the West Side Irrigation District at the hands of Miller & Lux, efforts to establish irrigation districts in California languished for almost ten years until the idea was revived by the passage of the Wright Act in March 1887. Enthusiasm for irrigation had been growing in the territory along the Tuolumne River, and in 1886 voters sent Modesto attorney C.C. Wright to Sacramento pledged to introduce an irrigation district bill. Despite opposition from Miller & Lux and other large landowners, Wright's bill sailed through the Assembly without a dissenting vote and won easy approval in the Senate. The act applied to any area that could be irrigated by a single system and on the petition of fifty property owners a county Board of Supervisors could hold hearings, adjust boundaries and call an election. Formation of an irrigation district required a two-thirds majority of all eligible voters, and once organized, it had the power to issue bonds, condemn property and water rights and collect a tax on all land and improvements in the district. By making all residents—not just landowners or irrigators—eligible to vote and by taxing all property, the Wright Act recognized that irrigation was a community benefit, and made water a community rather than a private resource.[165]

In June 1888, only weeks after the state supreme court had validated the Wright Act in a test case brought by the Turlock Irrigation District, an effort was made to revive the West Side Irrigation District as a Wright Act district. At a meeting in Hills Ferry, sentiment clearly favored the Wright Act and steps were taken to begin the organization process. Plans were soon drawn up for a diversion from the San Joaquin River twenty-three miles upstream from the canal company's dam at Mendota and for a canal that would initially run southwest to tap a branch of the Kings River before swinging north near Summit Lake to follow the line of William Hammond Hall's 1876 survey for a high-line route to Tracy. In early August a large crowd heard C.C. Wright

---

[165] Pisani, *From the Family Farm to Agribusiness*, 251-255; Alan M. Paterson, *Land, Water and Power: A History of the Turlock Irrigation District, 1887-1987* (Glendale, CA, The Arthur H. Clark Co., 1987): 53-58.

enthusiastically endorse the 250,000-acre district, and a committee was appointed to finalize its boundaries. Once again, however, great hopes came down to nothing more than meetings and oratory.[166]

It may be that the failure to organize a new district on the west side was a blessing in disguise. Only a handful of the forty-nine districts formed under the Wright Act succeeded, and then only after enduring legal and financial challenges. Many districts were poorly conceived and some were nothing more than the work of speculators who wanted to make a quick profit from the sale of overvalued water rights or the promise of irrigated land. A sad case in point was the Sunset Irrigation District, which covered a narrow strip of land from Mendota south to Tulare Lake. The territory was virtually uninhabited so promoters had to give away small acreages just to get enough residents to sign the petition and then approve a large bond issue, the proceeds of which benefitted only the district's backers. Legitimate problems as well as outright frauds like the Sunset district prompted the legislature to repeal the Wright Act in 1897 and put in its place an irrigation district law that established much higher barriers to district formation, so high in fact that no additional districts were organized until 1909. By that time it had become clear that public districts had an important role to play in California irrigation development. In 1911 a state Irrigation District Bond Commission was established to certify the bonds of districts judged to be feasible by the state engineer, providing a measure of state oversight and paving the way for a rapid expansion of irrigation district activity.[167]

While controversy swirled around the Wright Act districts, the west side witnessed the beginning of a protracted contest between the canal company and its customers over the cost of water. It started in Stanislaus County, at the northern end of the canal system where the influence of Miller & Lux was weakest. In 1893 Thomas Crow successfully challenged the canal company's right to charge for surplus or "waste" water used for irrigation. In cooperation with E.S. Wangenheim, the managing partner of the Simon Newman Company, Crow founded a Water Users Association to push for lower rates. When the canal company refused a request for reduced rates, the consumers

---

[166] *Pacific Rural Press*, July 7, 1888; *Pacific Rural Press*, August 18, 1888.
[167] Pisani, *From the Family Farm to Agribusiness*, 266-278, 353-356; Frank Adams, *Irrigation Districts in California, 1887-1915*, California Department of Engineering, Bulletin No. 2 (1916), 36-37.

took their complaint to the Stanislaus County Board of Supervisors, which had authority under an 1885 statute to set irrigation rates. The supervisors conducted a hearing and lowered the alfalfa rate from $2.50 per acre to $1.50. Miller & Lux fought back by filing suit in federal court alleging that the county, and the 1885 state law, had violated the Constitution's contract clause and the protection of property provided by the Fourteenth Amendment.

The company's contract argument hinged on an 1862 California law, in effect at the time the canal was built, that dictated that rates be based on "the capital actually invested" rather than the 1885 requirement that rates should reflect the value of property "actually used in and useful to" irrigation deliveries. The canal company listed a book value of one million dollars for its assets, but Stanislaus County engineers had calculated the actual value at about one-third of that amount. In 1904 the U.S. Supreme Court ruled that the 1862 law did not constitute a contract and had been superseded by the 1885 statute. In regard to the applicable value of the canal company's property, the decision cited the company's own minutes in which "a shareholder said there had been a waste in the management of the affairs of the company amounting to $350,000, which was caused by the chief engineer who had been in charge of the canal, and that his mistakes had cost the company a good deal of money. There would seem to have been more of a dispute as to who was responsible for this loss than over the fact of the loss." That finding verified the opinion of observers like James Schuyler that the canal's original cost had been excessive. The Court found no reason to intervene and Stanislaus County's rate was allowed to stand.[168]

The Supreme Court did leave a significant loophole in its decision; if the combined rates in the three counties served by the canal returned less than the minimum 6 percent required by the 1885 law the canal company could renew its attack on Stanislaus County. Although it had originally had a single rate structure for the entire system, Miller & Lux now concluded that rates should reflect the cost of service to the point of delivery, which meant that consumers closer to the headworks at Mendota should pay less than those further away. At the company's suggestion, Merced and Fresno counties reduced their rates, and pushed the total rate of return to under 6 percent. When Stanislaus County

---

[168] Miller, *Flooding the Courtrooms*, 46-50; *San Francisco Call*, October 21, 1896; *County of Stanislaus v. San Joaquin & Kings River Canal & Irrigation Co.*, 192 US 201, the quoted passage is on page 214.

predictably refused to grant the canal company's request for an increase to $2.25 per acre, the stage was set for another legal contest. This time the canal company claimed that its water rights were part of its property and had a monetary value that had to be added to the cost of its physical properties when calculating rates. Before that concept could be fully tested a fresh controversy broke out between the canal company and its customers.[169]

After it got an injunction in 1908 suspending the new county rates the canal company imposed an entirely different rate structure based on the amount of water actually used. Under annual per-acre pricing irrigators had had no incentive to conserve water but with its diversions restricted to 760 second-feet by the Stevinson injunction the canal company had good reason to want to eliminate waste and inefficient use. And water had not been used carefully. Farmers commonly reduced the number of field ditches by running water from one check to another before draining off the excess water ponded in the upper checks. To enforce greater efficiency the company defined a flow of one second foot for a twenty-four-hour period (equivalent to just under two acre-feet) as the unit of measurement, and priced it at $1.25 in Fresno County, $1.90 in Merced County and $2.35 in Stanislaus County. Irrigators did become more careful in their water use and some put in additional ditches to improve the distribution of water but as the cost of irrigation increased, sometimes significantly, more and more of the company's customers joined the Water Users Association. Farmers, especially those in Fresno and Merced counties whose rates had actually been reduced during the legal battle with Stanislaus County, became increasingly suspicious of the company.[170]

Angry water users appealed to the counties to reimpose acreage-based rates and by July 1911 all three had enacted new rates; Stanislaus County even increased its rate to $2.00 per acre, although that still fell short of what the canal company wanted. Federal Judge William Morrow rejected the canal company's arguments on the valuation of its water rights in September 1911 and lifted the injunction against county rates. Determined to pursue the issue,

[169] Miller, *Flooding the Courtrooms*, 50-55.

[170] Miller, *Flooding the Courtrooms*, 58-59; F.W. Roeding and Samuel Fortier, *Irrigation in California*, U.S. Department of Agriculture, Office of Experiment Stations, Bulletin No. 237, (Washington, D.C.: Government Printing Office, 1913), 56; Bailey, "Irrigation Under the San Joaquin and Kings River Canal and Irrigation Company," 7-8; Cone, *Irrigation in the San Joaquin Valley*, 41. Cone cited slightly different rates of $1.10, $1.75 and $2.25 in Fresno, Merced and Stanislaus counties respectively.

the company appealed the decision and the rate case was once again before the U.S. Supreme Court. This time the company was successful. The Court ruled in 1914 that the canal company did own water rights and those rights had a value that had to be recognized. By 1914 rate-making authority had shifted from the counties to the state Railroad Commission, and the canal company then dropped its efforts to charge for measured use and petitioned the commission for rates of $1.25 and $1.75 per acre in Fresno and Merced counties, respectively, which were the same rates that those counties had adopted in 1911. In Stanislaus County it requested a rate of $2.25 per acre, which the commission denied when more than thirty irrigators protested. The Railroad Commission reversed its decision the following year when the company was able to show that all consumers in Stanislaus County had actually signed contracts at the $2.25 per acre rate. By 1915 rates were lower than they had been ten years earlier but the canal company had established important legal principles.[171]

The furor over the canal company's abrupt and unpopular change to volumetric rates in 1908 led to a revival of interest in a public irrigation district. Congressman J.C. Needham, for example, proposed having the U.S. Geological Survey plan an extension of the canal into San Joaquin County, and he urged the establishment of a Wright Act district that could condemn and purchase the San Joaquin & Kings River canal system. In early 1911 reports surfaced of plans for a massive district from Summit Lake to Tracy; plans that Miller & Lux attorney E.F. Treadwell dismissed as unnecessary. A few months later, meetings were held from Mendota to Crows Landing to consider formation of a 370,000-acre district. All of these irrigation district proposals were vague and short-lived and are important only as evidence of a simmering distrust of Miller & Lux and its canal company.[172]

Irrigation district activity intensified in 1918 when plans were unveiled for the organization of a district of over 426,000 acres that included extensive areas of dry land north of Crows Landing as well as the Stevinson colony on the east side of the San Joaquin River. That proposal was quickly defeated when canal

---

[171] Miller, *Flooding the Courtrooms*, 47, 59-66; *San Joaquin & Kings River Canal & Irrigation Co. vs. Stanislaus County*, *233 us 454*; Railroad Commission of the State of California (hereafter cited as Railroad Commission), Decision 2022, December 22, 1914; Railroad Commission, Decision 2657, August 3, 1915.
[172] *Pacific Rural Press*, June 5, 1909; *San Francisco Call*, January 22, 1911; *San Francisco Call*, February 12, 1911; *San Francisco Call*, February 12, 1911; *Pacific Rural Press*, July 1, 1911.

company superintendent J.F. Clyne orchestrated a campaign to convince existing San Joaquin & Kings River customers that a district would saddle them with higher bills. Opposition also arose to the proposed expansion of the canal's service area that would have the effect of spreading an already limited summer water supply across a greater acreage to the detriment of its current users. [173]

Revisions to the irrigation district law soon set the stage for a more serious challenge to Miller & Lux. In 1919 the legislature passed a bill authored by Senator J.L.C. Irwin of Hanford to substantially loosen the requirements for organizing an irrigation district. While a petition for the formation of a district had formerly needed the signatures of a majority of the landowners representing a majority of the assessed value, it would now require only the names of five hundred residents with twenty percent of the assessed value, and instead of a two-thirds vote of eligible electors a district could now be formed on a simple majority vote.[174] Miller & Lux attorney Edward F. Treadwell feared that "The formation of these districts is likely to ruin the company. They can be formed without the company, and when formed will be governed irrespective of it."[175] Opponents forced a referendum on the law, which suspended its operation until the November 1920 general election. The same legislative session also approved the California Irrigation District Act, which provided for an entirely different kind of irrigation district; one in which acres rather than people voted.

On November 5, 1919 members of the Cottonwood Farm Center (part of the local Farm Bureau) voted to pursue the formation of an irrigation district and named a five-man committee to meet with a similar committee from Dos Palos. Their intention was to take over the San Joaquin & Kings River canals and "probably extending the system into a storage proposition."[176] At the same time, Miller & Lux took advantage of the new California Irrigation District Act to set up the Western Irrigation District; a district with boundaries drawn to include mainly Miller & Lux land. The district was one of several set up by the

[173] Miller, *Flooding the Courtrooms*, 125-126, Paul E. Vandor, *History of Fresno County, California, with Biographical Sketches of the the Leading Men and Women of the County Who have been Identified with its Growth and Development from the Early Days to the Present* (Los Angeles: Historic Record Company, 1919), 437-438.
[174] Miller, *Flooding the Courtrooms*, 126; *Gustine Standard*, May 30, 1919.
[175] Edward F. Treadwell to J.F. Clyne, May 20, 1919, in Miller, *Flooding the Courtrooms*, p. 126-127.
[176] *Gustine Standard*, November 7, 1919.

corporation to obstruct Wright Act districts, and the move took local irrigation district advocates by surprise. When the organizing committee for the new irrigation district met in Los Banos in early December they were faced with the choice of trying to join the Miller & Lux district or forming an independent and overlapping district. A vote of those in attendance favored a Wright Act district, although observers noted that about a third of the group abstained. It was reported that "There was no animosity expressed toward the Canal Company or Miller & Lux, on the contrary there were many expressions of friendliness towards the big corporation which has developed the West Side by their energy and far seeing capability, but the irrigators of the West Side feel that a new condition is arising which they must meet and solve for their best interests."[177] The "new condition" facing the irrigation district committee was a heightened concern over the adequacy of their water supply at a time when farmers in other parts of the valley were increasing their irrigated acreage and planning storage reservoirs to insure more reliable summer irrigation. The Western Irrigation District only added to their unease; as the *Gustine Standard* put it, "Miller & Lux have always taken care of them [local irrigators], and perhaps Miller & Lux always will, but they don't know that for a certainty."[178]

The circulation of petitions for the formation of the West Joaquin Irrigation District began in January 1920. The district would cover about 208,000 acres of the land irrigated from the San Joaquin & Kings River system, which the new district would have to acquire, by condemnation if necessary. At the same time, W.E. Bunker and A.P. Miller, acting as trustees for the proposed district, filed a water right application claiming 2,500 second-feet for direct diversion and 400,000 acre-feet of storage at a still undetermined location.[179] Miller & Lux reacted angrily, sending a circular letter to canal company customers claiming, among other things, that "for years we have been practically GIVING water to the consumers of the company" and threatening to raise rates if an irrigation district was formed.[180] In reply, the local committee reiterated that "We are seeking no quarrel with the canal company or Miller & Lux. ... But the prosperity and development of the West

---

[177] *Gustine Standard*, December 12, 1919.
[178] *Gustine Standard*, November 21, 1919.
[179] *Gustine Standard*, January 9, 1920; State Water Commission, Application No. 1638, received January 21, 1920.
[180] *Gustine Standard*, March 5, 1920.

Side require a better water supply, and if the company will not provide it for us, we believe we have a right to get it for ourselves."[181] In August Miller & Lux won an injunction preventing the filing of the West Joaquin district petition with the Merced County Board of Supervisors because the district overlapped the corporation's Western Irrigation District. The victory was short-lived, however, because the California Irrigation District Act was overturned by the state supreme court and the Miller & Lux districts formed under it were dissolved.[182]

With their plan to use company-controlled irrigation districts as protection against Wright Act districts defeated, Miller & Lux opened negotiations with backers of the West Joaquin district. Bunker and Joseph Pfitzer met with Miller & Lux president J. Leroy Nickel, and there were legal discussions between Edward F. Treadwell and irrigation district attorney A.L. Cowell. Miller & Lux was now promoting a larger district that would include all of the company's west side acreage, but Treadwell insisted that it be controlled by landowners. Until the details could be worked out, Miller & Lux urged that the process of forming the West Joaquin district be halted. While proponents were willing to defer briefly, they soon decided to push ahead, bolstered by confirmation of the Irwin bill, under which the West Joaquin district would be organized, at the November 1920 election. Miller & Lux filed a series of legal motions to impede the process, joined by the Southern Pacific Railroad, which sought, like Miller & Lux, to have its property excluded from the district. By the end of 1921, the legal maneuvers had been rejected, and Miller & Lux was once again forced to bargain.[183]

The big cattle company was still a force to be reckoned with on the west side but its wealth and power were declining. Miller & Lux had risen to prominence in a regional market isolated from potential competitors in the east and midwest. The wall of distance that separated Miller & Lux from the rest of the country was first breached in 1890 when the American Cattle Trust, a combination of powerful Chicago packinghouses, bought the Baden estate from Charles Lux's widow. The trust then established the Western Meat Company and built a modern slaughterhouse and processing plant that could

---

[181] *Gustine Standard,* March 5, 1920.
[182] *Gustine Standard,* August 6, 1920.
[183] *Gustine Standard,* September 24, 1920, October 8, 1920, June 10, 1921, December 9, 1921.

challenge Miller & Lux for dominance on the west coast. Henry Miller fought back by organizing the San Francisco meatpackers and launching a surprisingly successful propaganda campaign against the supposed dangers of the refrigerated technology used at the Baden plant. The Western Meat Company nevertheless made inroads into Miller & Lux's markets, and its plant survived the 1906 earthquake and fire that destroyed Miller & Lux's bay-side facility. Although it rebuilt using the same modern technology it had been criticizing, Miller & Lux found compliance with the increasing federal regulation of meatpacking costly, and continued to lose market share to the better capitalized eastern packers.[184]

The company's stock raising empire fared no better. Improved transcontinental rail service made it cheaper for Miller & Lux to import grain-fattened midwestern hogs and cattle than to raise cattle on grass and alfalfa maintained by costly irrigation systems; by 1913 eastern meat made up more than half of Miller & Lux's business. In 1913, too, a change in tariff policy allowed cheap Australian refrigerated beef to enter west coast markets, and the price of cattle fell. Facing declining revenues, Miller & Lux reduced wages, laid off workers and cut back on its irrigation construction program. Wages rose in the manpower shortage during World War I followed by a drop in commodity prices during the agricultural depression that followed the war, squeezing Miller & Lux even more. Increasingly dependent on borrowed money for its operations, the company had no choice but to begin selling land; in January 1920, for example, surveyors were at work on the subdivision of a 9,000-acre tract near Dos Palos. Land and water were becoming the company's most important assets.[185]

In its negotiations with the West Joaquin district Miller & Lux had a new tool: a 1921 law authorizing the formation of water storage districts. This new type of district had several features that appealed to Miller & Lux. It was controlled by landowners, with one vote for each $100 in assessed valuation, and landowners did not have to live in the district to vote. Unlike an irrigation district, in which costs were spread evenly across all property in the district, taxes in a water storage district could vary in proportion to the benefits received by different parts of the district. Finally, a water storage district

---

[184] Igler, *Industrial Cowboys*, 159-169.
[185] Igler, *Industrial Cowboys*, 180; Miller, *Flooding the Courtrooms*, 119-121; *Pacific Rural Press*, January 3, 1920.

dominated by Miller & Lux could purchase the company's canals and water rights, providing much needed cash without actually surrendering control of those rights. In January 1922, J. Leroy Nickel told a meeting in Gustine that he had previously opposed any organization that could take Miller & Lux water or water rights but that he had been wrong, and he now saw the necessity of a district big enough to build the storage that the west side needed. Although Miller & Lux would be able to control a water storage district, company attorney Treadwell assured the farmers that Miller & Lux would choose three directors, the other landowners could choose three and the six directors would jointly choose the seventh.[186]

The West Joaquin organizers were clearly interested in the proposition because storage was one of their primary goals and they realized that Miller & Lux would continue to do everything it could to defeat or delay a Wright Act district. Moving fast, Miller & Lux hired W.F. Hume to organize a publicity campaign for "the big district" and petitions for its formation began circulating immediately. The proposed district would include the territory served by the San Joaquin & Kings River system, the San Luis Canal Company, the Firebaugh Canal Company, the Gravelly Ford Canal Company and other Miller & Lux canals. E.S. Wangenheim wanted to include the dry land in the southern part of the proposed West Stanislaus Irrigation District near Crows Landing, but Nickel distrusted Wangenheim and wanted to present an uncomplicated proposal for approval by the state engineer. A petition for the formation of the West Side Water Storage District was filed in April and that summer preliminary hearings were held in Los Banos and the state engineer began a study of its engineering and financial feasibility.[187]

Another irrigation district dispute broke out east of the San Joaquin River where Miller & Lux had been locked in an on-and-off battle with Madera County irrigators for more than thirty years. The first incarnation of the Madera Irrigation District was organized in 1888 but it faced such stubborn opposition from large landowners including Miller & Lux that it was dissolved

[186] Pisani, *From the Family Farm to Agribusiness*, 390-391; Miller, *Flooding the Courtrooms*, 131-133; *Gustine Standard*, January 6, 1922, January 13, 1922.

[187] Miller, *Flooding the Courtrooms*, 133-134; *Gustine Standard*, January 6, 1922, January 13, 1922, January 27, 1922, February 24, 1922; W.C. Hammatt, "Map of West Side Storage District Showing Areas Under Various Sources of Supply," May 1922; *Report of the Department of Public Works of the State of California, First Biennial Report*, November 1, 1922 (Sacramento, California State Printing Office, 1922), p. 26.

in 1896, and diversions by the Madera Canal & Irrigation Company from the Fresno River became the target of Miller & Lux litigation in the early twentieth century. As irrigation development in California intensified, a new Madera Irrigation District was proposed, and in 1916 its promoters applied for storage rights on the San Joaquin River at the Friant dam site. Miller & Lux initially explored cooperation with the Madera district on the storage project but in the end it remained fundamentally opposed to any interference with its water rights and to the potential tax burden on the company's lands that were inside district boundaries. As it did west of the river, Miller & Lux set up its own irrigation districts in 1919 to frustrate the establishment of a Wright Act district. The Madera Irrigation District was organized in 1920, and quickly won the backing of sympathetic state officials for its plans to utilize the waters of the San Joaquin River for crops rather than the flooding of pastures. Fighting back, Miller & Lux filed numerous suits to stop preliminary work on the dam and to challenge the legitimacy of district assessments and other actions. Litigation notwithstanding, there was considerable interest, both publicly and privately, in reaching a settlement, and on September 7, 1922 Miller & Lux, the Madera Irrigation District and the committee of the proposed West Side Water Storage District signed a memorandum of agreement to resolve their differences and proceed with the development of the Friant project.[188]

The way to bring the parties together was to create an even bigger water storage district. The San Joaquin River Water Storage District would include all of the land in the West Side Water Storage District and the part of the Madera Irrigation District south of the Chowchilla River that was determined to be "susceptible to economical irrigation" by surveyors chosen by Miller & Lux and the irrigation district. The district would be governed by a nine-member board, and following the pattern established with the West Side district, Miller & Lux would choose four of the directors and Nickel, the company's president, became president of the storage district board. The state engineer had to approve the formation of the district, and although Nickel wanted to move quickly, State Engineer W.F. McClure balked. Although presumably neutral, McClure had been an ally of the Madera district, and he and Nickel regarded each other with mutual suspicion. McClure thought the

---

[188] Adams, *Irrigation Districts in California*, 25-27; Miller, *Flooding the Courtrooms*, 24-30, 124-129, 134-135; *Pacific Rural Press*, March 25, 1922.

proposed 933,000-acre district was too big and that it contained too much alkali and hardpan land that could not benefit from irrigation. Miller & Lux agreed to remove a substantial acreage of its least productive land, and the formation of a 549,000-acre district was approved in November 1923.[189]

Now began the hard work of determining exactly which properties and rights the water storage district would buy from Miller & Lux and how much they were worth. The task initially fell to Harry Barnes, the engineer for the Madera Irrigation District who became the engineer for the water storage district, and Miller & Lux consulting engineer W.C. Hammatt. To make a detailed appraisal two other engineers were hired, Fred H. Tibbetts for Miller & Lux and Augustus Kempkey for the water storage district, and not surprisingly their valuations reflected the interests of their clients. Although significant issues remained to be settled, the water storage district board informally submitted a plan to the state engineer on May 22, 1925 and McClure rejected it a week later. S.T. Harding, a consulting engineer who worked closely with McClure, promptly undertook an examination of the flaws in the district's plan.[190]

The issues identified in Harding's September 1925 report were familiar to Miller & Lux and others involved in the water storage district negotiations. One of the basic premises on which the district was founded was that Miller & Lux would transfer the water and water rights used on its low-value pastures, referred to as the grasslands, to the district so that the water could be used to irrigate higher value crops on more productive land elsewhere. To accomplish that, the rights used by the grasslands had to be segregated from other Miller & Lux rights, which meant dismantling the complex integrated water system that the corporation had spent decades assembling. Reliable records were often missing. For example, excess water from the San Joaquin & Kings River system delivered to Miller & Lux grasslands through waste gates in the canal had never been measured. The San Luis Canal Company diverted water at both Temple Slough and Mendota Dam via the Helm Canal, but at times when there was not enough water in the river to support the Helm diversion, the San Joaquin & Kings River system was called upon to make up the difference. As W.C.

[189] "Memorandum of Agreement for Adjustment of Differences Between Miller & Lux Incorporated, Proposed West Side Water Storage District and Madera Irrigation District," September 7, 1922; Miller, *Flooding the Courtrooms*, 135-138.
[190] Miller, *Flooding the Courtrooms*, 141-145.

Hammatt explained in 1925 the grasslands were "a roving acreage, different lands probably coming in this class each year." Deliveries through the San Luis system also had to be apportioned between croplands and grasslands, and between riparian and non-riparian land. As part of this process of sorting out diversions through its various canal systems, Miller & Lux formed a new mutual water company in 1926, the Poso Canal Company, to take over the part of the San Luis system supplied by the Helm Canal. The byzantine complexity of the process of segregating lands in the water storage district is probably best illustrated by maps that show up to eighteen different classifications.[191]

There was relatively little controversy over the water rights of the San Joaquin & Kings River system. S.T. Harding found that the canal company's right to divert 1,360 second-feet, established in a 1917 judgment against the Fresno Slough riparian claims of Jefferson James, was uncontested except by the Stevinson interests. Actual mean monthly diversions had been as high as 1,700 second-feet, the difference being credited variously to the San Luis system or grassland irrigation. The San Joaquin & Kings River canal also had the most senior right, although the Chowchilla Canal (jointly owned by Miller & Lux and the California Pastoral & Agricultural Company) had an intervening right to 120 second-feet when the flow of the river exceeded 760 second-feet. Valuation was more complicated. Kempkey had appraised the canal company's physical properties—canals, weirs, gates, section houses and Mendota Dam—at the cost it would take to reproduce them, which resulted in a May 1925 estimate of $2,762,300. The appraisal of water rights was fraught with legal issues, but by the time the district submitted its plan to the state engineer Kempkey had settled on a figure of $2,421,000 for the canal company's rights. In all, Kempkey determined that the water storage district should pay Miller & Lux and its subsidiaries a total of $13, 733,100 for its properties and rights. McClure and Harding insisted that the cost was unjustified and exorbitant, and assessments on district farmers would be so high that the whole project would be uneconomical. [192]

---

[191] Miller, *Flooding the Courtrooms*, 141-142; S.T. Harding, "Report on the Proposed Plan of the San Joaquin River Water Storage District," September 1, 1925. The letter from W.C. Hammatt to Harry Barnes, July 17, 1925 is quoted on page 72; "Exhibit A: Map Showing Lands Heretofore Irrigated by the Respective Water Rights and Acreages of Same," c. 1928.
[192] Harding, "Report on the Proposed Plan," 61-62; A. Kempkey, "Appraisals as to Value of Physical Properties and Water Rights to be Acquired by Purchase by the San Joaquin River Water Storage District as per the District's Plan, No. B-1," revised to May 27, 1925, 1-33;

Supporters of the West Joaquin district had made storage and a more secure water supply one of their primary goals, but because the canal already had the most senior rights it was assumed that the land served by the San Joaquin & Kings River system would need relatively little additional water from the planned Friant reservoir and would thus have some of the lowest assessments in the water storage district. Nevertheless, those assessments would increase the cost of irrigation, and local water users protested appraisals that seemed designed to primarily benefit Miller & Lux. Harding's report estimated that canal company customers would incur a cost of about $45 per acre, and interest payments alone would be more than existing water rates. Unless the price of acquiring Miller & Lux assets could be reduced, San Joaquin & Kings River water users would be better off without the water storage district.[193]

The water storage district story played out against a backdrop of increasing financial stress for Miller & Lux. The stubborn post-war agricultural depression continued, keeping meat and commodity prices low. An outbreak of foot-and-mouth disease in 1924 coincided with a severe drought, which meant that quarantined livestock could not be moved to better pastures when the grass dried out so Miller & Lux had to buy high-priced feed to maintain its herd. The company sharply reduced its workforce and stopped its canal-building projects but still struggled to control its cash flow. In debt to bondholders for $25 million by 1925, Miller & Lux arranged a major refinancing but at the price of a commitment to accelerated land sales and the addition of bondholder representatives to its board of directors. As part of the reorganization, J. Leroy Nickel was replaced as president by James E. Fickett, whose primary concerns were economy, land sales and retirement of the firm's debt. The importance of its cattle business declined and the company's defeat by the Chicago packing interests it had battled since the 1890s was complete when it sold the HH brand—an iconic symbol of Henry Miller's empire—to a subsidiary of Swift along with its breeding herd in 1930.[194]

In the three years that followed Harding's 1925 report, negotiations between Miller & Lux and the San Joaquin River Water Storage District were continuous and inconclusive. The district wanted a precise description of what

[193] Harding, "Report on the Proposed Plan," 15-16; Miller, *Flooding the Courtrooms*, 145.
[194] Miller, *Flooding the Courtrooms*, 146-149; Igler, *Industrial Cowboys*, 180-181.

it was buying but many of Miller & Lux's water rights were based on legal theories that could still be challenged, and the company did not want negotiations with the district to undermine legal positions it had established over decades of tenacious litigation. The ownership and use of water released from power company reservoirs proved especially difficult. In an effort to resolve questions about the appraisals that had been challenged by McClure and Harding, a panel of three well-respected engineers was chosen to conduct an independent review. H.L. Haehl, B.A. Etcheverry and F.C. Hermann reduced the total valuation by more than a third to $8,332,000; a figure that was too small for Miller & Lux to accept and too high to convince farmers that they would be able to afford storage district assessments. Worried San Joaquin & Kings River water users appealed to the Railroad Commission, which had to approve the transfer of the canal company to the district. Their pleas were rebuffed, and in approving the anticipated sale in 1928 the commission made it clear that it had no authority over decisions made by the directors of a public district.[195]

In the spring of 1928 the district accepted Miller & Lux's price of $9,326,150 and a sales contract was signed. Numerous details, however, still had to be worked out as other riparians demanded concessions and dissatisfied canal company consumers carried an appeal of the Railroad Commission's decision to the state supreme court. As delays mounted, Miller & Lux announced that if the district's plan was not completed and forwarded to the state engineer by the end of 1928, the sales agreement would be canceled. Consummation of the water storage district was, and probably always had been, impossible; the goals of the interests involved were too different and the legal and engineering issues were too complex and entangled. In December 1928 the district's directors admitted that they could not meet the deadline imposed by Miller & Lux and soon began the process of dissolving the district.[196]

After the failure of the water storage district, the canal company petitioned the Railroad Commission for a rate increase. There had been no change in rates since the Stanislaus County rate had been adjusted in 1915, probably because

---

[195] Miller, *Flooding the Courtrooms*, 150-160; Railroad Commission, Decision 19376, February 17, 1928.
[196] Miller, *Flooding the Courtrooms*, 160-161; Harry Barnes to Board of Directors, San Joaquin River Water Storage District, April 23, 1928.

the company had spent most of the intervening years trying to win the support of its customers. The primary issue before the commission was setting a rate that would insure a reasonable return on the company's assets, and the biggest problem, as it has been in the water storage district negotiations, was putting a price on those assets. The canal company's own appraisal, provided by A. Kempkey, exceeded $4 million including $1.4 million for water rights, a valuation that was based on nothing more than Kempkey's own opinion as to what a reasonable figure should be. The commission agreed that the company was entitled to higher rates but used a rate base of $2 million, which reflected its own engineers' appraisal of physical properties and a less generous allowance for the value of the company's water rights. In March 1930 the commission did away with the practice of charging different rates in each county and set the rate for general crops at $2.75 per acre, $1.50 per acre for grain and $7.50 per acre for rice. The canal company suggested it would like to charge for the amount delivered rather than by the acre, a proposal that the commission enthusiastically endorsed but which drew predictable opposition from the Peoples Protective Association, representing local irrigators. Along with the new acreage-based rate schedule the commission also approved a measured rate of $1.15 per acre-foot but it went unused.[197]

Also before the Railroad Commission was the question of defining the canal company's service area, and more specifically the fate of the "overlap area" served interchangeably by San Luis Canal Company rights or by deliveries from the San Joaquin & Kings River canals which might or might not include the newly organized Poso Canal Company. The canal company considered the 50,500 acre Poso territory to be part of its service area even though water was delivered through the Miller & Lux-owned Helm Canal. For Miller & Lux confirming that the Poso Canal was part of the San Joaquin & Kings River system was an opportunity to transfer its San Luis rights to other properties, but to the Peoples Protective Association the expansion of the service area by up to 50 percent threatened to overburden an already inadequate water supply.[198]

---

[197] Railroad Commission, Decision 22228, March 19, 1930.
[198] Railroad Commission, Decision 22228, 15-17; Stephen W, Downey, "Before the Railroad Commission of the State of California, Application 15271, Brief of Peoples Protective Association," January 17, 1930, 63-83.

The commission agreed that under the natural flow rights of the San Joaquin & Kings River canals there was not enough water to meet irrigation demands in the summer and fall, especially for alfalfa and the expanding acreage of cotton. Miller & Lux claimed exclusive ownership of the water released from power company reservoirs although it had at times shared that supply with the canal company and could potentially offset the additional requirements of the Poso area by regularly allocating some of the storage releases to San Joaquin & Kings River diversions. During the commission proceedings Miller & Lux, the canal company, the Protective Association, the Farm Bureau and the commission staff negotiated a flow schedule that promised power company releases to the canal company in exchange for the use by Miller & Lux of part of the canal company's natural flow rights early in the irrigation season when there was typically water available in excess of the needs of the San Joaquin & Kings River system. While the flow schedule agreement applied only to 1930, the commission expressed its hope that it would prove so beneficial that it would be extended. Based on the extra summer water available to the canal company the commission allowed the expansion of the service area, and in 1935 it authorized the canal company to assume ownership of the Poso Canal Company's delivery system. The same 1935 decision allowed the canal company to take over the privately constructed Sullivan Extension of the Outside Canal and to connect it to the Main Canal.[199]

The canal company's consumers lodged a variety of complaints with the Railroad Commission about the quality of service they received, particularly "incomplete or delayed deliveries." The commission concluded that blame could be placed on the "archaic methods of water distribution which apparently have been little improved since the company first commenced operating in the eighties. All distribution of water should be scheduled and controlled directly through the main office of the company, discarding the present inefficient practice of permitting the various section foremen and ditch-tenders to function independently."[200] The commission required the canal company to adopt new rules and regulations to provide equitable and reliable service, including an approximately thirty-day rotation system when

---

[199] Railroad Commission, Decision 22228, 15-20; agreement, Miller & Lux and SJ&KRC&I Co., February 15, 1929; Railroad Commission, Decision 28340, November 12, 1935, 1-6.
[200] Railroad Commission, Decision 22228, 29.

water supply conditions required it. However the canal company was not entirely to blame for delivery problems; farmer-owned laterals were often too small and weed-choked, and water was wasted on land poorly prepared for irrigation. The commission urged the company to take control of the laterals, but in the meantime it promised to approve a rule denying service to consumers whose ditches were in such poor condition that they would waste water or delay delivery to other users.[201]

Litigation between Miller & Lux and the Madera Irrigation District had been suspended during the attempt to form a water storage district, and even after the district scheme collapsed there was an effort to reach a negotiated settlement under which Miller & Lux would sell the Madera district a block of water. That plan encountered many of the same obstacles that had doomed the water storage district. Its success would have required concessions that Miller & Lux was unwilling to make and money the irrigation district would have had trouble raising, and when the deal fell apart in 1930 litigation was revived. Two suits against the Madera Irrigation District—one involving the rights of the San Joaquin & Kings River Canal & Irrigation Company and the other pressing the claims of Miller & Lux—were tried simultaneously before Judge Charles G. Haines.[202]

It was the penultimate test of Miller & Lux's San Joaquin River rights; a battle that the company had tried to avoid by negotiation but was now necessary to protect the value of the property it was trying to sell. In the canal company case, key questions included what percentage of the 146,000 acre service area would be irrigated in any one year and how much water crops would actually require. Attorney J.E. Woolley advised company officials "to determine the maximum quantity of land that can be devoted to alfalfa, on the theory that eventually this quantity of land will be planted to that crop, and as alfalfa requires more water than any other crop except rice, this information may be the basis of giving the utility a larger water right than otherwise."[203] Testimony on historic and projected diversions and demands, on the extent of Miller & Lux's riparian lands and on the release of water from power company reservoirs went on for months. In March 1932 Haines issued a decision that

[201] Railroad Commission, Decision 22228, 20-21.
[202] Miller, *Flooding the Courtrooms*, 164-165.
[203] J.E. Woolley to T.C. Mott and A.R. Olsen, January 26, 1931.

represented a major victory for Miller & Lux, favoring the company in almost all of its arguments including its ownership of the power release water. The canal company's claim to 1,360 second-feet was confirmed and monthly diversions reflecting its historic use of water were given judicial recognition and protection. Weary of litigation, the Madera district did not appeal and the Haines decision became the rule of the river.[204]

Following the decision, a new flow schedule setting out the operational priorities of the San Joaquin & Kings River canal, Miller & Lux and the mutual canal companies had to be drawn up. There was some concern within the Miller & Lux organization that the schedule gave the San Joaquin & Kings river system too much water at the expense of mutual companies, while the Farm Bureau, representing canal company customers, took the opposite position because the schedule gave the mutual companies some power release water in July, August and September before the company reached its full 1,360 second foot diversion. The Railroad Commission, however, found that the arrangement struck a reasonable balance.[205] It noted that "The record shows that the service rendered by the applicant [the canal company] has improved materially during the months of July and August since the diversions have been made in accordance with the flow schedule" approved by the commission in 1930.[206] In regard to the new schedule, the commission admitted that while it "permits the invasion by the mutual canal companies of the utility entitlement to the extent of certain minor quantities during the summer months, it is equally true that in compensation therefor this utility should be enabled to provide adequate irrigation deliveries to all of its consumers throughout the entire irrigation season."[207] After two decades of uncertainty and controversy, the water supply for the west side had been stabilized, but by 1933 a new chapter in the story of regional water development was already beginning.

---

[204] Miller, *Flooding the Courtrooms*, 165-170. An example of the evidence introduced at the trial is found in "Miller & Lux vs. Madera Irrigation District and San Luis Canal Company vs. Madera Irrigation District, Brief on Behalf of Plaintiff, Part I—Argument on the Facts," undated.
[205] TRM to J.E. Woolley, August 22, 1932; Railroad Commission, Decision 26153, July 17, 1933, 6
[206] Railroad Commission, Decision 26153, July 17, 1933, 6
[207] Railroad Commission, Decision 26153, 7

Charles Lux
Photo courtesy of the Milliken Museum

Henry Miller
Photo courtesy of the Milliken Museum

Outside Canal Construction 1897
Photo courtesy of the Milliken Museum

Canal construction near Santa Nella, circa 1900
Photo courtesy of the Gustine Historical Society

Miller & Lux workers putting up hay for the winter
Photo courtesy of the Milliken Museum

Center Street, Dos Palos 1910
Photo courtesy of the Milliken Museum

Main Canal River Slough 1920
Photo courtesy of the Milliken Museum

Milk cans waiting for the train at the Gustine depot
Photo courtesy of the Gustine Historical Society

Delivering cream for the shipment from Gustine
Photo courtesy of the Gustine Historical Society

"He bought what he already had!"

THE WATER WATCHERS

EXECUTIVE COMMITTEE

EDWARD LEWIS, CHAIRMAN DOS PALOS	E. E. BUNKER GUSTINE	ROLLO SPINA LOS BANOS
WESLEY UNDERHILL NEWMAN	CLYDE HOUK DOS PALOS	R. E. DES JARDINS FIREBAUGH

Ads courtesy of the Milliken Museum

Ads courtesy of the Milliken Museum

Fishing from the Mendota Dam, circa 1919
Photo courtesy of the Milliken Museum

Irrigation discharge
Photo courtesy of the Milliken Museum

Sugar beet irrigation, circa 1965
Photo courtesy of the Milliken Museum

Tomato harvest circa 1968
Photo courtesy of the Milliken Museum

8

The Central Valley Project

Only a few weeks after his arrival in California in 1871 Robert Brereton set out on a reconnaissance that soon led to a bold plan to irrigate the entire San Joaquin Valley through a system of more or less coordinated canals. The Alexander Commission offered, at least on a conceptual level, the same kind of grand vision for the whole Central Valley but its emphasis on professional, centralized planning was well ahead of its time. The same might be said of California's first state engineer, William Hammond Hall. The engineer for the doomed West Side Irrigation District before his appointment to the state position in 1878, Hall had an ambitious agenda that included a comprehensive study of irrigation and the first measurements of the flow in California streams. Unfortunately, his effort to formulate a state-wide water plan was short-lived. The legislature slashed Hall's funding in 1881 amid controversies over mining debris dams and water rights. Hall struggled on until making an embittered exit in 1889, and California was left without a central engineering office for a decade.[208]

When William Hammond Hall left state service, he joined the U.S. Geological Survey at a time when that agency was adding hydrographic surveys to its program of topographical mapping. During the 1890s Geological Survey engineers and surveyors in California identified reservoir sites and investigated irrigation practices, resulting in reports like C.E. Grunsky's three volumes on irrigation in the San Joaquin Valley published in 1898 and 1899. The service also set up gauging stations to establish a record of streamflow; a prerequisite for irrigation planning that had been largely ignored during the pioneer period. The 1890s also saw a growing movement across the west in support of federal financing of irrigation projects that culminated in the passage of the Newlands Act in 1902 establishing an irrigation development program managed by the Reclamation Service, later renamed the Bureau of Reclamation. California formed a partnership with the Geological Survey and

---

[208] see Pisani, *From the Family Farm to Agribusiness*, 155-190 for background on the first state engineer.

began to build its own engineering capability as a series of Progressive Era reforms gave the state increased responsibility over the administration of water rights and the supervision of irrigation districts. Taken together, the expanding role of government agencies brought new levels of technical expertise and centralized planning to California water development.

California's first big water projects—ones that moved large quantities of water long distances and from one from river basin to another—were built not by federal or state agencies but by the state's two largest metropolitan areas. In 1905 Los Angeles city engineer William Mulholland unveiled plans to tap the Owens River over two hundred miles to the north. The Reclamation Service had been planning an irrigation project for the remote area east of the Sierras, but the head of the Service in California, J.B. Lippincott, was sympathetic to the city and actively furthered its plans, risking scandal and contributing to the controversy surrounding Los Angeles's activities in the Owens Valley. The Los Angeles Aqueduct was completed to the San Fernando Valley in 1913. To the north, San Francisco city officials expected demand to exceed what the Spring Valley Water Company could supply from local sources and in 1901 set in motion a plan to dam the Tuolumne River at Hetch Hetchy in Yosemite National Park. The proposal faced determined opposition from nature-lovers who wanted to preserve the scenic valley and from the Turlock and Modesto irrigation districts who wanted to protect their own water supply. The city received congressional permission in 1913 to build the reservoir and an aqueduct to serve San Francisco and suburban communities, but Hetch Hetchy water did not reach the city until 1934. Although both projects generated heated disputes that linger to this day, they demonstrated the feasibility of large inter-basin transfers.[209]

A plan for a much bigger project was introduced in September 1919 by Robert Bradford Marshall, whose long career in the U.S. Geological Survey included topographic mapping in California from 1891 to 1902 before taking regional and national administrative posts.[210] As Marshall saw it, irrigation was necessary to fully develop the Central Valley, to turn it into "the world's

---

[209] Norris Hundley, Jr., *The Great Thirst: Californians and Water, 1770s-1990s* (Berkeley and Los Angeles: University of California Press, 1992), 139-190 provides a general overview of the Los Angeles and San Francisco projects.
[210] Pisani, *From the Family Farm to Agribusiness*, 394-395.

greatest garden," and only a comprehensive plan could achieve that end. "My solution of the whole problem," he wrote, "is to turn the Sacramento River into the San Joaquin Valley."[211]

The centerpiece of Marshall's proposal was a dam on the Sacramento at Iron Canyon, just north of Red Bluff, supplemented by a diversion from the Klamath River to the Sacramento. From Iron Canyon a "Grand Canal" would run along the hills on the west side of the Sacramento Valley to Benicia, where it would be carried beneath the Carquinez Straits in an inverted siphon. From Martinez the canal would take a circuitous route to the Walnut Creek area, rounding Mount Diablo and running south to a point near Dos Palos. A branch canal would run to the Santa Clara Valley and north to San Francisco. On the east side, a second large canal would run from Iron Canyon to the San Joaquin River, picking up water from tributary streams along its course. Another canal from the Stanislaus River would terminate south of Tulare Lake and a final San Joaquin Valley canal would begin on the San Joaquin River at an elevation of 1,000 feet and follow a high line to the southern end of the valley and then north to Dos Palos to complete the irrigation of the entire valley. Finally, the Kern River would be diverted to Los Angeles through the Mojave Desert before joining the route of the Owens Valley aqueduct.[212] Marshall acknowledged the immense scope of his plan: "The plan is a large one, larger by many times than the entire program of the US Reclamation Service in the 16 public-land States, but it is in keeping with the State, for small ideas have no place in California."[213] It was a sentiment that William C. Ralston would have appreciated.

Marshall's plan was intended to promote California's general prosperity by providing millions of acres of newly irrigated land and homes for thousands of people, but the state soon faced water shortages that threatened existing livelihoods. During the 1920s the limits of the San Joaquin Valley's natural water supply were becoming painfully apparent, especially in parts of the Tulare Lake basin. With limited surface water, farmers turned to groundwater, using increasingly powerful electric and gasoline pumps. At the epicenter of the problem in Tulare County the total horsepower in electric pumps rose

[211] Robert Bradford Marshall, *Irrigation of Twelve Million Acres in the Valley of California* (Sacramento: California State Irrigation Association, November 1921), 5.
[212] Pisani, *From the Family Farm to Agribusiness*, 396-399; Marshall, *Irrigation of Twelve Million Acres*, 7.
[213] Marshall, *Irrigation of Twelve Million Acres*, 4.

nearly five-fold between 1914 and 1924. As a result the water table dropped, the depth to water falling between five and thirty-five feet from 1920 to 1924, and as pump lifts increased so did the cost of irrigation. By the late 1920s more acres were being irrigated by more pumps as farmers took advantage of high cotton prices. A groundwater overdraft of that magnitude could not be sustained, and there were reports of farms being abandoned due to water shortage or because their owners could not afford deeper wells or bigger pumps. Without relief, thousands of acres of irrigated land could be lost.[214]

Another significant problem emerged in the Delta region at the junction of the Sacramento and San Joaquin rivers. Decades of reclamation had turned the one-time tule marsh into a productive agricultural landscape of leveed islands irrigated from the surrounding channels. The Delta sat at the upper, freshwater end of the San Francisco Bay estuary, where the flow of the rivers balanced the daily tidal pulses that pushed ocean salinity upstream. In times of flood Suisun Bay would fill with fresh water but in seasons of low streamflow salinity could move into the western Delta. By 1917 the State Water Commission worried that the appropriation and diversion of additional water would reduce summer inflow to the Delta to the point that tidal salinity would reach further into the Delta and threaten irrigation there. That happened in the summer of 1920 when expanded rice planting in the Sacramento Valley coincided with a drought. Salinity above the limit considered safe for irrigation pushed north of Rio Vista, and the City of Antioch, located just below the mouth of the San Joaquin River, filed suit against Sacramento River diverters. The city lost its case but an even more severe dry year in 1924 and a deeper penetration of salinity into the central Delta brought additional litigation, beginning with the Holland Land Company case that pitted 143 Delta plaintiffs claiming riparian rights against hundreds of diverters in the Sacramento and San Joaquin watersheds, including Miller & Lux. Clearly, the salinity threat had ramifications far beyond the Delta.[215]

---

[214] San Joaquin Valley Water Committee, *The San Joaquin Valley in the Statewide Water Problem of California*, 1930, 25-46; California Department of Public Works, Division of Engineering and Irrigation, Bulletin No. 9, *Supplemental Report on Water Resources of California* (Sacramento: California State Printing Office, 1925), 13.

[215] For additional information on the salinity problem in the Delta see W. Turrentine Jackson and Alan M. Paterson, *The Sacramento-San Joaquin Delta: The Evolution and Implementation of Water Policy, An Historical Perspective* (Davis, California: California Water Resources Center, 1977), 5; Vincent J. McGovern, Memorandum to Mr. Olsen, August 17, 1936, 5-6.

Inspired by the sweeping vision of the Marshall plan and facing a growing list of water problems, the legislature in 1921 authorized a study of California's water resources and the development of a plan for irrigation and flood protection. In a report issued two years later as Bulletin No. 4, state engineers summarized patterns of streamflow, estimated the ultimate irrigation requirements for all parts of California, and provided an outline of a comprehensive plan to maximize irrigated acreage at the least cost. For the Central Valley, water would be collected by large reservoirs at Iron Canyon and at a new site where the Pit River flowed into the Sacramento, and supplemented by a diversion from the Trinity River watershed. Several canals would serve the west side of the Sacramento Valley but unlike the Marshall plan, water to be transferred to the San Joaquin Valley would flow down the channel of the Sacramento River to the Delta, which would be protected from salinity by a dam across the Carquinez Straits. A two hundred-mile canal with nine pumping plants along its route would run from the Delta to Tulare Lake on the level plains west of the San Joaquin River, making it less expensive to build than a higher-elevation canal along the foot of the Diablo Range but additional pump lifts would be required to distribute water to large areas of the west side lying above the state canal. The southern San Joaquin Valley would be supplied by canals beginning at the Stanislaus and Kings rivers and from the Tulare Lake reservoir. Robert Marshall served on the consulting board for the state plan, which resembled a scaled-down version of his grand design.[216]

The legislature declined to fund additional work on the comprehensive plan but in September 1924 the San Francisco and Los Angeles Chambers of Commerce agreed to pay for studies of the physical works that could provide water to areas where the need was greatest, especially Tulare County. A report written several years later presented the problem in starkly simple terms:

> There are now about half a million acres in the southern San Joaquin Valley supporting prosperous communities, that are either overdrawing their underground supplies or are approaching this condition. These areas are constantly growing larger. ... There is no way to stop the sinking of new wells. All the overlying lands have the legal right to pump from underground sources if they choose. The construction of storage

---

[216] California Department of Public Works, Division of Engineering and Irrigation, Bulletin No. 4, *Water Resources of California* (Sacramento: California State Printing Office, 1923), 46-49, Plate IV.

reservoirs on local streams would help temporarily but little new water would be created thereby because four-fifths of the mean flow in the streams is already in use. … Therefore, a permanent solution to the water problem of the southern San Joaquin Valley can only be attained by the importation of a large supply from some outside source.[217]

Robert Marshall's dream of adding millions of acres of irrigated land had not been abandoned, and state engineers emphasized that all of their work was consistent with the long-term comprehensive plan, but the focus was shifting to the rescue of regions already facing critical shortages.

Bulletin No. 9, released in 1925, was more specific in its recommendations. The location of the Sacramento River dam was moved to Kennett (the future site of Shasta Dam). The salt water barrier in the Carquinez Straits, which had attracted enthusiastic support in communities around Suisun Bay, was determined to be unnecessary during the first phase of the plan when controlled releases from Kennett would be sufficient to repel salinity but the barrier was still considered necessary in the long run to fully utilize the Sacramento River. Instead of a separate canal south of the Delta, a series of dams, each about ten feet high, would be built in the channel of the San Joaquin River and water would be lifted from pool to pool by pumps. The initial phase would have six dams and pumping plants on the river and a cut from Salt Slough with another three pumping lifts to deliver 1,000 second-feet to the San Joaquin & Kings River canal near Los Banos. Ultimately the pumping system would be extended to Fresno Slough and expanded to deliver 3,000 second-feet.[218]

Bulletin No. 9 also introduced the concept of an exchange of waters, with imported Sacramento River water replacing the San Joaquin River as the irrigation supply for land below Mendota Dam. The San Joaquin River could then be diverted at Friant to the Kings River to supply that stream's users, and a canal from the Kings River to Earlimart would supply Tulare County. It was assumed that the Friant reservoir planned by the San Joaquin River Water Storage District and the Pine Flat Dam proposed by the Kings River Water

---

[217] California Department of Public Works, Division of Engineering and Irrigation, Bulletin No. 12, *Water Resources of California and a Coordinated Plan for Their Development* (Sacramento: California State Printing Office, 1927), 35-36.
[218] California Department of Public Works, Division of Engineering and Irrigation, Bulletin No. 9, *Supplemental Report on Water Resources of California* (Sacramento: California State Printing Office, 1925), 15-21, 45-48.

Conservation District would be incorporated into the state system.[219] While institutional and legal issues were not specifically addressed, water users were assured that "These exchanges would all be made by delivering an equivalent supply, both in time and in volume, to the lands receiving other water in place of their customary and rightful supply."[220]

Investigations continued, plans were refined and issues of money and water rights, and political realities, were debated until State Engineer Edward Hyatt presented the completed State Water Plan to the legislature in 1931. Its initial units included the Kennett reservoir, San Joaquin River exchange system, Friant Dam, the Madera Canal and a single canal from Friant to Kern County instead of the two-stage transfer system suggested in 1925. A canal from the western Delta to serve Contra Costa County farms and industries replaced the salt water barrier, which had finally been discarded in favor of salinity control releases from Kennett. Difficulties with the Friant dam site, including the great length of the dam and the large amount of unusable storage below the elevation of the canal outlets, prompted engineers to consider the upstream Temperance Flat site as an alternative. Unfortunately, a dam at Temperance Flat would require relocation of the Kerckhoff powerhouse and when that cost was added it was found that Friant would be cheaper at any reservoir capacity below 700,000 acre-feet. In assessing the availability of water, state planners assumed that the Miller & Lux grassland rights would be acquired for the project and that delivery to crop lands would generally follow the flow schedule worked out during water storage district negotiations and modified by the Railroad Commission. Looking beyond its initial stage, the State Water Plan included a long list of additional dams in the Central Valley watershed and a transfer of water from the Trinity River.[221]

A detailed analysis of the San Joaquin Valley elements of the plan in Bulletin No. 29 introduced an engineering problem that had not been discussed in any depth previously—how to get water across the Delta from the Sacramento River to the San Joaquin pumping system. The San Joaquin River side of the Delta was larger in area and in water use than the Sacramento section but had less inflow so there was a natural north-to-south cross-Delta

[219] Bulletin No. 9, 17-19.
[220] Bulletin No. 9, 19.
[221] Pisani, *From the Family Farm to Agribusiness*, 416-434; California Department of Public Works, Division of Water Resources, Bulletin No. 29, *San Joaquin River Basin*, 1931, 56-57, 171, 244-249.

flow, mostly through Georgiana Slough. The amount of water carried by the slough from its head near Walnut Grove varied depending on river flow and tidal conditions, but was usually between 2,000 and 3,000 second-feet. Under ultimate development of the State Water Plan, salinity repulsion flows would have to be distributed across the Delta and the Sacramento River would be called on at times to meet irrigation requirements and channel losses in the southern Delta and the export demands of the Contra Costa Canal and the San Joaquin River pumping system, up to 12,000 second-feet in all. To deal with the deficit in transfer capacity the state plan envisioned a diversion dam on the Sacramento River near Hood and a cut to connect the river to Snodgrass Slough running south to the Mokelumne River and other sloughs that joined the San Joaquin River west of Stockton. From that point existing channels would carry water to the pumping system and distribute it for other uses in the southern and central Delta.[222]

Plans for the San Joaquin River pumping system had also been modified by 1931. There were now five dams and pumping plants in the river, the last one just below the mouth of the Merced River. From the final pool a canal, with three more pumping plants in a distance of seven miles, would run southwest, passing south of Newman with delivery connections to the Main and Outside canals. Two more pumping plants five miles west of Los Banos would bring the canal to an elevation where it could flow by gravity to Mendota Dam. By 1936, the canal route had been further refined to put the final lift west of Gustine and add more connections to existing canals, including one that would carry up to 500 second-feet directly to the Arroyo Canal. The initial capacity of the pumping system was expected to be 3,000 second-feet with eventual expansion to up to 8,000 second-feet to supply the hundred-mile long Mendota-West Side pumping system that would ultimately carry water as far south as the Elk Hills west of Bakersfield.[223]

The legislature passed the Central Valley Project Act in August 1933, authorizing $170,000,000 in revenue bonds for the construction of initial units of the State Water Plan. Fearing that state construction of transmission lines

---

[222] Bulletin No. 29, 286-289.
[223] Bulletin No. 29, 52, 289-293; Water Project Authority, *Reports on Acquisition of and Plan of Exchange of Waters for the San Joaquin River, Report No. 2, Plan of Exchange of Water Supplies by and through San Joaquin Pumping System of the Central Valley Project, Physical Works and Source of Substitutional Supply,* August 1936, Plate 1 "Plan for Exchange of Water Supplies Through San Joaquin Pumping System, July 1936."

from the project's hydroelectric plants would open the door to public power competition, Pacific Gas & Electric and its private power allies forced a referendum election in December 1933. The project survived, but only by a narrow margin as southern Californians voted heavily against a plan that offered few benefits for their part of the state. Facing stricken financial markets in the depths of the Depression, the state never tried to sell its project bonds, instead it made a concerted effort to win federal funding.[224]

The federal government had long had an interest in the state's plans. A Bureau of Reclamation engineer had made the first thorough feasibility study of the salt water barrier, and in 1929 the Hoover-Young Commission, named for the president and governor who appointed its members, was created to coordinate federal and state planning. The national government had preeminent authority over navigation and flood control, and California officials had always expected contributions based on the benefits to those functions that the Central Valley Project could provide. It was for that reason that members of the Senate Committee on Irrigation and Reclamation visited California in 1932. They were greeted on their arrival in Los Angeles by State Engineer Hyatt and after meeting Louis B. Mayer and touring the MGM studio the senators traveled through the southern San Joaquin Valley where they were shown orchards abandoned due to a lack of water. They stopped at the Mendota Dam where "The present developments at this point were inspected and explained to the committee and the proposed plans for improvement in the interest of navigation and irrigation were discussed" before crossing a section of the grasslands on their way to Merced.[225]

By the time the Central Valley Project Act had been approved it appeared that funding might be available under New Deal programs like the National Industrial Recovery Act, and during the referendum campaign supporters urged voters to support President Roosevelt's jobs program by casting their ballot for the project. California's efforts were rewarded in 1935 when Roosevelt transferred relief funds to the Bureau of Reclamation to begin construction, and Congress made additional funding available in the interest of navigation and flood control. Two years later the Central Valley Project was

---

[224] Pisani, *From the Family Farm to Agribusiness*, 434-437.
[225] Pisani, *From the Family Farm to Agribusiness*, 424-428; *Report on Investigation and Inspection Trip to Great Central Valley Project of California by United States Senate Committee on Irrigation and Reclamation* (Washington, D.C.: Government Printing Office, 1933), 3.

formally reauthorized by Congress as a reclamation project. Although the state's Water Project Authority continued its work, the Central Valley Project was now firmly in federal hands and took its place alongside Grand Coulee Dam and the Tennessee Valley Authority as an example of regional planning and monumental construction.

Shortly after the Bureau of Reclamation received authorization to begin construction, Thomas C. Mott, chief engineer for Miller & Lux and its canal companies, summarized the companies' position:

> We have been watching this situation very closely and we do not believe that up to the present time there is anything to cause us any undue alarm because in the event that the Dam is built at Friant the State or the Federal Government will be compelled to allow our crop water to come on down the river to Mendota Dam in the same manner that it has in the past until such time as they may provide water from another source, namely, the Sacramento River through the meeting of the Kennett Dam and the pumping system along the San Joaquin River.[226]

Mott acknowledged that Miller & Lux could not stop the Central Valley Project, and might even find it advantageous, depending on arrangements for the exchange of waters.

Before the exchange could take place, water rights had to be defined. Crop land rights were fixed by the flow schedule, approved by the Railroad Commission, that generally reflected the terms of the Haines Decision. In fact, Thomas Mott found that for the Miller & Lux canal companies—the San Joaquin & Kings River Canal & Irrigation Company, the San Luis Canal Company, the Columbia Canal Company and the Firebaugh Canal Company—the flow schedule was actually more favorable than a strict interpretation of the judicial decision might have been. Miller & Lux executives considered demanding an increase of 10 to 15 percent in crop water allotments to better protect their canal companies, but Mott advised against it. He believed that the companies already had an entitlement to all the water they needed, and in dry years there was not enough water in the river to meet even the existing allocation. Later, there was a suggestion that Miller & Lux should reserve certain grassland rights, averaging almost 51,000 acre-feet per year, to

---

[226] Thomas C. Mott to Fred G. Lyon, December 31, 1935.

increase crop land deliveries in the late summer, but instead the company agreed to make the widely accepted flow schedule the basis for the exchange agreement. Having made that concession, the company hoped to improve its water supply by negotiating with the Bureau of Reclamation for minimum dry year deliveries based on a percentage of the regular flow schedule.[227]

The state's Water Project Authority, which conducted preliminary negotiations with Miller & Lux under an agreement with the Bureau of Reclamation, defined three classes of water rights on the San Joaquin River: crop land rights, "controlled" grassland rights covered by the flow schedule and delivered through the various canal systems and "uncontrolled" grassland rights for land flooded by the natural overflow of the river. The Central Valley Project intended to acquire all of the grassland rights owned by Miller & Lux and its affiliated companies for diversion at Friant to the east side of the valley. Miller & Lux grasslands irrigated by canals under the flow schedule totaled 156,102 acres, including 37,420 acres from the Main and Outside canals and 58,776 acres of San Luis grasslands served by the Helm and Poso canals. Friant Dam was also expected to capture most of the water in excess of the flow schedule that would otherwise have flooded riparian grasslands, so the owners of those lands were entitled to compensation for damages. Miller & Lux owned 46,800 acres of such riparian land. The Department of the Interior appointed a three-man board of appraisers to set a price for the Miller & Lux water rights to be purchased by the project. They applied three different approaches that yielded essentially similar valuations, and concluded that the reasonable fair market value of the rights was $2,450,000. That sum was only $50,000 below Miller & Lux's asking price, and on July 8, 1937 Secretary of the Interior Harold Ickes was able to announce substantial agreement with the company at the appraised price.[228]

Miller & Lux and its affiliated companies did not sell their rights to receive San Joaquin River water for their crop lands, but they agreed to allow the Bureau of Reclamation to divert that water at Friant in exchange for a

---

[227] T.C. Mott to J.E. Woolley, October 2, 1936; J.B. Lippincott, "San Joaquin Demand for Crop Land Canals," September 2, 1937.

[228] Water Project Authority, *Reports on Acquisition of and Plan of Exchange of Waters for the San Joaquin River, Report No. 4, Valuation of Rights to the Waters of the San Joaquin River proposed to be Acquired for Diversion to Upper San Joaquin Valley,* March 1937, see especially the map of grassland properties on Plate I; B.A. Etcheverry, F.C. Hermann, Curtis Walker, "Appraisal of Miller & Lux Grass Land Water Rights and Damage to Miller & Lux Riparian Rights," December 12, 1936, I-III, 1-5; U.S. Department of the Interior, "Memorandum for the Press," July 8, 1937.

substitute supply equal in quantity and quality. As soon as a deal had been struck for the purchase of the grassland rights and, by extension, for the definition of the crop land rights that the canal companies would retain, attention turned to the details of the contract for an exchange of waters. In August 1937 Miller & Lux hired well-connected Los Angeles consulting engineer J.B. Lippincott with instructions to focus on the question of the quality of the water that would be delivered to the canal companies. Miller & Lux already had doubts about the San Joaquin River pumping system. State planners assumed that the stair-step series of dams in the river would collect and recirculate drainage from irrigated lands, and that doing so would reduce the amount of water that had to be pumped through the system from the Delta and lower San Joaquin River tributaries. However, drain water carried salts from the soil it had passed through, and if applied in a high enough concentration those salts could damage crops. The state believed that salinity levels in the pumping system would be safe but Miller & Lux was unconvinced and began to collect its own water samples from the river and from wells.[229]

The company's suspicions were soon confirmed. In a November 1937 report Lippincott's associate S.A. Kerr concluded that the salinity of water delivered by the pumping system would reach 300 parts per million of total dissolved solids compared to 39 parts per million in the existing San Joaquin River diversion. Kerr expected the concentration to rise over time as water, and salt, from the Delta were imported into the region and little or no salt was allowed to escape. Long experience had shown that drainage and the maintenance of a favorable salt balance were essential to the sustained success of any agricultural region.[230] The Bureau of Reclamation arranged for a panel of three water quality experts from the University of California and the U.S. Department of Agriculture to examine the reasonable limits of salinity in the substitutional supply, but at a meeting in Riverside Deputy State Engineer A.D. Edmonston did not allow Kerr's report to be submitted for their consideration. Lippincott was outraged. In a visit to Sacramento he first made his case to Walker Young, project manager for the Bureau of Reclamation, and then went

[229] A.R. Olsen to J.B. Lippincott, August 26, 1937; A.R. Olsen to J.B. Lippincott, November 4, 1937; Bulletin No. 9, 20.
[230] S.A. Kerr, "Quality of Water to be Supplied to Mendota Canals under Proposed Exchange Agreement," November 22, 1937.

to the state engineer's office. State Engineer Edward Hyatt was noncommittal but Lippincott reported that "After a long but friendly discussion Edmonston admitted to me that the state pumping plan as originally submitted was wrong."[231] The state was by then considering a plan for a drainage channel that would run from above the mouth of the Merced River to a point in the Delta far enough west of the pumping system to avoid any recirculation of drainage. Returning to Walker Young's office, Lippincott "sensed the feeling that Mr. Young was relieved to find that the original State plan was not only opposed by us but admitted by Edmonston to be wrong."[232] Meanwhile, one of the water quality consultants saw Kerr and got a copy of his report.

The consultants—W.P Kelley, Warren R. Schoonover and Frank M. Eaton—made an investigation of conditions on the west side and submitted their report in February 1938. They emphasized the importance of drainage, which was already needed in some areas where the water table was within five feet or less of the surface. The necessity for drainage would become more urgent if water of a higher salinity was introduced to the area and on less permeable soils salt accumulation could worsen and possibly hasten the abandonment of some land. They concluded that on permeable soils a concentration of 300 parts per million total dissolved solids would be acceptable and might prove to be satisfactory on soils of lower permeability, but added that "This conclusion is based upon the assumption that adequate drainage will be provided and maintained for the area as a whole." They recommended that the maximum salinity of the exchange water supply should not exceed 300 parts per million on a five-year moving average, but believed that higher values were acceptable for a short time including a one-year average of up to 400 parts per million and a one-month maximum of 600 parts per million.[233] Lippincott thought 300 parts per million was too high but was prepared to accept an annual average of 225 parts per million.[234]

The Bureau of Reclamation had already been investigating an alternative plan for a pumping plant on the Old River branch of the San Joaquin near

---

[231] J.B. Lippincott to A.R. Olsen, December 8, 1937, 2.

[232] Lippincott to Olsen, December 8, 1937, 3.

[233] W.P. Kelley, Warren R. Schoonover, Fred M. Eaton, "Report of Committee of Consultants on the Suitability of a Proposed Substitutional Water Supply for Part of the Central Valley Project," February 5, 1938. The quotation is on p. 9-10, emphasis in original.

[234] J.B. Lippincott to A.R. Olsen, February 21, 1938; J.B. Lippincott to A.R. Olsen, April 1, 1938.

Tracy and a gravity canal to Mendota with delivery points connected directly to west side canals, a scheme that Miller & Lux favored. Following the rejection of the state's in-river pumping system, the Bureau was uncertain how it could best solve the exchange water quality problem and briefly contemplated a diversion from the San Joaquin River between Stockton and Lathrop and a canal route along the east side of the valley to Mendota so that Old River could become the drainage channel for the valley. At the same time, draft contracts were being circulated that included a proposal to require delivery to the Miller & Lux canals of water with an annual average of total dissolved solids no more than 35 percent higher than the annual average in the Sacramento River at the mouth of Snodgrass Slough. Lippincott urged acceptance since his preliminary estimate showed an average of only 132 parts per million total dissolved solids under that plan. Miller & Lux agreed, but T.C. Mott reported that the mutual canal companies wanted the additional protection of a specific maximum salinity limit and had in mind the 225 parts per million value that Lippincott had suggested. In response Bureau engineer E.B. Debler proposed limits of 300 parts per million for July through September and 200 parts per million the rest of the year and that offer too was accepted and added to the Snodgrass Slough provisions, although Debler soon became concerned that fluctuations in water quality in the Sacramento River might make the monthly standard hard to meet.[235]

In November 1938 Secretary of the interior Ickes gave his approval to the completed purchase and exchange contracts. Reclamation Commissioner John Page commented that:

> Nothing in the prior experience of the Bureau of Reclamation has compared with the complexity of completing arrangements for the San Joaquin division of the Central Valley Project. Whenever existing conditions are disturbed in so vast and highly developed a community, especially in one where water is far more precious than the most productive of its lands, the working out of a satisfactory arrangement, fair to all parties concerned, is difficult and time consuming. It is believed that these two contracts will be satisfactory to everyone.[236]

---

[235] J.B. Lippincott to A.R. Olsen, April 1, 1938; J.B. Lippincott to A.R. Olsen, May 17, 1938; Thomas C. Mott to J.B. Lippincott, August 10, 1938; J.B. Lippincott to A.R. Olsen, August 11, 1938; J.B. Lippincott to A.R. Olsen, August 30, 1938.
[236] *Gustine Standard*, November 17, 1938.

The two contracts were the Purchase Contract and the Exchange Contract. The first covered the sale of Miller & Lux grassland rights for $2,450,000 and defined the remaining crop water entitlements. For the Miller & Lux canals those rights, expressed as a mean daily flow for each month, were shown in Schedule 1. The amounts reflected the seasonal pattern of irrigation demand, ranging from under 500 second-feet for the months of November through February to a maximum of 2,316 second-feet in July. The rights of other diverters were listed in Schedule 2. The Bureau of Reclamation was obligated to deliver the flow of the San Joaquin River, as modified by the operation of the power companies' reservoirs, up to the sum of Schedule 1 and Schedule 2 to water users below Friant. When the flow, as measured at the Whitehouse gauge above Mendota Dam, fell below the amounts specified, the Bureau was required to pass through the entire inflow to Friant.[237]

The Exchange Contract between the Bureau and the Miller & Lux canal companies provided for the interception of Schedule 1 water at Friant for diversion into the Madera and Friant-Kern canals and the provision of a substitute supply through what became known as the Delta-Mendota Canal, subject to the water quality requirements negotiated with Miller & Lux. In addition, to protect the canal companies during dry years, the contract required a minimum delivery equal to 72 percent of Schedule 1. In the event that the Bureau of Reclamation could not deliver the full contractual entitlement from the Delta it would have to release water from Friant to make up the difference.[238]

The contracts could not become final until the Exchange Contract was accepted by the shareholders of the mutual companies and the San Joaquin & Kings River company received authorization from the Railroad Commission. At a hearing in the Los Banos grammar school auditorium in January 1939 T.C. Mott claimed that when the 72 percent guarantee became effective irrigators would have an improved and reliable water supply under almost all conditions, and J.B. Lippincott confirmed that the project could actually provide the benefits it promised. Frank Eaton, one of the members of the salinity consulting board, told the commission that even though the substitute supply would have four times the salts it would still be among the best

[237] U.S. Department of the Interior, "Contract for Purchase of Miller & Lux Water Rights," July 27, 1939.
[238] U.S. Department of the Interior, "Contract for Exchange of Waters," July 27, 1939.

irrigation water in the west. The Railroad Commission enthusiastically approved the Exchange Contract and a new flow schedule for the division of water between the four canal companies to take effect when delivery of Sacramento River water began. The contracts were signed on July 27, 1939, and the future of the San Joaquin River, and of the water supply for the San Joaquin & Kings River canals, was placed in the hands of the Bureau of Reclamation.[239]

---

[239] *Gustine Standard,* February 2, 1939; Railroad Commission, Decision 31861, March 20, 1939.

9

The Birth of CCID

In 1939 the west side, like the rest of the country, was emerging from the Depression. The annual acreage irrigated by the San Joaquin & Kings River system had declined in the early 1930s under the pressure of a series of dry years and economic dislocations including efforts by the New Deal Agricultural Adjustment Administration to restrict planting of cotton and other crops. Prior to 1931 the canal had routinely irrigated 100,000 acres in a service area that had been defined as approximately 146,700 acres by the Railroad Commission in 1930. Irrigated acreage dropped to 78,933 in 1931 and stayed below 100,000 acres until 1937. Alfalfa remained the predominant crop, covering over three-quarters of the irrigated acreage in the early 1920s but its acreage had fallen dramatically by 1939 when it accounted for about 44 percent of crop acreage. Grain also continued to be important, especially during the early 1930s when drought conditions prevailed. Cotton acreage had risen to over 18,000 acres at the beginning of the Depression before dropping to only 755 acres in 1932. Acreage increased gradually in the following years but exploded to over 20,000 acres in 1937 before falling back to around 10,000 acres annually. Rice acreage was smaller but more consistent, ranging from about 3,000 to 5,700 acres during the 1930s. In 1939 those four crops accounted for over 80 percent of the total acreage irrigated by the canal company.[240]

In calculating the canal company's expected earnings under an acreage-based rate the Railroad Commission had assumed that an average of 114,000 acres, or about 78 percent of the authorized service area, would be irrigated each year but instead crop acreage declined and so did revenue from water sales. A survey by the canal company identified approximately 6,263 acres in 132 parcels that had not taken water for at least five years and were unlikely to

---

[240] The San Joaquin Canal Company (hereafter "SJCC"), "Record of Acreages Irrigated Annually Segregated by Crops," undated; Central California Irrigation District (hereafter "CCID"), "Various Crops, Total Acreage Irrigated (Including double cropping)," c. 1979.

do so in the future because alkaline soil or drainage problems had rendered the land unfit for irrigation. In 1937 it asked for permission to exclude those parcels and substitute a roughly equal acreage that had requested water service. A number of owners with idle acreage promised to properly level their land for irrigation or take other steps that would enable them to use water, and those parcels, some four hundred acres, were allowed to remain in the service area. The Railroad Commission approved the company's request for exclusion and matching inclusion on the remaining acreage in order to maintain its income without raising rates and to put its water rights to maximum beneficial use. In its written opinion, however, the commission worried that some of the lands requesting inclusion were no better than those being removed and observed that "As most all the good quality lands under the canal system have already been served for many years and are now within the service area as established, by far the larger portion of the new lands asking for water lies adjacent to and above the Outside Canal." The commission also felt that it had a duty to warn water users that "an alarmingly large number of acres may soon be forced to discontinue the use of water for irrigation through the excessive water-logging of the lands" due to over-irrigation or lack of drainage.[241]

As a new decade began the San Joaquin River's future was taking shape at Friant. Secretary of the Interior Harold Ickes, an enthusiastic supporter of the Central Valley Project, spoke at the ceremonial start of construction on November 5, 1939, only a little more than four months after the Purchase and Exchange contracts had been signed. Construction contracts had been awarded in October that required the completion of the dam in 1,200 days. With foundation work completed, the first concrete was poured in July 1940 and by March 1941 four giant mixers were making up to 5,500 cubic yards of concrete per hour, carried in four-cubic-yard buckets running on a steel trestle above the dam site. The last of over two million cubic yards of concrete was placed on June 16, 1942. At 319 feet high, 267 feet thick at its base and two-thirds of a mile long at its crest, Friant was the fourth largest concrete dam in the world, behind only three other Bureau of Reclamation projects—Grand Coulee, Shasta and Hoover. Its size and the speed of its construction made it

---

[241] Railroad Commission, Decision 29501, February 1, 1937. The quotations are on pages 5 and 6.

one of the symbols of the era of heroic construction that transformed western river basins.[242]

Ironically as the first concrete was being placed at Friant, Mendota Dam suffered a major failure: a washout at its foundation. At Friant, the massive dam was anchored to bedrock but there was no such solid footing below the sandy bottom at the mouth of Fresno Slough. Begun in 1917 and completed in 1919 at a cost of over $182,000, the concrete Mendota Dam was built, like its brush and timber predecessors, on a foundation of pilings driven deep into the river bed. According to chief engineer Thomas C. Mott the July 16, 1940 incident was not a complete failure but "it could well have been that serious."[243] The washout revealed that the original pilings were poorly driven and in places a layer of sand several inches thick had been left on top of the pilings so that the concrete structure was not tied to its foundation. Mott believed that the dam had been built with a profile too narrow and with an insufficient number of pilings. All new sheet pilings were installed using 346 steel pilings and large quantities of heavy timber and additional concrete to tie the structure together at a cost of nearly $40,000.[244]

The security of the newly repaired dam was very much a concern in the days after Pearl Harbor when acts of sabotage were widely feared. Guards were posted, and it was suggested that a cable or some sort of screen should be extended across the river above the dam to intercept explosive devices sent floating downstream. T.C. Mott warned his superiors that the plan was entirely wrong. "It is impossible," he wrote, "for one not familiar with the situation to imagine the quantity of trash such as leaves and brush, to say nothing of logs and whole trees that come floating down the river during high water." He predicted that any screen that would be effective against floating bombs would fill in trash in a few hours "and would then become an extreme menace in itself" and the amount of debris reaching the Helm headgate in lower flows indicated the problem was not limited to floods.[245]

---

[242] Robert Autobee, "Friant Division, Central Valley Project," (U.S. Bureau of Reclamation, 1994), 7-14.

[243] Thomas C. Mott to F.L. Humphrey, April 13, 1945.

[244] F.L. Humphrey to T.C. Mott, April 4, 1945. Company records used by Humphrey gave the final completion date as 1921 but 1919 is generally accepted as the date of construction of the present dam; T.C. Mott to R.S. Calland, October 11, 1945; "Job 291, Cost Analysis of Inspection and Repairs to Mendota Dam Resulting from Washout July 16, 1940," c. 1940.

[245] T.C. Mott to J. Leroy Nickel, Jr., March 12, 1942.

Another war-time problem emerged during the 1942 irrigation season. Designated "enemy aliens," non-citizen Italian and German immigrants, were subject to travel restrictions and a curfew from 8:00 p.m. to 6:00 a.m., which prevented them from irrigating at night. Mott compiled a list of fifty-eight enemy alien canal company customers, almost all Italian, and in a letter to Miller & Lux president J. Leroy Nickel, Jr. noted that "you will recognize the names of at least 90 percent of them who are old Miller & Lux employees and purchasers of Miller & Lux lands."[246] The largest number were in the Los Banos Main Canal section on the Badger Flat and Johnson Field laterals where irrigation had become especially difficult. The problem was brought to the attention of the military authorities and in August special permits were issued to allow an exception to curfew regulations. A few months later Italians were removed from enemy-alien status. Rationing of gasoline, tires and some construction material, as well as labor shortages resulting from military service and the lure of higher paying jobs in defense industries, had a minimal effect on irrigation operations but left the canal company with a backlog of deferred maintenance when the war ended.[247]

The war also slowed work at Friant. The War Production Board ruled that the Central Valley Project was non-essential to the war effort, essentially shutting down work. Although the contractors managed to finish the dam itself, other work had to be suspended, including the installation of control valves in the four outlets to the San Joaquin River. Without those valves the river flowed freely through the dam except during high water in the winter of 1942 when it briefly backed up into the reservoir. Citing wartime agricultural needs, in July 1943 the War Production Board authorized installation of the control valves and completion of the Madera Canal. Two valves were borrowed from Hoover Dam in 1943 to begin work and on February 21, 1944 the outlet works were functional and controlled storage began.[248]

In the region south and west of the canal company's service area irrigation depended on groundwater. As early as 1910 land irrigated from artesian wells was advertised for sale near Mendota and the eight thousand-acre Oro Loma

[246] T.C. Mott to J. Leroy Nickel, Jr., July 2, 1942.
[247] SJCC, "List of Enemy Aliens Who Are Consumers of the Canal Company," c. 1942; Herman P. Goebel, Jr. to Judge D. Oliver Germino, August 13, 1942; Public Utilities Commission of the State of California (hereafter cited as PUC), Decision 41368, March 23, 1948, 5.
[248] Autobee, "Friant Division," 13-14; Vincent McGovern, "Memorandum to Mr. Nickel," October 3, 1947.

Farms tract four miles south of Dos Palos went on the market in 1913. By the late 1930s the irrigated acreage above the canal system was expanding and wartime demand accelerated the development of new crop land. Unfortunately, groundwater too often proved to be an unreliable water supply. In 1943 Sam Hamburg applied for canal company service on six thousand acres south and west of the Camp 13 area. The land was already partially irrigated from groundwater but the water table was dropping and the wells had become so saline that without an alternative source of water, farming would have to be abandoned. Hamburg requested service only from September 15 to the following June 15, placing no additional burden on the system at the peak of the irrigation season. There seemed to be no doubt that the canal company, now renamed the San Joaquin Canal Company, had enough water to provide the service and a year earlier T.C. Mott had suggested selling surplus water outside the company's service area. There was no significant opposition to the proposal, but the California Farm Bureau Federation, which often represented local agricultural interests at Railroad Commission hearings, succeeded in adding a stipulation that from May 15 to June 15 and from September 15 to October 15 water could be delivered to the Hamburg lands only when the requirements of existing consumers were fully met.[249]

The concern that water users had about any expansion of irrigated acreage was not a new issue; the water supply was limited, especially during the summer. There was also a lingering suspicion that Miller & Lux was willing to add acreage to increase the canal company's revenue regardless of the impact on existing users. The Hamburg request, and the canal company's apparent confidence that it had ample water to serve another six thousand acres in all but the three months at the height of the irrigation season, brought those latent fears to the surface. So it was that during a break in the Railroad Commission hearing on the Hamburg case a group of farmers gathered under a tree to discuss ways to more effectively present and protect their interests. From that informal discussion, and countless unrecorded meetings, came the organization of the Central California Mutual Water District on November 29, 1944. Membership was open to any landowner in the service areas of the San Joaquin Canal Company, San Luis Canal Company, and Columbia Canal

[249] advertisement, "Oro Loma Farms, $75 per Acre with Abundant Water", *Pacific Rural Press*, January 25, 1913; Thomas C. Mott to J. Leroy Nickel, Jr., March 24, 1942; Railroad Commission, Decision 36691, November 8, 1943.

Company. Members of the founding Board of Directors were Floyd E. Redfern, Harry G. Fawcett, Jack Duarte, Jack Bunker, Henry B. Wolfsen, Rudolph Lindemann, Joe P. Gomes, William Pfitzer and Herman H. Willis. For the first time in more than a decade, water users had an independent local voice.[250]

The organization's first test came when Sam Hamburg asked for additional service. Once Friant Dam began storing water in 1944, the Bureau of Reclamation could capture water in excess of the flows it was required to release to the Miller & Lux canals. Hamburg negotiated a contract with the Bureau for water during the summer months and he wanted to pay the San Joaquin Canal Company to deliver it. CCMWD objected. They claimed that carrying the additional 30 second-feet of water in the Outside Canal, and the difficulty of keeping track of it, could affect service to other consumers. Attorney C. Ray Robinson of Merced said that the group would oppose any plan to supply new agricultural land through the canal system and thereby dilute the rights of existing users. The canal company had anticipated such complaints and company president J. Leroy Nickel, Jr. had denied in June 1944 that it had any plan to expand its service area above the Outside Canal or to transport water for others. Now chief engineer Mott testified that at Oro Loma Road the capacity of the canal was 547 second-feet but the theoretical demand was only 342 second-feet, making it possible to deliver Friant water to the Hamburg pumping system. The Railroad Commission approved the request in October 1945, placing a rate of 25 cents per acre on the service and making the transportation of water subordinate to the needs of the canal company's regular service area.[251]

A similar situation involved the delivery of water to the grasslands. Often impregnated with alkali and poorly drained, the grasslands were suited only for pasture. Miller & Lux had flooded the expanse of shrub brush and grass with surplus water in the spring and again in the fall to produce feed, and in the process created a seasonal wetland habitat used by ducks, geese and other waterfowl migrating along the Pacific Flyway. Responsible sportsmen, but not the more destructive market hunters, were permitted to use the property. As part of its land sales campaign, Miller & Lux began selling its grasslands in the

---

[250] C.W. Bates, "Central California Irrigation District," June 11, 1979, 1; C.W. Bates, "History of Central California Mutual Water District," c. 1979; "By-Laws of the Central California Mutual Water District," c. 1945.
[251] *Los Banos Enterprise*, February 16, 1945; J. Leroy Nickel, Jr. to Richard E. Hyde, June 2, 1944; Railroad Commission, Decision 37712, March 13, 1945, 6-9.

1920s to duck clubs and cattlemen who continued the heritage of dual use. After they were sold, the grasslands tracts continued to receive their customary water supply, but Miller & Lux retained the water rights and it was those grassland rights that the company sold to the Central Valley Project. Once Friant Dam and the canals it supplied were completed, the grasslands would be without a water supply and a valuable waterfowl habitat would be lost.[252]

While the terms of the Purchase Contract were still being finalized in 1939, Secretary of the Interior Ickes and Reclamation Commissioner Page met with grasslands owners to discuss the possibility of getting water from the federal project. As a result, the San Joaquin Grass Lands Mutual Water Association was formed in March 1939 with board members including Henry Wolfsen and George Fink, president of the Gustine Gun Club and a long-time advocate for waterfowl protection. The association made little progress, but faced with an immediate water shortage the Cattlemans' Emergency Water Committee paid almost $13,000 in June 1944 for summer irrigation, making it the first organization to purchase Friant water. Two months later a new Grass Lands Water Association was formed and assumed responsibility for buying supplemental water. Water purchased from the Bureau of Reclamation was delivered by the San Joaquin Canal Company, and in 1945 the Railroad Commission approved the transportation of water to the grasslands and at the same time allowed the canal company to sell its surplus water for grassland irrigation at the standard pasture rate of 75 cents per acre per irrigation. As with the Hamburg lands, all deliveries to the grasslands were subordinate to the needs of regular consumers.[253]

In his testimony at the Railroad Commission hearing on the transportation of Friant water to the Hamburg lands, T.C. Mott spoke out against extending the same arrangement to any additional land. However, within months the Railroad Commission was confronted with over 130 applications for water service which, if granted, would add 50,000 acres to the canal company's service area. Thirty thousand of those acres were above the Outside Canal despite the fact that the Exchange Contract limited the canal company's expansion into that area to 15,000 acres, and 7,000 acres, including

[252] Philip Garone, *The Fall and Rise of the Wetlands of California's Great Central Valley* (Berkeley and Los Angeles, University of California Press, 2011), iBook edition, 182-186, 345-348.
[253] Philip Garone, *The Fall and Rise of the Wetlands of California's Great Central Valley*, iBook edition, 355-360; *Gustine Standard*, June 29, 1944; Railroad Commission, Decision 37712, 5-6, 8-9.

the Hamburg land, were already receiving water. According to the commission it was generally conceded that the willingness of the Bureau of Reclamation to store part of the canal company's entitlement early in the year when there was surplus water and deliver it during the summer had greatly improved the water supply situation. Of particular importance was a 40 percent increase in deliveries to irrigators from July through September. The canal company proposed bringing into the regular service area about 1,500 acres that had historically had temporary service, and that plan was supported by consumer groups, including CCMWD. Noting that negotiations to amend the Exchange Contract were on-going, the commission decided that it was impossible to know how much land could safely be added to the permanent service area so all requests were rejected except for a small acreage of exclusions and matching inclusions for existing irrigators.[254]

At the same hearing, the commission considered another, much larger request for transportation of water purchased from the Bureau of Reclamation. J.R. Hammonds and Panoche Farms were joined by other landowners in a plan to purchase 250 second-feet from Friant for use on 36,000 acres which, like the Hamburg acreage, had an unsustainable groundwater supply. There was not enough capacity in the Outside Canal to carry that much additional water, but the Main and Parallel canals offered an alternative way to deliver water to a pumping system beginning near Camp 13. The Railroad Commission approved the plan, but only to the extent that it did not interfere with service to other irrigators. By January 1946 Hammond and his associates told the canal company that they planned to reduce their purchase to no more than 150 second-feet and requested reconsideration of use of the Outside Canal in order to avoid the additional seventeen feet of pumping lift between the Main and Outside canals. Mott, however, wanted to keep 145 second-feet of excess capacity in the Outside Canal to continue the coordinated operation of the Main and Outside canals that had proven useful in the past, and that made the transportation of so much additional water difficult. In a November 1946 contract the Panoche Water Association agreed to increase the capacity of the Outside Canal by 170 second-feet and the canal company agreed to use 80 second-feet of existing capacity to carry a total of 250 second-feet, with

[254] Railroad Commission, Decision 37712, 6-7; Railroad Commission, Decision 38355, October 30, 1945, 1-9.

evaporation and seepage losses borne by the Panoche association. As improvements were made to the Main and Outside canals the company was able to abandon and fill in the Parallel Canal in 1949.[255]

The Central California Mutual Water District worked to establish itself as the voice of local water users but at first only a few farmers signed up as members, and recruiters working on a commission basis had little success in boosting membership. In May 1947 public meetings were held in Dos Palos and Los Banos in an effort to reinvigorate the organization and at Harry Fawcett's suggestion Charles W. Bates was hired as secretary. Bates visited farmers, sometimes accompanied by director Jack Duarte, and by July membership had increased from 25 to 312 representing 54,312 acres. A full-time engineer was hired to gather data for use at Railroad Commission hearings and to assist members, and a temporary office was opened at 554 I Street in Los Banos before moving to a permanent location at 919 6th Street. The high level of public engagement proved to be unsustainable and after less than a year on the job the engineer was let go and Bates began selling insurance part time, reducing his $400 per month CCMWD salary by half of his income from insurance sales. Half of the office space was subleased to a liquor store to cut down on expenses. Membership continued to increase, however, and the directors became increasingly active behind the scenes as their frustration with the canal company mounted.[256]

That frustration was evident during hearings in early 1948 on the canal company's application to increase its rates, which had not changed since 1930. At that time the Railroad Commission had based its rates on a 7 percent rate of return on invested capital of $2 million for a net annual income of $140,000. The company contended that its actual return had been far less, and analysis by the Public Utilities Commission, the successor to the Railroad Commission, generally confirmed that conclusion. Despite protests from CCMWD and the Farm Bureau, the commission approved the canal company's proposed rate schedule with only minor changes and calculated that in 1946 and 1947 the new rates would have yielded a net revenue in excess of $140,000, representing a rate of return of less than 6 percent on fixed capital of nearly $2.5 million.

[255] Railroad Commission, Decision 38355, 9-11, 13-14; J.E. Woolley to J. Leroy Nickel, Jr., January 29, 1946; Thomas C. Mott to J. Leroy Nickel, Jr., September 13, 1946; agreement, SJCC and Panoche Water Association, November 5, 1946.
[256] Bates, "History of Central California Mutual Water District," 2-5; C.W. Bates, untitled pages, c. 1979, 42; *Los Banos Enterprise*, June 6, 1947; *Los Banos Enterprise*, August 8, 1947.

The old rates ranged from 75 cents per acre for a single pasture irrigation to $7.50 per acre per year for rice with most other crops paying $2.75 per acre annually. The company argued, and the commission agreed, that applying the same rate to crops with different water requirements had the effect of subsidizing the more water intensive crops at the expense of growers who needed less water. The new rates reflected actual water needs. Only milo and field corn remained at the old rate while alfalfa went to $3.75 per acre. At the upper end of the scale were permanent pasture including ladino clover (a water hungry forage crop that had become popular in the San Joaquin Valley) at $5.50 and rice at $7.75. C.W. Bates later admitted that CCMWD "didn't do too good on this one," and there was a sense that the Public Utilities Commission had been too willing to accept the canal company's proposals.[257]

CCMWD was worried about more than the cost of water or the effects of bringing more land into the service area; there was also a persistent concern, evident as early as March 1946, that their basic water supply—the flow schedule based on Schedule 1 of the Purchase Contract—was inadequate, particularly in light of the increasing acreage of summer crops. In fact, Miller & Lux shared that concern and had already initiated talks with the Bureau of Reclamation. Those discussions did not produce any immediate solution, and CCMWD insisted that it should be a participant in any further water supply negotiations. A series of dry years in the late 1940s made the problem even more urgent, and T.C. Mott admitted in 1949 that there was just not enough water. On August 10, 1949 attorney C. Ray Robinson, C.W. Bates and the CCMWD directors went to Sacramento to meet with Bureau officials for a discussion of water problems, although the revision of the flow schedule was not specifically addressed.[258] CCMWD followed up that meeting with a resolution on August 22 calling for an investigation by the Bureau of Reclamation "to ascertain the present and ultimate requirements of the area, to the end that relief can be obtained through negotiation to adjust Schedule 1 water deliveries."[259] Although the Bureau was willing to consider a survey of water requirements, Acting Regional Director Phil Dickinson reminded

[257] PUC, Decision 41368, 1-7, Schedule No. 1 Flat Rate Irrigation Service; Bates, "History of Central California Mutual Water District," 4-5.
[258] Bates, "History of Central California Mutual Water District," 2-5; Phil Dickinson to T.C. Mott, October 11, 1949.
[259] Central California Mutual Water District, resolution adopted August 22, 1949.

CCMWD that the study as well as any negotiations would require the cooperation of the Miller & Lux canal companies. By late 1949, however, any hope of cooperation between CCMWD and Miller & Lux was becoming increasingly unlikely.[260]

Immediately after the rate hearing at the beginning of 1948, the CCMWD Board of Directors asked for its attorney's advice on the steps necessary to purchase the San Joaquin Canal Company. In April a committee was appointed to meet with company president J. Leroy Nickel, Jr. to discuss a possible sale, but it was agreed that they should move cautiously because the sentiments of their own members, to say nothing of the broader public, were unknown. Nickel replied that the canal company was not for sale because for the now much diminished firm of Miller & Lux it remained a good income property. The leaders of the CCMWD undoubtedly anticipated that response because even before they received Nickel's rejection they met with water attorney Stephen Downey at the Sutter Club in Sacramento to discuss ways to take over the canal company. At that June 2, 1948 meeting it was agreed that the best approach would be the formation of an irrigation district, which would have the power to condemn the canal system if negotiations for its purchase were unsuccessful. Rather than take immediate action, the district board decided on a policy of "watchful waiting."[261]

The final straw may have been a new proposal from Sam Hamburg. To insure a reliable summer irrigation supply for his land above the Outside Canal, Hamburg proposed drilling a series of wells that would pump water into the canal downstream from his property in exchange for gravity water from the canal company. CCMWD was strongly opposed and the Public Utilities Commission hearing on January 16, 1950 attracted such a large crowd of irate farmers that Nickel published "An Open Letter to Consumers of the San Joaquin Canal Co." in which he announced the withdrawal of the Hamburg petition and accepted responsibility for misreading the situation. By then it was already too late to avert a larger battle. CCMWD board president Rudolph Lindemann had died on December 29, 1949, and according to C.W. Bates, Lindemann had been reluctant to start a fight with Miller & Lux. His successor,

---

[260] Phil Dickinson to C. Ray Robinson, September 13, 1949.
[261] Bates, "History of Central California Mutual Water District," 4-5.

Lawrence Wolfsen, had no such reservations. At a meeting on January 9, 1950 the board voted unanimously to begin the formation of a Wright Act district.[262]

The first step in the organization of an irrigation district was the preparation of a petition that, with the signatures of at least five hundred district voters or landowners representing 20 percent or more of the district's assessed property value, would set the stage for an election. The proposed Central California Irrigation District would include only the land entitled to full irrigation service from the San Joaquin Canal Company, about 150,000 acres. Within days of announcing its intention to form an irrigation district, the CCMWD board gave engineer Fred Woolley, the brother of long-time Miller & Lux attorney W.E. Woolley, the task of drawing the boundary map to accompany the petition, which was complicated by the fact that the canal company served so many non-contiguous parcels. Meanwhile, C.W. Bates began the public promotion of the district.[263]

Proponents made three main arguments in the district's favor. The first was the claim that in seeking remedies to what had become an inadequate water supply a public district would be better positioned to deal with the Bureau of Reclamation or even to drill wells as a source of supplemental water than the private corporation. Unknown to CCMWD, the canal company did briefly consider a well drilling program but it could not afford the investment, and even if it could find the money it feared a backlash against the higher rates that would be needed to recover the cost. The second point was that the farmers themselves, not Miller & Lux or the Public Utilities Commission, should control their most vital resource. Local control and the promise of a better water supply had, of course, been fixtures in earlier attempts to form a public district on the west side. Finally, district proponents believed that the canal system could be acquired, by negotiation or condemnation, for the $2.5 million fixed capital value recognized in the 1948 rate case, and that private or government loans to cover the purchase price could easily be repaid without raising water rates by using the profit margin built into the rate structure. It was an optimistic assumption because although the canal company had been

---

[262] Bates, "History of Central California Mutual Water District," 5-6; Bates, "Central California Irrigation District," 2; *Los Banos Enterprise,* January 20, 1950; *Los Banos Enterprise,* January 27, 1950
[263] Bates, "Central California Irrigation District," 2.

willing to accept the $2.5 million valuation for the purpose of setting rates it claimed that the full value of the properties and rights was at least $4 million.[264]

At a CCMWD meeting in Los Banos on July 11, 1950 petitions were handed out to fifty volunteers who would gather the necessary signatures. Support came from local Farm Bureau and Grange chapters and from two dairy associations, and by the end of August the petitions had enough signatures but lacked the necessary valuation. It took several more months to finish the job but by the beginning of 1951 the petition had 738 names. J. Leroy Nickel noted that when the names of spouses were removed the petition carried the names of fewer people than CCMWD had claimed as members in the canal company service area in 1948. When the petition came before the Merced County Board of Supervisors on February 20, 1951 opposition came from attorney L.M. Linneman representing twenty-five farmers from the Dos Palos-Firebaugh area and from canal company officials, who pointed to discrepancies in the legal description of the boundaries. On a vote of four-to-one the supervisors accepted the petition and forwarded it to the state Division of Water Resources for an analysis of the district's feasibility. Rebuffed by the supervisors, Miller & Lux took their complaint to the courts. They claimed that the district map had left out a 980-acre tract and that even though the map showed 25 acres in Madera County the petition and notice of hearing had not been published in that county as the law required. They argued that those lapses were sufficient to invalidate the action taken by the Board of Supervisors.[265]

While the case made its way through the legal system, the canal company launched a public campaign against the district. It claimed that less than a quarter of its approximately 1,600 consumers had signed the irrigation district petition, suggesting a lack of enthusiasm for a public district. Following a company-sponsored meeting in June 1951 an opposition group called the Water Watchers was formed under the chairmanship of Edward Lewis of Dos Palos, and some landowners who had signed the petition switched sides and

[264] *Los Banos Enterprise*, January 13, 1950, March 3, 1950; *Gustine Standard*, February 2, 1950; J. Leroy Nickel, Jr. to T.C. Mott, January 29, 1951.

[265] Bates, "History of Central California Mutual Water District," 7; *Los Banos Enterprise*, July 14, 1950, February 23, 1951, July 6, 1951; J. Leroy Nickel, Jr. to T.C. Mott, January 30, 1951.

joined the opposition, including Floyd Redfern, CCMWD's first president.[266] Their major complaint was put in the form of a question directed to district backers: "How much is it going to cost us to bond our land so that we may raise the money to buy what we already have?"[267] In response CCMWD reiterated its belief that no bond would be necessary and in any event a bond issue would require a separate election. The district's petition returned to the Board of Supervisors on August 1. In an all-day hearing attended by none of the opponents, the supervisors corrected the district map, rejected Sam Hamburg's request for the inclusion of his 6,000 acres and set an election for October 9, 1951 to decide the fate of the Central California Irrigation District.[268]

Both sides were ready for a high-stakes contest. CCMWD had hired Sacramento publicist Ralph Clark a year earlier to supervise its advertising campaign.[269] An example of his work was an August 1951 newspaper advertisement that capitalized on the themes of absentee ownership and the demand for more water. A cartoon millionaire complete with top hat, cigar and diamond stick-pin was shown carrying buckets of "water profits" to San Francisco while the text highlighted "Big Profits — Little Water" and claimed that "Development of additional water would cut into the fat dividends of the San Francisco owners." An irrigation district, however, would use those profits to "increase water supplies to 100 per cent of the needs of the people."[270] In opposition the Water Watchers adopted a wise old owl as their logo along with the phrase "Why buy what we already have?" One advertisement challenged district backers to explain "How we can get something for nothing, How we can borrow 100% of the purchase price of this water system without a mortgage lien on our farm land for security." The answer, they suggested, was that farmers "would be bonded or assessed" and disparaged the "attempt to hoodwink us into believing the canal company could be bought or acquired through condemnation proceedings at the ridiculously low figure of 2-1/2 million dollars!"[271] Subsequent attacks by the Water Watchers sharpened the

[266] *Los Banos Enterprise*, June 29, 1951; Bates, "Central California Irrigation District," 3.
[267] *Los Banos Enterprise*, July 6, 1951.
[268] *Los Banos Enterprise*, July 20, 1951, August 3, 1951; *Gustine Standard*, August 2, 1951.
[269] Bates, "Central California Irrigation District," 3.
[270] *Los Banos Enterprise*, August 24, 1951.
[271] *Gustine Standard*, August 30, 1951.

emphasis on district tax assessments and the risk of foreclosure if assessments went unpaid.[272]

CCMWD was forced to answer their opponents' claims that an irrigation district would inevitably bring debt and tax assessments. In a shift in tactics, a mid-September CCMWD advertisement said "Let's find out—the American way! The only way we can intelligently determine whether it is good business for the farmers to own and operate the San Joaquin Canal Company is to form a legal water district at the October 9th election." Voters were reminded that "formation of the district does not authorize the issuance of one penny in bonds against any ranch or private property."[273] That theme remained prominent for the rest of the campaign. The Water Watchers fired back, asking "Why find out the hard way! Why form the CCID and then look at the bill! Is it the American way to leap before you look?"[274] Although it relied on the Water Watchers to lead the opposition the canal company ran ads of its own reminding voters that it had defended the region's irrigation rights for 80 years and asking pointedly "Do you remember the Depression days?" when farmers had to pay only for the acres they actually planted and the company, not the landowners, absorbed the risk of lower water sales.[275]

The fight for an irrigation district divided neighbors and even families; Jack Bunker was a prominent CCMWD director and E.E. Bunker joined the executive committee of the Water Watchers. Public meetings brought out large crowds that heard mostly respectful debates between representatives of CCMWD and the Water Watchers. At one meeting, however, CCMWD attorney James Cobey "enlivened the evening with 15 minutes of spirited oratory" that included calling the Public Utilities Commission "nothing but stooges for Miller & Lux" and on another occasion C.W. Bates became so enraged by what he believed were falsehoods that he called Water Watcher's chairman Edward Lewis "a God damn liar."[276] Besides meetings and newspaper advertisements, CCMWD used a series of radio broadcasts and mail pieces to reach voters. The final campaign mailing was ready to go to the post office

---

[272] *Los Banos Enterprise*, September 14, 1951.
[273] *Los Banos Enterprise*, September 14, 1951.
[274] *Los Banos Enterprise*, September 21, 1951.
[275] *Los Banos Enterprise*, September 28, 1951.
[276] *Los Banos Enterprise*, October 5, 1951; Bates, "Central California Irrigation District," 6.

when a store next to the CCMWD office caught fire on a night just before the election. Bates recruited on-lookers to help move the mailing and other records to the safety of a nearby bank. The office suffered only minor water damage.[277]

On election day both sides were well organized and ready to get their supporters to the polls. C.W. Bates remained at the office taking calls regarding the eligibility to vote, which was limited to actual residents of the canal company service area and therefore left out landowners who lived outside those boundaries. Like the rest of the election campaign the get-out-the-vote effort was intense. Bates later recalled that "Charley Machado told the story of going to one family where he found 3 of them were for the District, and 1 opposed. He managed to get the 3 into the car to go to the polls just about the deadline for voting, and swiped the boots of the 1 who was opposed so that he never left the house."[278] For the crowd gathered at the CCMWD office the first returns were discouraging; the Gustine precinct went against the district by a margin of more than two-to-one. The district won small majorities in the Newman, Dos Palos and Firebaugh areas but it took a two-hundred-vote plurality in Los Banos to put the district over the top. In the end, a total of 1,288 votes were cast in favor of the district with 1,201 votes against its formation. It had been a bruising fight but by the narrowest of margins, San Joaquin & Kings River farmers finally had an irrigation district.[279]

---

[277] *Los Banos Enterprise*, October 5, 1951; Bates, "Central California Irrigation District," 4.
[278] Bates, "Central California Irrigation District," 4.
[279] Bates, "Central California Irrigation District," 4-5; *Gustine Standard*, October 11, 1951.

10

Under New Management

At the October 9, 1951 election, voters also elected the directors of the new irrigation district. The directors—Frank L. Cerutti, J.P. Bunker, Harry G. Fawcett, Herman H. Willis and Lawrence C. Wolfsen—met for the first time on November 20, 1951. Wolfsen, who had been head of the CCMWD, was elected president and C.W. Bates was named secretary. At its first meeting the board resolved to do whatever it could to deal with the seasonal water shortage anticipated for the summer of 1952. In fact, however, their ability to do anything was limited. Miller & Lux promptly filed a new legal challenge that broadened the list of alleged irregularities in the proceedings before the Merced County Board of Supervisors that the company had pleaded in its first attempt to stop the organization of the irrigation district, a case that was still pending in a San Benito County court. Until the legality of its existence was finally settled, the district was forced to delay its plans to take over the canal company.[280]

A heavy snowpack in early 1952 gave irrigators a full supply in the spring and early summer but even though the flow in August was expected to be close to the Schedule I entitlement of the Miller & Lux canals, the San Joaquin Canal Company's share of the entitlement was not enough for its entire crop acreage, forcing service to be cut off to land with temporary or secondary contracts. As it had done in 1951, the company allowed consumers with wells to pump into the canal system for transfer to other lands holding regular water service contracts. In ruling against requests to add irrigated acreage to the service area, the Public Utilities Commission in February 1953 confirmed that the canal company now had an inadequate water supply from about mid-July to early September. It was against that background that Ralph Hammonds, whose family corporation owned land uphill from the canal in the Firebaugh area, made a proposal to the CCID board in January 1953. Hammonds offered to develop approximately seventy wells in the canal company service area capable

---

[280] Bates, "History of Central California Mutual Water District," 8; *Los Banos Enterprise*, December 14, 1951.

of supplying up to 22,000 acre-feet per month in exchange for secondary water service on 9,100 acres. George Nickel, Jr., Henry Miller's great-grandson, had helped negotiate the deal as a way to increase revenue by selling surplus water, and T.C. Mott believed that the well drilling program would do no damage to existing wells. Although undoubtedly skeptical about plans to increase the service area even with the promise of a supplemental water supply, the CCID board took a neutral position and got George Nickel, Jr. and canal company engineer William Raznoff to agree to a mail ballot to gauge landowner support for Hammonds' proposal. The results were unfavorable, but by that time other events had intervened.[281]

The San Joaquin Canal Company had always been a valuable asset to Miller & Lux. Although the big cattle company had initially feared regulation by the Railroad Commission, it discovered, as had other utilities, that regulation had distinct advantages, including an assurance of reasonable profits. In 1952 for example, water sales of half a million dollars yielded a before-tax profit in excess of $157,000. And as long as it was a profitable business, Miller & Lux executives saw no reason to sell the canal company to CCID. The irrigation district could launch condemnation proceedings and let a jury determine the valuation of the company, but CCID attorney C. Ray Robinson knew that the process could be long and costly. It was also risky because the valuation might turn out to be more than the landowners were willing to pay. Instead, Robinson quietly negotiated the sale of the company with J. Leroy Nickel, Jr. and in March 1953 the CCID board learned that a deal had been struck to purchase the canal company for $4.2 million. The price was far above the $2.5 million estimate that irrigation district supporters had optimistically used during the organization election but was only about half the figure advanced by the Water Watchers and was less than what most observers expected. A preliminary agreement was soon signed and the sale was announced to the public at a dinner meeting of the CCID board at the Canal Farm Inn. Announcement of the sale surprised local residents because the legal

[281] W.A. Raznoff to J. Leroy Nickel, Jr., June 19, 1952; Vincent J. McGovern to T.C. Mott, March 25, 1952; Public Utilities Commission, Decision 48294, February 17, 1953, 4-5; CCID, "Minutes of the Board of Directors" (hereafter cited as CCID Board Minutes), 1: 36 (January 6, 1953); *Los Banos Enterprise*, January 30, 1953; George Wilmarth Nickel, Jr., *Following the Cattle King: A Lifetime of Agriculture, Water Management and Water Conservation in California's Central Valley* (Berkeley: Bancroft Library, Regional Oral History Office, 2002), 61, 63; CCID Board Minutes, 1: 38 (February 3, 1953); Bates, "History of Central California Mutual Water District," 9.

battle over the district's formation was not yet resolved. The district's opponents had lost in the lower court and their appeal was still pending. Miller & Lux and several of the individual plaintiffs withdrew from the case when terms of the sale were finalized but over a dozen landowners continued the fight until July 1953 when the appellate court ruled in favor of the district.[282]

When CCID directors announced their agreement to buy the canal company, they also revealed plans for a bond issue to pay for it. Bonds offered the lowest financing cost, and because bonds required a public election they fulfilled a campaign promise to let the people decide whether the cost of acquiring the canal system was reasonable or not. By early June 1953 an engineer's report in support of the bonds had been forwarded to the California District Securities Commission, which gave its approval by the end of the month. Petitions calling for an election were circulated and in less than a month had over six hundred signatures representing one-third of the assessed value of property in the district. The election was scheduled for September 2.[283]

At public meetings, engineer John C. Luthin of Santa Cruz, the author of the bond analysis submitted to the state, noted that prior to the agreement to sell the system, the canal company had applied to the Public Utilities Commission for a substantial rate increase. Under the company's proposal the cost of alfalfa irrigation would rise from $3.75 per acre to $5.75 per acre, cotton would climb from $3.00 per acre to $4.55 per acre and other crops would face similar increases. By comparison, CCID's plans called for a rate of $2.30 per acre plus an additional $2.00 per acre-foot for entitlement water delivered during the peak months of July through September. Pump water, when developed, was expected to cost about $2.50 per acre-foot. Luthin found that the CCID rate would be cheaper than the canal company's proposal for every crop, and after operating expenses and bond repayment the district would have a surplus that could be used to acquire additional water and improve the canal system.[284] A pro-bond pamphlet summed up the district's case: "Now is our

---

[282] John F. Forbes & Co., "San Joaquin Canal Company, Statement of Income and Earned Surplus for the Years Ending December 31, 1953 and 1952, and Comparison," May 13, 1954; Bates, "Central California Irrigation District," 7; CCID Board Minutes, 1: 45 (March 6, 1953); *Los Banos Enterprise*, March 27, 1953; *Los Banos Enterprise*, July 3, 1953; CCID Board Minutes, 1: 62 (July 8, 1953).

[283] *Los Banos Enterprise*, March 27, 1953; CCID Board Minutes, 1: 65-73 (July 27, 1953).

[284] *Los Banos Enterprise*, August 14, 1953.

chance to get the water we must have … at rates we can afford."[285] On election day, the bonds carried easily on a vote of 1,508 to 226, and even the Gustine precinct, which had opposed formation of the district two years earlier, supported the bonds by a margin of almost three-to-one.[286]

The canal company had agreed to take the bonds as payment at an interest rate of 4 percent, but instead the district advertised the bonds in hopes of getting a lower rate. The only bidder was a syndicate led by Bank of America that offered 3.85 percent, a rate that disappointed district officials but eventually proved to be a bargain. After the bonds had been printed, and after district president Wolfsen and secretary C.W. Bates had spent an entire day signing all 4,200 bonds, it was discovered that the cost of an armored car to transport them to the Bank of America office in San Francisco would be prohibitive. Instead, Bates put the now fully negotiable bonds in the trunk of his car on the early morning of January 15, 1954 and with his wife headed for San Francisco followed by a constable in another car. The bonds were safely delivered and later that day the directors of the Central California Irrigation District gathered in the office of Miller & Lux to hand over their check and sign the final documents that brought to a close the oldest major private irrigation enterprise in California, and once again reconnect the ownership of land and water. In its final years as owner of the canal system Miller & Lux had been a capable steward but changing times required more than business as usual. Those present and future challenges, and the heritage of the great canal, now belonged to the district.[287]

Even though the formal sale of the canal company was not completed until January 15, the district took operational control of the canal system on January 1, 1954. CCID intended to retain virtually all of the San Joaquin Canal Company's employees but its top managers in Los Banos—Thomas Mott and William A. Raznoff—also managed the three Miller & Lux mutual water companies. Miller & Lux agreed to continue paying Mott's salary with CCID contributing its proportional share while the district employed Raznoff and billed Miller & Lux for the time he spent working for the mutual companies. A similar arrangement covered southern division superintendent Ed Mulkey,

---

[285] Water user's Vote "Yes" Committee, "Let's Talk About Local Ownership of the Irrigation System." 1953.
[286] CCID Board Minutes, 1: 81-82 (October 9, 1953).
[287] Bates, "Central California Irrigation District," 7-8.

who had one-third of his time billed to the drainage-only Poso Canal Company. Miller & Lux continued to provide engineering services to CCID, and it was not until 1959 that the district board instructed the manager to buy a good level so that CCID could do more of its own routine engineering and surveying. As part of the now-amicable transition, the irrigation district moved its office into the Miller & Lux building, where it leased space for $200 per month, all expenses included except long-distance telephone.[288]

CCID found it necessary to clean up some rare abuses by individual canal operators. Only the widely disliked head canal tender in the Colony section was removed when CCID took over, but within a year a canal tender in the Orestimba section was fired because he had made a habit of accepting bribes. CCID assessor-collector-treasurer R.C. Osburn recalled that "we never got water until we slipped him a $20 bill. That wasn't too bad, we got used to it, but what irked us was that as soon as he collected from me, he went upstream on the ditch and collected another $20 [from] another farmer for the privilege of stealing the water being sent down to me."[289] At about the same time, a canal tender at Badger Flat was dismissed for the same reason, setting off a short-lived furor among irrigators who had become comfortable with a certain level of corruption that CCID was determined to stamp out.[290]

In 1954 the Central California Irrigation District was the state's fifth largest, with a gross area of 144,322 acres. It operated 263 miles of canals regulated by 240 check structures or weirs, half of them still made of wooden timbers. There were fifteen outlets to farmer-operated lateral canals and over 1,300 gates for delivery to farm ditches. Alfalfa was still the most important crop at over 50,000 acres in 1954, followed by 23,000 acres of grain and about 13,000 acres for both rice and cotton. Permanent pasture rounded out the top five crops with nearly 12,000 acres. CCID continued improvement and maintenance work started by Miller & Lux including the installation of an automatic radial headgate on the Outside Canal designed to maintain consistent flow into the canal when the water level in the pool behind Mendota

[288] CCID Board Minutes, 1: 117 (November 13, 1953); CCID Board Minutes, 1: 121-122 (December 2, 1953); CCID Board Minutes, 2: 241 (February 11, 1959).

[289] Bates, "Central California Irrigation District", 9-10. The quotation in on p. 9.

[290] Bates, Central California Irrigation District, 9; CCID, *Financial Statement and Annual Report for the Year Ending December 31, 1954* (hereafter cited as CCID Annual Report for 19__), 10.

Dam rose or fell, and in 1955 a similar manually-operated gate went in at the head of the Main Canal.[291] One of the most important changes initiated by the district in its first year was putting two-way radios in most district vehicles, a program that officials believed quickly "paid for itself many times over in improved service and water savings."[292] New technology helped but the district also had to contend with all of the mundane and longstanding problems of operating the canal system like weed control, cattle trampling down canal banks and muskrats undermining them. In 1958 farmers were informed that "The Muskrat control problem continues to plague your District, and all water users desiring a little target practice are urged to travel the canal banks about dusk and try their aim."[293]

Another perennial problem involved the places where the Main and Outside canals crossed the creeks that flowed out of the Diablo Range. To prevent damage to the banks, the canals were closed in the winter and the stream channels were opened, and in the spring the process was reversed and the creeks were plugged to allow canal water to pass. Spring storms could force canal operators to halt irrigation and open the creeks, often more than once. During the campaign for the bond issue in 1953, CCID directors made a commitment to build siphons to carry the canals safely under creek channels and permit uninterrupted irrigation. Los Banos Creek was the most important because so much of the district's service area was north of it. Following a destructive flood in December 1955, CCID worked with Merced County to clean out the Los Banos Creek channel to improve flood passage, and in February 1956 a siphon was completed on the Outside Canal. The situation was more complicated at the Main Canal crossing because the canal followed the creek bed for over two hundred yards. To install a siphon the creek had to be realigned to intersect the canal at a right angle. It took until 1971 to reach agreement with neighboring landowners on the relocation of the creek and the following spring the five-barrel Main Canal siphon was finished. To the north, a small siphon was run under San Luis Creek on the Outside Canal to provide limited service until the creek was plugged in late spring but it was the construction of San Luis Dam that eliminated the flood threat on that creek.

---

[291] CCID Annual Report for 1954, 8-10.
[292] CCID Annual Report for 1955, 10.
[293] CCID Annual Report for 1958, 15.

Garzas Creek was not a significant threat but Orestimba Creek was, and the district had to haul dirt for several weeks to restore the banks washed out by a 1958 flood. A siphon was finally built during the 1972-1973 winter construction season.[294]

Some situations were unexpected. About 1947 the canal company had noticed that a section of the Outside Canal south of Dos Palos was not able to carry as much water as it had in the past. At first, engineers thought it was partially blocked by silt but on closer inspection they discovered that the canal and the ground around it had dropped eighteen inches in elevation. The cause was not immediately apparent, but it turned out to be an example of subsidence. On the land lying above the canal, irrigation relied on pumping from deep wells. The rapid expansion of agriculture in the late 1930s and 1940s led to an equally rapid groundwater overdraft. Not only did the depth to water in the wells drop quickly but the land itself collapsed into the dewatered strata. In some areas south and west of Mendota surface elevations dropped by as much as ten feet. By 1960 subsidence in the vicinity of Oro Loma reached six inches per year and CCID was forced to continually raise the height of the canal banks to keep water flowing through the low spot. Following years of negotiations, the district was able to get permission from the Bureau of Reclamation in 1963 to construct a bypass from the Delta-Mendota Canal to the Outside Canal downstream from the subsidence area to help maintain flow through the system.[295]

The changes made to the canal system improved service to growers but the overarching problem was getting enough water at the times when it was needed. Securing a "100 percent supply" had been a central theme of the campaign for district formation and it would remain a constant concern. The district's basic water supply was defined by the 1939 Exchange Contract. The four Exchange Contractors (CCID, San Luis Canal Company, Firebaugh Canal Company and Columbia Canal Company) were entitled to a substitute supply equal to the flow reserved to them by Schedule 1 of the Purchase Contract, as measured at the Whitehouse gauging station northeast of Mendota. In May

---

[294] Bates, "Central California Irrigation District," 10-13; CCID Annual Report for 1956, 12; CCID Annual Report for 1957, 13; CCID Annual Report for 1958, 10-11; CCID Annual Report for 1971, 15-16; CCID Annual Report for 1972, 14.
[295] Ralph L. Milliken, notes from talk with Thomas Mott, January 11, 1955; CCID Annual Report for 1957, 14; CCID Annual Report for 1959, 13; CCID Board Minutes, 2: 329 (April 27, 1960); CCID Annual Report for 1963, 13.

1943 Bureau of Reclamation engineer Courtlandt Eaton wrote to T.C. Mott that he was "much interested in discussing with you a new and simplified Schedule 1. Also the transfer of Whitehouse to Kerckhoff thus avoiding a lot of future mathematics."[296] Eaton's letter showed that the Bureau was beginning to grapple with the operational realities of the Purchase and Exchange contracts, which required daily calculation of a constantly variable flow entitlement that was a combination of natural runoff and the storage and release of water for upstream power generation. Those were the mathematics that Eaton was worried about, and it would be simpler to base any calculation on the actual flow of the river into Friant (measured below the Kerckhoff powerhouse) than to use a location downstream from Friant that would often have little or no actual flow once the Central Valley Project was in full operation. Bureau officials later underscored that they were "interested in revising the schedule primarily for the reason that we want to circumvent the administrative difficulties inherent in Schedule-1."[297]

T.C. Mott was less concerned about the mechanics of calculating the Schedule 1 entitlement than he was about matching Exchange Contract deliveries with seasonal irrigation demand. Schedule 1 represented historic crop water rights based on river flows that peaked in the spring and early summer and then dropped later in the summer. The shortage of summer water had been an issue since the early twentieth century but the shift from grain and pasture irrigation to summer crops made the problem even more acute. Presented with an opportunity to revisit Schedule 1, Miller & Lux hoped to trade a reduction in the Bureau's total water supply obligation for a more favorable seasonal distribution. Mott drew up a new schedule of monthly deliveries that shifted water to the summer months but gave up some unneeded water at other times of the year. Mott proposed an annual delivery to the contracting companies of about 790,000 acre-feet, later revised to 804,277 acre-feet, which was less than the original Schedule 1 entitlement. Courtlandt Eaton responded with a proposal for 690,000 acre-feet, and by 1946

[296] quoted in SJCC, "Summary of Negotiations Between Bureau and Four Contracting Companies for Revision of Schedule 1," September 30, 1952, 2.
[297] R.S. Calland to T.C. Mott, December 4, 1947.

Bureau engineers had unofficially suggested a 712,500 acre-foot schedule of deliveries no longer dependent on San Joaquin River flow calculations.[298]

After the Bureau of Reclamation rejected Mott's first attempt at revising Schedule 1, he drew up a new 795,000 acre-foot plan but the mutual water companies objected and by the time their demands were incorporated and the San Joaquin Canal Company's share had been placed on the same basis the schedule had ballooned to over 859,000 acre-feet. During 1949 Miller & Lux drafted a proposal referred to as "Schedule X" that would provide a minimum delivery of 712,000 acre-feet and maximum of 830,000 acre-feet, with each year's specific quantity based on an estimate of San Joaquin River runoff. The plan was submitted to the Bureau in late December 1949 and was rejected in March, with the observation that while Schedule X would slightly reduce the total amount of water the Bureau was obligated to deliver the increased summer deliveries would require larger releases from Sacramento River storage and a consequent reduction in water sales to other users. Discussions continued between Miller & Lux and the Bureau of Reclamation but by the spring of 1951 there were no signs of progress.[299]

The first water delivered by the Delta-Mendota Canal reached the Mendota Pool on July 15, 1951. Unexpectedly high levels of salinity were immediately detected and prompted a protest from Miller & Lux. The basic problem, which had been under almost continuous study for more than a quarter century, was finding a way to move low salinity Sacramento River water across the Delta to the pumping plant near Tracy that minimized contamination from higher salinity San Joaquin River flows. The state had planned to divert water from the Sacramento River to Snodgrass Slough and let it flow south through interior Delta channels. The Bureau of Reclamation initially preferred a completely isolated conveyance around the edge of the Delta with a siphon under the San Joaquin River. That plan was much more expensive and encountered local opposition, so after tests on a hydraulic model of the Delta in the Bureau's Denver laboratory attention returned to

---

[298] SJCC, "Summary of Negotiations," 3-4; Courtlandt Eaton to T.C. Mott, April 6, 1944; Thomas C. Mott to J. Leroy Nickel, Jr., January 17, 1947 and attached undated Bureau of Reclamation memorandum.

[299] SJCC, "Summary of Negotiations," 4-8; Vincent J. McGovern, "Memorandum re: An Amendment to the Exchange Contract So As To Provide for a Definite Monthly and Annual Schedule of Water Deliveries to the Contracting Canal Companies," April 18, 1949; Vincent J. McGovern, "Proposed Diversion Schedule with Bureau Modifying Existing Commitments Under Exchange Contract," August 10, 1949; Thomas C. Mott to Richard Boke, December 28, 1949; Richard L. Boke to T.C. Mott, March 2, 1950.

through-Delta options. Instead of the elaborate diversion system envisioned by state engineers, a 4,200-foot dredged cut with control gates—called the Delta Cross-Channel—connected the Sacramento River to Snodgrass Slough at Walnut Grove. The cross-channel was not yet in operation when the Delta-Mendota Canal began deliveries, but even after it was the salinity limits in the Exchange Contract were frequently exceeded.[300]

As soon as CCID took control of the canal system in January 1954, T.C. Mott resubmitted his December 1949 Schedule X proposal, which he believed remained the best starting point for negotiations. The final paragraph of his letter to the Bureau of Reclamation pointedly noted that "The resubmission of this plan is based on the assumption that it will be possible for the Bureau to deliver water of the quality specified in the Exchange Contract."[301] Mott's plan was again quickly rejected, but Acting Regional Director R.S. Calland expressed a willingness to negotiate the kind of delivery schedule sought by CCID and the other contracting companies but one determined without reference to flow on the San Joaquin River and with less stringent salinity requirements. The salinity issue was particularly important. Calland wrote that "it should be possible to arrive at new water-quality provisions which would assure delivery of water acceptable for agricultural purposes while providing benefit to the Project in compensation for the advantages accruing to you under the other changes."[302] After ten years of on-again, off-again talks, it was the unachievable salinity limits in the Exchange Contract that gave the contractors the leverage they needed to reach a deal with the Bureau of Reclamation.

The question, of course, was how much salinity was "acceptable for agricultural purposes." To get an answer the three water quality experts who had reviewed the terms of the original contract in 1938 were asked to revisit the issue and make recommendations. On a visit to the region in July 1954 they found that conditions had improved since 1938 and that the application of water with a higher salt content had actually increased the permeability of some soils. They emphasized the importance of leaching—the application of

---

[300] T.C. Mott to A.R. Olsen, July 24, 1951; Vincent J. McGovern to T.C. Mott, July 26, 1951; Jackson and Paterson, *The Sacamento-San Joaquin Delta*, 42-44; "Contracting Entities: Salinity of Water Delivered During 1954 Compared with Allowable Salinity," October 15, 1954.
[301] Thomas C. Mott to Clyde H. Spencer, January 21, 1954
[302] R.S. Calland to T.C. Mott, February 15, 1954

sufficient water to flush dissolved salts from the crop root zone—along with drainage to maintain a salinity balance and keep the water table at a safe depth. In fact, Warren Schoonover and W.P. Kelley concluded that "As was the case at the time of the previous report, we still hold that leaching and drainage, rather than the quality of the Delta water, are the primary problems in the area under consideration."[303] As to acceptable salinity levels in water delivered by the Bureau of Reclamation, Schoonover and Kelley simply reiterated their previous opinion that it would be safe to apply water with a five-year average of 300 parts per million total dissolved solids, a one-year average of 400 parts per million and a one-month average of not over 600 parts per million. The third member of the committee, Frank M. Eaton, reached similar conclusions but insisted on using a leaching formula that his colleagues found unconvincing.[304]

Negotiations were concluded in 1955, and on March 17, 1956 the Amended Exchange Contract was signed in a ceremony at the Canal Farm Inn in Los Banos. Missing from the gathering was Thomas C. Mott, the architect of both the original contract and its replacement, who had died unexpectedly the previous year. The new agreement made a number of fundamental changes. Instead of an entitlement that fluctuated with flow on the San Joaquin River, the new schedule was fixed at 855,000 acre-feet in normal years and 665,000 acre-feet in critical years, with a monthly distribution that increased availability in the summer months. The designation of critical years was based on inflow to Shasta Lake, reflecting the dependence on the Sacramento River as the ultimate source for deliveries through the Delta-Mendota Canal. However, in the event that the Bureau could not provide enough water from the Delta, CCID and the other contracting entities retained all of their rights on the San Joaquin River as recognized in the 1939 contracts. The contractors also gained considerable flexibility in scheduling water delivery within each month as well as a limited ability to carry over unused water to the following months. In terms of water quality, the new contract promised "suitable irrigation water" and set maximum average salinity levels of 400 parts per

---

[303] W.P. Kelley and W.R. Schoonover, "Evaluation of the Salinity of the Water Delivered Through the Delta-Mendota Canal," September 8, 1954, 9.
[304] Kelley and Schoonover, "Evaluation of the Salinity of the Water Delivered Through the Delta-Mendota Canal," 8; W.P. Kelley to G.H. Spencer, October 7, 1954.

million over five years and up to 800 parts per million daily. Except for a monthly average of 600 parts per million, the new salinity limits exceeded the consultants' recommendations but Schoonover assured CCID that the higher values would still be satisfactory.[305] The amended contract recognized that circumstances had changed since 1939 and it provided important benefits for both the Bureau of Reclamation and the San Joaquin River Exchange Contractors. For CCID it seemed that, except for years of statewide water shortage, "an adequate water supply appears assured."[306]

The Amended Exchange Contract provided for renegotiation of any of its provisions after five years. In October 1960 the four Exchange Contractors announced their intention to seek modifications that would give them greater flexibility in scheduling adjustments to the monthly delivery schedule, and they acknowledged that the Bureau of Reclamation would require "some compensating advantages."[307] What the Bureau wanted was for the Exchange Contractors to surrender some of their winter water, initially asking for 24,000 acre-feet. It took until 1966 to reach agreement on a plan that would have the contractors give up 15,000 acre-feet of their November-March entitlement, reduce the daily maximum delivery during those months and make other operational concessions. In return, CCID and its partners got substantially greater scheduling flexibility throughout the year, including the elimination of the so-called "change of status" provision that hampered their ability to shift water between months when the Bureau was drawing down Shasta storage as well as the opportunity to exceed the maximum delivery rate of 2,316 second-feet for short periods of time. The Second Amended Exchange Contract was finalized in late 1967, giving CCID an opportunity to more closely match its entitlement water supply to each year's unique climate and crop demands.[308]

In the early 1950s when CCID was preparing to take control of the canal system, renegotiation of the Exchange Contract was still only a hopeful possibility but the need for a supplemental water supply during the summer months was already a pressing necessity. With the bond election behind them,

[305] *Merced Sun-Star*, March 19, 1956; U.S. Department of the Interior, "Amended Contract for Exchange of Waters," March 17, 1956; Warren R. Schoonover to William A. Raznoff, May 11, 1955.
[306] CCID Annual Report for 1955, 9.
[307] W.A. Raznoff to H.P. Dugan, October 18, 1960.
[308] CCID Board Minutes, 2: 460 (March 28, 1962); CCID Annual Report for 1967, 12-13; U.S. Department of the Interior, "Second Amended Contract for Exchange of Waters," December 6, 1967.

CCID directors in October 1953 discussed well drilling as a way to provide an immediate supplemental water supply, and they prepared to ask private well owners if they would be willing to lease their wells to the district. During its first season eight district-owned wells were placed in operation, and although some farmers expressed concerns about the effect that CCID pumping could have on their own wells, the generally high water table under the district seemed likely to permit a safe expansion of groundwater pumping. A drought from 1959 to 1961 accelerated the well program and by 1966 CCID had thirty-eight of its own wells and twelve leased private wells, and had access to another twenty-six wells on a water credit basis when needed to meet short-term requirements. The wells, along with eight low-lift pumps that returned drainage water to the canal system, produced 73,506 acre-feet in 1966 or about 14 percent of the water delivered to consumers. Facing increasing demands, the district continued to add new wells and refurbish old ones, reaching fifty-three wells in 1976.[309]

CCID needed even more water to keep pace with increasing crop demands. As a result of double- and triple-cropping, by 1960 the reported crop acreage exceeded the gross area of the district. Alfalfa acreage continued its long decline as the dairy industry gave way to diversified row-crop production, and in 1974 a spike in cotton planting finally toppled alfalfa from its decades-long position as the area's leading crop. The 588,040 acre-feet delivered to irrigators in 1974 was second only to 1972 during an irrigation season that stretched from late January into December. Even with the flexibility offered by the twice-amended Exchange Contract, CCID had to purchase 34,563 acre-feet that year, including 13,500 acre-feet directly from the Bureau of Reclamation and smaller amounts from other Central Valley Project contractors as well as over 11,000 acre-feet from private pump owners. The district's own pumps contributed 82,673 acre-feet to the water supply. Although weather and the acreage planted to various crops varied from year to year, 1974 was a fairly typical season, and as in most years the Exchange Contractors traded water among themselves to balance supply and demand. As the Bureau of Reclamation increased its sales to other water agencies, both

[309] J. Leroy Nickel, Jr. to T.C. Mott, January 29, 1951; CCID Board Minutes, 1: 105 (October 14, 1953); CCID Annual Report for 1954, 8; CCID Board Minutes, 1: 169 (April 14, 1954); CCID Annual Report for 1966, 11; CCID Annual Report for 1976, 20.

along the Delta-Mendota Canal and from the Mendota Pool, its excess capacity diminished and CCID and the other Exchange Contractors realized that in the future it would be difficult to purchase supplemental water or increase peak season deliveries.[310]

The water shortage that CCID feared arrived sooner than expected. A severe drought began in 1976, but unlike the situation in other Central Valley river basins inflow to Shasta remained high enough to avoid a critical year designation under the Exchange Contract. Dry conditions increased irrigation demand, and CCID delivered a near-record amount of water in 1976 by shifting all of its November and December entitlement to earlier in the year and buying water from the Broadview and San Luis water districts and from wells in the Firebaugh Canal Company service area. For perhaps the first time, there was no supplemental water available from the Central Valley Project.[311]

The Bureau of Reclamation, like most water agencies in California, gambled that the next year would be better and met most contract commitments by reducing carryover storage in its reservoirs. It was a bet that failed. The winter of 1976-1977 was exceptionally dry, prompting the director of the Department of Water Resources to comment in January 1977 that "prior to six weeks ago I don't think anyone in their right mind would have predicted that we would be saying that 1976 wasn't so bad after all."[312] Faced for the first time with a critical year water supply, CCID crop acreage dropped slightly. Under the Second Amended Exchange Contract, CCID received about 79 percent of its normal entitlement, but the Bureau of Reclamation was able to reduce the impact of restricted deliveries by giving the district additional latitude in moving water from month to month. The district's own groundwater production declined as the owners of most of the leased wells took them back to irrigate their own farms. Normally growers were not subject to a fixed limit on water use, but at the beginning of 1977 the district imposed a maximum allocation of 3 acre-feet per acre. By June efforts to conserve water, heavy use of groundwater and the scheduling flexibility for Delta-Mendota Canal deliveries allowed the CCID Board to relax its strict limits and deliver additional water. The district also permitted growers to transfer their

---

[310] CCID Annual Report for 1974, 11-12.
[311] CCID Annual Report for 1976, 12-13.
[312] "Statement of the Department of Water Resources for the Dry Year Hearings," January 20, 1977 in Jackson and Paterson, *The Sacramento-San Joaquin Delta*, 184.

entitlement to other land within district boundaries, but no transfers outside the district were allowed. Fortunately, the drought ended with heavy rain and snowfall the next winter and water supply conditions quickly returned to normal.[313]

In 1977 the district had been in charge of the canal for almost a quarter century. It had matured as an organization, and one visible symbol of that maturity was its office. Maintaining continuity of operations, CCID had rented space from Miller & Lux in the downtown Los Banos office built in the early 1920s when the company still dominated the west side. When the district learned in 1964 that Miller & Lux was being dissolved the board considered the renovation of the former Bank of America building or the construction of a new office in conjunction with the other Exchange Contractors before deciding in 1967 to build an office of its own on West I Street next to the Main Canal. Its new building, finished in 1968, was designed by Frank Lloyd Wright protege Robert Beharka and incorporated recognizable elements of Wright's modern style.[314]

Many of the people who had been instrumental in founding CCID remained on the job until the early 1980s. C.W. Bates stepped down as manager in 1979 but he continued to serve as secretary until the spring of 1983. Bates was succeeded as manager by Timothy McCullough and then by Mike Porter in 1983. William Raznoff, who had begun his career with Miller & Lux and had played a key role in negotiations with the Bureau of Reclamation, retired in 1980. The Board of Directors had little turnover, and in 1980 two of the original directors—J.P. Bunker and Herman H. Willis—were still in office. On June 25, 1983 the district reached another milestone when a bond burning party was held at the Wolfsen ranch near Dos Palos to celebrate the final payment of the debt incurred to purchase the canal company. That event, along with the transfer of management to a new generation, marked the end of CCID's founding era.[315]

---

[313] CCID Annual Report for 1977, 12-15.
[314] CCID Annual Report for 1964, 16; CCID Annual Report for 1968, 16.
[315] CCID Board Minutes, 5: 217 (July 25, 1979); CCID Board Minutes, 5: 275 (February 27, 1980); CCID Annual Report for 1990, 5.

11

Drainage and Ducks

Drainage is irrigation's unglamorous stepchild. The Exchange Contract water quality consultants had bluntly reminded local water users of the importance of adequate drainage, and failure to understand just how critical it was had doomed ancient irrigated civilizations from Mesopotamia to the American southwest. Drainage serves two closely related purposes. The first is to keep excess water from drowning crop roots. The second, more insidious hazard of a high water table is the accumulation of harmful salts in the root zone. All soils contain salts and all irrigation waters carry dissolved salts. Plants utilize only pure water and water is also lost to evaporation from the soil surface; both processes leave behind salts that can build up to hazardous levels unless enough additional water is applied to flush them through the soil profile. The maintenance of a beneficial salt balance depends on maintaining an outlet for the excess water and salt. The alternative is crop loss and eventually abandonment of the land itself.

Seepage from the new San Joaquin & Kings River canal was responsible for an immediate rise in groundwater elevations of as much as thirty feet, bringing water to the surface in a few places. In 1879 engineer James Schuyler predicted that water levels would continue to rise unless the rate of percolation from the canal and newly irrigated fields slowed. He concluded that "The necessity for scrupulous attention to drainage in connection with irrigation has forced itself emphatically upon the irrigators along the line of the San Joaquin and Kings River Canal, particularly those who till the adobe soils."[316] Apart from the care needed to prevent water from standing on the surface, drainage did not become an important problem on most of the lands irrigated by the canal until the rapid expansion of irrigated acreage that accompanied the construction of the Outside Canal and the dairy boom. By 1911 the water table was within five to eight feet of the surface generally, higher in some spots, and still rising. Water continued to leak from the canals—losses were estimated at 30 percent

---

[316] Schuyler, "Report on Works and Practices of Irrigation," 172.

in the 1930s—but as irrigated acreage rose over-irrigation became a major contributor to the growing drainage problem. The Railroad Commission cautioned farmers against excessive use and urged, without success, the replacement of per-acre pricing with a charge for the amount of water actually used, which the commission believed would lead to more efficient use and reduce water-logging.[317] The problem persisted and even in 1948, at a time when the canal company struggled to supply enough late summer water, a local road district had to warn irrigators around Gustine that "The practice of using irrigation water carelessly, thereby flooding the roads, as well as the practice of diverting waste waters onto the roads, has become so widespread that it is a serious problem," and it threatened to penalize offenders.[318]

In a 1922 report on drainage, former Miller & Lux engineer W.C. Hammatt noted several problem areas including one running from north of Los Banos to east of Gustine, mainly between the Main Canal and Los Banos Creek. Conditions were especially critical west of Volta "where the ground has become so alkaline by lack of drainage that many tracts formerly farmed have been abandoned."[319] Badger Flat, just east of the area identified by Hammatt and one of the first areas irrigated from the canal, was also becoming waterlogged. Acting against advice given by T.C. Mott as early as 1926, farmers had dammed unused Miller & Lux irrigation ditches running through the area that could have served as drainage conduits. Mott thought that if some of those ditches were cleaned out and deepened, "possibly the greater part of the land which is now out of production would be brought back into production, at least for shallow-rooted crops and as time went on it might even be possible to get a fairly good stand of alfalfa in some places."[320] Drainage works were part of the plan for the San Joaquin River Water Storage District, and when that comprehensive approach failed local farmers set up their own organizations. The 10,000-acre Dos Palos Drainage District was established in 1932 and used twelve to fifteen drainage wells to maintain the water table at a depth of four

[317] Cone, *Irrigation in the San Joaquin Valley*, 41; George Trowbridge, "Vandervort et.al., Plaintiff vs. Southern California Edison Company, Ltd., Defendants, Digest of Defendant Miller & Lux Witnesses," June 1936, 3; Railroad Commission, Decision 22228, 21; Railroad Commission, Decision 29501, February 1, 1937, 6.
[318] advertisement, "Notice to Irrigators," *Gustine Standard*, August 19, 1948.
[319] W.C. Hammatt, "Report on Drainage of Irrigated Lands in San Joaquin River Water Storage District," December, 1922, 10.
[320] T.C. Mott to G.H. Russell, August 4, 1938.

to six feet, which was still considered too high for full alfalfa production. A similar district was organized at Gustine in 1938 and by 1950 had twenty-two wells in operation. In Dos Palos the pumped water was put into irrigation canals for reuse while the Gustine district discharged its drainage to Mud Slough in the grasslands. Proposals for drainage were also discussed in Los Banos in 1939 after 2,000 acres had already been lost to water-logging.[321]

Natural drainage from the west side plains moved downhill toward the valley trough, often following the beds of the intermittent creeks. In the grasslands, the creeks met the northward flowing Mud and Salt sloughs, which carried the San Joaquin's seasonal overflow back to the river. Miller & Lux shaped and reshaped the flood plain during decades of excavation and levee-building, creating a complicated network of natural and man-made canals and drains. North of Firebaugh, Poso Slough was one of the company's early irrigation diversion sites but it was later closed off from the river and turned into a major drain running northwest and connected to feeders like the Holland Farm and Silaxo drains. Further west the Camp 13 drain was used for both irrigation and drainage. A waste gate in the Main Canal released surplus water for grassland irrigation, regulated by structures in the Camp 13 drain, while at other times the drain carried excess water from the "Camp 13 swamp" to Mud Slough. The Gadwall Canal branched off from the Camp 13 drain and had the same dual purpose, providing an alternative drainage outlet to Mud Slough when irrigation water was running in the Camp 13 drain. Those were just two examples of the extensive system of surface drains used to manage the flow of water across thousands of acres of low-lying crop and grasslands and carry excess water to the valley's ultimate drainage outlet, the San Joaquin River.[322]

Drainage from surrounding farm land passed through the grasslands, and in 1939 T.C. Mott told the Railroad Commission that even though the grassland water rights had been sold to the Bureau of Reclamation he believed there would be enough drainage from surrounding farm lands to take care of the needs of the duck clubs. Mott was probably too optimistic, and in any event the timing of drainage discharge did not necessarily match the requirements

---

[321] U.S. Department of Agriculture, *Soil Survey of the Los Banos Area, California* (Series 1939, no. 12, January 1952), 94-95; University of California, *Drainage Problems in the San Joaquin Valley*, 1958, 74-76; Trowbridge, "Vandervort et.al.,", 4; *Gustine Standard*, March 9, 1939.
[322] Hammatt, "Report on Drainage of Irrigated Lands," 4-8.

for fall flooding of waterfowl habitat. Beginning in 1944, grassland interests were able to buy water from Friant on a year-to-year basis, but once the Central Valley Project became fully operational there would be no extra water for sale to the grasslands. A study of the problem by the Bureau of Reclamation and the U.S. Fish & Wildlife Service resulted in an October 1950 report that promised Central Valley Project water to present and expanded state and national refuges but offered the privately-owned duck clubs only a three-year transitional supply of 30,000 acre-feet in 1951, 20,000 acre-feet in 1952 and 10,000 acre-feet in 1953.[323]

The plan gave grassland users a limited time to develop alternative supplies from drainage and groundwater, if those sources were available or adequate. A bill introduced in Congress in 1952 to aid the grasslands made little progress, but that fall when water-short grassland managers delayed flooding, ducks descended instead on rice fields near Dos Palos. Facing heavy crop damage, state officials negotiated the delivery of additional water to create temporary habitat on private land, and similar programs were employed in 1953 and 1954, underscoring the value of maintaining the grasslands as a haven for waterfowl. Following a federal-state conference convened by Governor Earl Warren, a bill reauthorizing the Central Valley Project and adding fish and wildlife conservation to the list of project purposes was passed in 1954. Among its provisions was a specific authorization for contracts with public agencies like the newly formed Grassland Water District, which got 50,000 acre-feet of fall water. CCID delivered the federal water through its canals, and in 1955 agreed to provide the Grassland district with three ditchtenders and a watermaster to manage the grassland distribution system, an operating arrangement that continued for more than two decades.[324]

The increase in irrigated acreage above the San Joaquin Canal Company service area added to the drainage problem. In 1948, T.C. Mott opposed the delivery of interim federal water to land near Dos Palos because the area was already suffering from a high water table and more water would only aggravate the situation and threaten more productive land nearby. It should not have

---

[323] *Gustine Standard,* February 2, 1939; Garone, *The Fall and Rise of the Wetlands of California's Great Central Valley,* iBook edition, 356-367.

[324] Garone, *The Fall and Rise of the Wetlands of California's Great Central Valley,* iBook edition, 367-382; Jayne Philpott Casey, ed., *The Grasslands Water Summary* (Grasslands Water District, undated), 3-5, 11, 13, 44-45; CCID Board Minutes, 1: 194 (July 28, 1954; CCID Board Minutes, 1: 263 (June 8, 1955).

come as no surprise then that drainage conditions changed dramatically after the completion of the Delta-Mendota Canal in 1951. Tens of thousands of acres that had been dependent on limited, often saline groundwater received a reliable supply of surface water, and the volume of drainage moving downhill toward CCID steadily increased. The Central Valley Project brought more than additional water to the west side, it also brought salt pumped from the Delta. Miller & Lux and then CCID had routinely taken drainage into the canal system, primarily at Camp 13, to increase the irrigation supply but by the mid-1950s water quality was deteriorating. Imported salts were not the only problem; the presence of elevated levels of sulphates and boron suggested that salts native to west side alluvial fan soils, and salts deposited by earlier groundwater irrigation, were being mobilized and added to the drainage flow. In 1956 the CCID Board of Directors put upslope interests on notice that the district would not accept potentially hazardous drainage into its canal system, and the following year a siphon was installed under the Main Canal at Camp 13 to bypass drainage to the grasslands when it was too salty for blending with water from the Mendota Pool. As drainage flows continued to increase, CCID reached agreements with neighboring districts including the San Luis Water District, Broadview Water District, Panoche Drainage District and Charleston Drainage District to use new or existing facilities to transfer upslope drainage through its territory directly to the Grassland Water District.[325]

Soon after CCID took over the canal system, and before drainage from higher land had become a critical issue, the 1954 consultants' report on Exchange Contract water quality warned of a new threat. Schoonover and Eaton noted that "when the San Luis Reservoir is completed, considerable areas lying above the Delta-Mendota Canal will likely be brought under irrigation. After these dry lands have been under irrigation for a few years, it is very likely that the depth to ground water in the area below the Canal will be affected."[326] In fact, thousands of acres on the plains south of Mendota were already irrigated and had been since the late 1930s but it had quickly become

---

[325] *Los Banos Enterprise*, June 18, 1948; Warren R. Schoonover, "Quality of Water, Central Valley Project, California: A Report on Water Quality in Lower San Joaquin River as Related to Agriculture," (U.S. Bureau of Reclamation, October 1963), 85; CCID Board Minutes, 2: 40 (May 9, 1956); CCID Annual Report for 1957, 15; CCID Board Minutes, 2: 401 (May 24, 1961); CCID Board Minutes, 3: 371 (March 22, 1967); CCID Board Minutes, 4: 350 (November 26, 1973); CCID Board Minutes, 4: 481 (December 24, 1975); CCID Board Minutes, 5: 315 (December 24, 1980).
[326] Kelley and Schoonover, "Evaluation of the Salinity of the Water Delivered Through the Delta-Mendota Canal," 9.

apparent that the underlying aquifer was not a sustainable water supply. In 1942 the Westside Landowners Association was formed to lobby for a new water project, and it helped fund a Bureau of Reclamation study of water delivery options. As a result, the Bureau proposed the construction of an 816,000 acre-foot reservoir on San Luis Creek where surplus winter and spring Sacramento River flows, delivered by the Delta-Mendota Canal, would be stored for use during the irrigation season along a canal extending south to the Kettleman Hills. The 400,000-acre Westlands Water District was organized in 1952 to contract for San Luis water, and following a favorable feasibility report in 1955, work began to secure congressional authorization of the project.[327] By then CCID realized that it had its own stake in the San Luis plan. As the CCID Board explained later:

> These lower lands have already experienced drainage difficulties from the new higher elevation lands brought under irrigation from the Delta-Mendota Canal commencing in 1951. This area, under the District's predecessor at that time, did not take proper action to protect itself from the drainage problems arising from the Delta-Mendota Canal, and it is your Board of Director's sincere opinion that we cannot afford to make the same mistake the second time.[328]

It was a struggle that would last for decades.

The increase in drainage salinity that alarmed CCID was also felt in the lower San Joaquin River. Salt concentrations increased significantly after 1951, threatening downstream irrigators in the Patterson, West Stanislaus and Banta-Carbona districts. Studies by state agencies of the worsening San Joaquin Valley drainage problem began in the mid-1950s and coincided with planning for a new State Water Project that would deliver water from northern California to coastal cities and southern San Joaquin Valley farms. The concept of a master drain for the valley soon emerged as a solution to a regional problem too big for local agencies to solve by themselves. The drain would collect subsurface runoff, separate it from the San Joaquin River and discharge

---

[327] U.S. Department of Interior, *Central Valley Basin: A Comprehensive Report on the Development of the Water and Related Resources of the Central Valley Basin for Irrigation, Power Production, and Other Beneficial uses in California, and Comments by the State of California and Federal Agencies*, 81st. Congress, 1st. Session, Senate Document 113, August 1949, 67, 130; Ed Simmons, *Westlands Water District: The First 25 Years, 1952-1977* (Fresno: Westlands Water District, December 1983), 24-43.
[328] CCID Annual Report for 1962, 15-16.

it to tidewater at the western edge of the Delta. CCID saw the master drain as an answer to its own problems, but only if it was built soon enough to prevent additional damage to lower-lying lands. The district and the other Exchange Contractors adopted a basic policy that any project importing water into the valley must be able to remove its drainage from the valley, and irrigation and drainage facilities had to be built at the same time instead of waiting until uncontrolled drainage became a problem. The district and manager C.W. Bates took a leading role in lobbying for the inclusion of drainage guarantees in the federal legislation authorizing the San Luis Unit.[329] They succeeded, and the act passed in 1960 required that:

> Construction of the San Luis Unit shall not be commenced until the Secretary [of the Interior] has ... received satisfactory assurance from the State of California that it will make provision for a master drainage outlet and disposal channel for the San Joaquin Valley, ... which will adequately serve, by connection therewith, the drainage system of the San Luis Unit or has made provision for constructing the San Luis Interceptor drain to the Delta designed to meet the drainage requirements of the San Luis Unit.[330]

The State Water Project, approved by voters in 1960, included plans for a larger, two-million acre-foot San Luis Reservoir that would be shared with the Central Valley Project, giving the CVP 45 percent of the joint project. The San Joaquin Valley drain was also authorized but with its plans still indefinite the state informed the Bureau of Reclamation in June 1961 that it could not provide the assurance required by the San Luis Unit Authorizing Act that the drain would be available by the time irrigation service was expected to begin in the new federal service area. The Bureau therefore announced that construction of the San Luis Interceptor drain would begin in January 1966. Notwithstanding that commitment, by the time President John F. Kennedy arrived for the ceremonial groundbreaking at San Luis Dam in August 1962 CCID was becoming increasingly uneasy about the Bureau's intentions. There had been talk of interim facilities such as an evaporation basin near Tranquility

---

[329] Ronald Loren Nye, "Visions of Salt: Salinity and Drainage in the San Joaquin Valley, California, 1870-1970," Ph.D. dissertation, University of California, Santa Barbara, 1986, 230-239; University of California, *Drainage Problems in the San Joaquin Valley*; Schoonover, "Quality of Water," 37-45; CCID Board Minutes, 2: 176 (January 8, 1958).
[330] San Luis Unit Authorizing Act, quoted in CCID Annual Report for 1962, 15.

or even a desalinization plant, but construction of irrigation facilities seemed to be moving forward without any evidence of similar progress on the drain.[331] The district complained that "Repeated requests for information as to the Federal Government's provisions for drainage facilities have met with either cold silence, or else vague plans for 'future investigations' as to 'alternate' disposal of drainage waters from the federal service area."[332]

On November 7, 1962, attorney C. Ray Robinson wrote to Secretary of the Interior Stewart Udall to forcefully remind him that drainage was required by the time water was delivered. When they received no immediate response, CCID and several neighboring irrigation and drainage entities filed suit in federal court on December 20 seeking an injunction against construction of the San Luis Unit until there was a definite plan for drainage facilities. Udall's January 1963 reply to Robinson's letter stressed that Congress had been informed of the pending construction of the interceptor drain following California's withdrawal and that the Bureau of Reclamation was following the steps required by law to provide drainage when needed.[333] Judge M.D. Crocker concluded that the federal government did, in fact, intend to build the drain and declined to intervene but added "However, should it later appear that the defendants [the Department of the Interior] have not provided a drainage system as required by the Act, and that plaintiffs are threatened with injury, they may again ask this court for an injunction."[334] If nothing else, the suit made it clear that CCID would remain vigilant on the matter of San Luis Unit drainage.

The litigation turned out to be no more than a prelude to a period of more intense controversy. No sooner had the Bureau renewed its pledge to build the interceptor drain than the Department of Water Resources asked for reconsideration of a joint federal-state master drain. The state service area at the southern end of the valley would eventually need drainage and the construction of a single joint drain would be cheaper than separate drains running side by side to the Delta. Unfortunately, the state's plan was still not ready so a cooperative venture would mean suspending work on the San Luis

[331] CCID Board Minutes, 2: 453 (February 14, 1962); Nye, "Visions of Salt," 245-246; CCID Board Minutes, 2: 479-480 (June 27, 1962); CCID Board Minutes, 3: 20 (October 10, 1962).

[332] CCID Annual Report for 1962, 15.

[333] Nye, "Visions of Salt," 246-248; Stewart Udall to C. Ray Robinson, January 15, 1963.

[334] quoted in CCID Annual Report for 1963, 15.

drain without a definite alternative. The Bureau believed that interim measures would provide sufficient relief in the early years of San Luis Unit operation when drainage volumes were expected to be small. Drainage could be routed to evaporation ponds or to a holding reservoir where it could be diluted and released down the San Joaquin River.[335] When the Bureau agreed in early 1964 to seek a delay, reaction from the west side was predictable. "This is precisely what the interests I represent were afraid of when we sought ironclad guarantees through the courts," fumed C. Ray Robinson.[336] Faced with opposition it surely must have expected, the Bureau returned to work on the interceptor drain until California offered its official assurance in June 1964 that it would provide a master drain capable of handling San Luis Unit drainage on a timetable only a year or two later than the Bureau's own target date.[337]

A different kind of obstacle to drainage planning appeared in late 1963. Both state and federal drainage plans had always contemplated a terminus at the western edge of the Delta near the Antioch Bridge, but Contra Costa County officials now became increasingly vocal in their opposition to the introduction of a new source of pollution at a location just upstream from urban and industrial intakes. Characterizing the project as a "sewer" they were concerned not only with the salts flushed from valley farms but with pesticide residues and fertilizer-derived nutrients like nitrogen. In December 1963 the U.S. Public Health Service announced that its preliminary studies suggested that the drain could be a pollution hazard and that location of its outfall required further study.[338] CCID now found it "necessary to fight and fight hard" to advance the drainage program.[339] Warren Schoonover, an expert familiar with west side drainage issues since his service on the water quality board in 1938, was hired as a consultant to gather facts and help present the area's case while C. Ray Robinson contemplated a return to court. Contra Costa was fighting hard too. In June 1964 Congressman John Baldwin attached an amendment to the public works appropriation for the 1965 fiscal year that prohibited any expenditure of funds for construction of a San Luis drain

---

[335] Nye, "Visions of Salt," 248-249, 256-259; CCID Annual Report for 1964, 14.
[336] *Fresno Bee*, January 10, 1964.
[337] Nye, "Visions of Salt," 263-264.
[338] Nye, "Visions of Salt," 250-253, 265-267; *Oakland Tribune*, May 9, 1964.
[339] CCID Annual Report for 1964, 14-15.

discharge east of Port Chicago on Suisun Bay, a point well downstream from the Antioch Bridge. Because only studies and not construction would take place in 1965 the amendment had little immediate impact but it nevertheless set a worrisome precedent.[340]

Now that it was committed to a joint drainage project, California faced the problem of paying for its 40 percent share of the section from Kettleman City to the Antioch Bridge. State guidelines required that financing for three-quarters of total project cost had to be available before construction, which meant finding a way to collect money from the drain's beneficiaries. In order to spread the cost as broadly as possible and to avoid the complicated task of identifying specific users, the Department of Water Resources proposed formation of a valley-wide drainage district. Opposition from sections of the valley that did not have a drainage problem quickly confirmed that the idea of an omnibus district was politically impractical. As an alternative in late 1965 the state sent draft drainage service contracts to entities like CCID that carried a price tag of $15 to $18 per acre-foot discharged to the drain, plus whatever additional costs might eventually be needed to move the outfall point to someplace other than the Antioch Bridge or build other facilities to solve pollution problems. Those open-ended provisions were enough to keep CCID from giving the proposal serious consideration, and in general potential users complained that even the base rate was more than farmers could afford to pay. The following year the state made its third offer, reducing the price to $6 per acre-foot plus a $6.00 per 100 acre-foot stand-by charge for the first ten years of operation. At that price, water users quickly signed up for all of the projected capacity. CCID contracted for 20,000 acre-feet per year as a form of insurance, to be used by the district or transferred to individuals and drainage districts if and when it became impossible to continue drainage discharges directly or indirectly to the San Joaquin River.[341]

While the cost of drainage got most of the attention, design work continued. CCID advocated locating the drain next to the Main Canal to utilize excess district land and reduce the amount of private land needed for the right-of-way. The location of a regulating reservoir was a bigger problem. In 1965 the district took a position against a reservoir site on 5,500 acres four

---

[340] CCID Annual Report for 1964, 14-15; Nye, "Visions of Salt," 265-267.
[341] Nye, "Visions of Salt," 267-270, 277-279; CCID Annual Report for 1966, 17.

miles southwest of Dos Palos, suggesting that less valuable land further north in the grasslands would be a better option. By the next year the size of the planned South Dos Palos reservoir had been reduced to 3,200 acres situated just north of the Main Canal between the Agatha Canal and Camp 13, with a secondary reservoir at the 6,000 acre Kesterson site northeast of Gustine.[342]

Although there had been an agreement in principle in 1964 on construction of a single master drain, the terms of the contract between the state and federal partners still had to be worked out, a task made more difficult by the on-going controversy surrounding the ultimate location of the outfall. CCID remained involved in all aspects of the process, and on May 4, 1966 all of its directors and drainage counsel C. Ray Robinson, along with representatives of other local agencies, met in Washington with Reclamation Commissioner Floyd Dominy. No new assurances were given but the meeting definitely pin-pointed the remaining bottlenecks before actual construction could commence, and also placed the Bureau of Reclamation and State Department of Water Resources on notice that the District and Companies vitally affected by drainage from the application of new water on the Federal service areas would not acquiesce in further delays and procrastination evidenced by Federal and State Officials and Agencies.[343]

As 1966 drew to a close the success of the Department of Water Resources' contract offer removed the final roadblock to signing the long-awaited agreement. According to DWR Director William E. Warne, the agreement had been approved by the Secretary of the Interior and was scheduled to be signed in Sacramento by Warne and Bureau of Reclamation Regional Director Robert Pafford, Jr. Pafford had been hospitalized but arranged for an ambulance to take him to his office for the signing. On the night of December 18, Warne received word that final clearance from Washington had not been received so the signing was rescheduled for December 27 in Washington. Just before Christmas, the Department of the Interior informed Warne that a "hold" had been placed on the contract by the White House and nothing more could be done until President Lyndon Johnson returned from his Texas ranch in January. No reason was given for the delay, which may have been related to

---

[342] CCID Annual Report for 1965, 15; CCID Board Minutes, 3: 224 (June 9, 1965); CCID Board Minutes, 3: 290 (March 9, 1966); CCID Annual Report for 1966, 17.
[343] CCID Annual Report for 1966, 16.

budget considerations, and the contract was finally cleared for signature on January 17, 1967. However, on January 2, 1967 Ronald Reagan became governor, and his new director of the Department of Water Resources, William Gianelli, wanted to reopen the question of state reimbursement. Gianelli quickly determined that Warne's $6 per acre-foot contracts could recover only operating costs and interest but would repay little, if any, of the state's capital costs of drain construction. A poll of potential drainage contractors found them unwilling to pay the $16 to $20 per acre-foot that Gianelli believed the state needed to collect, so on March 10, 1967 California officially withdrew from the San Joaquin Valley drain.[344]

Remarks made by Gianelli in January 1967 had already convinced CCID that the state was planning to abandon the drain. With deliveries to the Westlands Water District from San Luis Reservoir scheduled to begin in early 1968 and no apparent progress on drainage, the district and nine other entities filed a new suit in February 1967 seeking an injunction against water deliveries until adequate drainage was available. However, in April the Bureau of Reclamation announced plans to have the drain completed to the Kesterson holding reservoir in late 1969, with later development of the South Dos Palos reservoir if needed. Because work on the federal drain had resumed, no injunction was issued but the case remained open until the suit was finally dismissed in 1973. CCID did whatever it could to expedite construction of the drain, from testifying in support of funding to right-of-way easements and property transfers. Construction was underway near Dos Palos in 1969 and the initial 85-mile drain was completed in 1975 to a temporary terminus at Kesterson reservoir[345]

Plans to extend the drain to the Delta remained mired in controversy. A report by the Federal Water Pollution Control Administration in early 1967 identified nitrogen as the most important pollutant because it could induce algae blooms that posed a threat to fish as well as to recreational and industrial water uses. That finding was contradicted by a subsequent study but experiments in nitrogen and salinity removal continued at a cooperative research station near Firebaugh. Beginning in 1965 a rider was attached to the Central Valley Project's annual appropriations requiring agreement on

[344] William E. Warne to C. Ray Robinson, January 5, 1967; Nye, "Visions of Salt," 279-282.
[345] Los Banos Enterprise, May 11, 1967; CCID Annual Report for 1967, 13; Nye, "Visions of Salt," 286-287.

protective water quality standards prior to the selection of an outfall location. In 1975 the Bureau of Reclamation, Department of Water Resources and State Water Resources Control Board established the San Joaquin Valley Interagency Drainage Program in yet another effort to find an acceptable solution to the drainage problem, leading to a recommendation for a drain ending at Chipps Island, downstream from Antioch. The release of drainage at any point in the estuary required a pollution discharge permit, and in 1981 the Department of the Interior began a planned three-year study to develop the data needed for a permit application.[346]

The first phase of Kesterson reservoir covering 1,280 acres was completed in 1971, and acting on the assumption that the four-foot-deep ponds would provide waterfowl habitat the nearly 6,000 acre reservoir site was designated by the U.S. Fish & Wildlife Service as the Kesterson National Wildlife Refuge in 1970. At first water was supplied to the refuge by the Grassland Water District. The drainage collector system in the Westlands Water District began sending subsurface runoff to Kesterson in 1978 and by 1981 it made up most of the reservoir inflow. With progress on extension of the drain to the Delta stalled, the Bureau of Reclamation was forced to convert Kesterson from a regulating reservoir to a storage and evaporation site with the intention of releasing water to the San Joaquin River during periods of high flow.[347]

When the Bureau of Reclamation began the latest round of studies in 1981 high levels of trace elements, including selenium, were found in drainage water but the finding caused no immediate alarm. Selenium, boron and other trace elements and salts originated in the ancient marine sediments of the Diablo Range that over thousands of years had eroded and washed into the valley, where they were concentrated in the soils of the alluvial fans of Panoche and other creeks. Irrigation flushed selenium into the shallow groundwater collected by the San Luis drain. In 1982 selenium levels in mosquito fish in Kesterson were found to be one hundred times higher than fish in the nearby Volta Wildlife Area. Fish & Wildlife Service biologists conducting a survey of resident waterfowl during the summer of 1983 made the first discovery of dead

[346] CCID Annual Report for 1968, 13; Jackson and Paterson, *The Sacramento-San Joaquin Delta*, 142-144; San Joaquin Valley Drainage Program, "Preliminary Planning Alternatives for Solving Agricultural Drainage and Drainage-Related Problems in the San Joaquin Valley," August 1989, 1-10-1-11.
[347] Garone, *The Fall and Rise of the Wetlands of California's Great Central Valley*, iBook edition, 435-441; "Kesterson Reservoir" (undated public information document).

or sometimes grotesquely deformed chicks in 10 percent of the nests they examined. The abnormalities were quickly linked to selenium and a U.S. Geological Survey analysis confirmed significantly elevated levels of selenium at Kesterson, in the drain and in the shallow groundwater that flowed into the drain. As increasing numbers of affected birds were found in 1984, the Bureau of Reclamation provided an extra 11,000 acre-feet of Delta-Mendota water, delivered to the Grassland Water District by CCID, to create attractive habitat in other parts of the grasslands to reduce waterfowl exposure to Kesterson. Meanwhile concern for human risks led to warnings by state authorities against consumption of ducks from the Kesterson area, and neighboring landowners appealed to the State Water Resources Control Board, citing evidence of environmental damage to their property. Although the Bureau of Reclamation disputed many of its findings, the state board issued an abatement and clean-up order in February 1985. The following month the television program *60 Minutes* brought the Kesterson story to a national audience. Days later at a congressional hearing in Los Banos the Department of the Interior announced that Kesterson and the San Luis Drain would be closed and the subsurface drainage lines on 42,000 acres in the Westlands Water District would be plugged. The discharge of drainage to Kesterson ended in 1986 and the now-notorious reservoir was dewatered, its low spots filled and its contaminated vegetation destroyed.[348]

The impact of the selenium tragedy was not limited to Kesterson. Increasing volumes of upslope drainage—70,000 to 90,000 acre-feet per year— were flowing into the grasslands where it was used by private duck clubs and federal and state wildlife refuges. After Kesterson, drainage went from being an important source of wetland water supply to a toxic liability. CCID was caught, quite literally, in the middle. The district had developed cooperative relationships with drainers and had taken some of their discharges into its system as a supplemental supply when salts and boron were within acceptable levels for irrigation use and passed what it could not use through to the Grassland Water District. Some agencies, including the Panoche and Charleston drainage districts, had contracts for the delivery of drainage

---

[348] Garone, *The Fall and Rise of the Wetlands of California's Great Central Valley*, iBook edition, 448-457, 469-476; CCID Board Minutes, 6: 115 (December 12, 1984); "Testimony by David G. Houston, Regional Director - Mid-Pacific Region, U.S. Bureau of Reclamation Presented to California Water Resources Control Board," January 8, 1985.

directly to the Grassland Water District. In early 1985 CCID determined that the Main Drain at Camp 13 was the only source of selenium entering the CCID system, and stopped further use of that water for irrigation. At the same time, it developed a plan for supplying management units in the southern grasslands with freshwater in place of drainage water. The district, the entities draining into the grasslands basin and the Grassland Water District worked together to route drainage directly to the San Joaquin River using existing canals in a "flip-flop" arrangement in which the Camp 13 Drain and the Agatha Canal alternately carried drainage to the river and freshwater to wetland areas. While the practice reduced the exposure of waterfowl to selenium, it was inefficient and it limited delivery of water made available from the Delta-Mendota Canal because grassland conveyance facilities were often filled with drainage.[349]

By 1989 the local agencies were working on a plan to use a portion of the San Luis Drain—idle since 1986—to separate drainage from grasslands channels and deliver it to the northern reach of Mud Slough where it would flow into the San Joaquin River. It took until 1995 to negotiate an agreement with the Bureau of Reclamation for use of the drain and to obtain approval from state water quality regulators for the Grassland Bypass Project. To participate in the bypass project the Broadview Water District, Charleston Drainage District, Firebaugh Canal Water District, Pacheco Water District, Panoche Drainage District, Widren Water District and the Camp 13 drainage area in the CCID service area formed a regional drainage entity (administered through the San Luis and Delta-Mendota Water Authority) that covered nearly 100,000 acres. A new four-mile ditch connected the Panoche Drain and the Main Drain to the Bureau's San Luis Drain southwest of Dos Palos. Permits for the bypass project required reductions in the amount of selenium and other harmful drainage constituents reaching the San Joaquin River, which would initially be accomplished by increasing irrigation efficiency in the drainage problem area and by on-farm drainage recycling. By the end of its first five years in operation the project had reduced total drainage volume by 47 percent, selenium discharges by 56 percent, salt by 28 percent and boron by 41

---

[349] Norman D. Coontz, "Agricultural Drainwater Management Organizations in the Drainage Problem Area of the Grasslands Area of the San Joaquin Valley," prepared by Ebasco Services for the San Joaquin Valley Drainage Program, March 1989, 4-3-4-13; CCID Board Minutes, 6: 124 (January 9, 1985); CCID Board Minutes, 6: 140 (March 13, 1985); Nigel W.T. Quinn, Joseph C. McGahan, Michael L. Delamore, "Innovative Strategies to Reduce Selenium in Grasslands Drainage," *California Agriculture* 52, no. 5 (1998), 12-13.

percent. Having demonstrated its value, the bypass project was extended to 2009 and then to 2019 with a mandate to virtually eliminate the discharge of selenium and salt. To do that, drain water had to be recycled until it became too saline for most commercial crops and it was then collected and used to irrigate 6,000 acres of salt-tolerant crops including forage and pistachios. By 2014 selenium had been reduced by 90 percent and salt by 87 percent, and several water treatment systems were being tested in the hope that agricultural production could be maintained with essentially zero drainage discharges.[350]

CCID's decades-long effort to manage drainage from upslope irrigation began with a concern about the accumulation of excess water and waterlogging district farms, but the hazards associated with salts, boron and selenium carried by drainage discharges soon became an equally critical problem. Those local drainage issues unfolded against a background of broader regulatory action on San Joaquin River water quality. Growing concern about the health of America's rivers and lakes was reflected in the passage of the Water Quality Act of 1965 and the subsequent efforts by the Central Valley Regional Water Quality Control Board to develop enforceable water quality standards for the protection of beneficial uses in valley rivers and the Delta. The major water quality problem in the San Joaquin River was elevated salinity, part of the drainage problem that was already one of CCID's major worries. The district expressed its frustration with early plans for salinity control in the 1968 annual report: "At the present time, the preliminary interim objectives set for water quality standards on agricultural drainage are somewhat ridiculous, in that in some instances, and in some stretches of the San Joaquin River, for example, the standards for water quality of waste water is higher than the initial quality of the water supply before it is used for the first time!"[351] The proposed standards were never finalized because new laws, notably the state's Porter-Cologne Act in 1969 and the 1972 federal Clean Water Act, imposed different and more comprehensive regulatory requirements.

[350] Qunin, et. al., "Innovative Strategies," 13-14, 17-18; San Joaquin River Exchange Contractors Water Authority, Broadview WD, Panoche Water District, Westlands Water District, "Westside Regional Drainage Plan," May 2003, 7-8; U.S. Bureau of Reclamation-San Luis & Delta Mendota Water Authority, "Grassland Bypass Project, 2010-2019 Environmental Impact Statement and Environmental Impact Report, Final," August , 2009, 1-1-1-3, 2-9-2-11; *Fresno Bee*, August 2, 2014.
[351] CCID Annual Report for 1968, 14.

The Clean Water Act required dischargers of agricultural drainage to obtain a National Pollutant Discharge Elimination System (NPDES) permit from state authorities, and to make the process more manageable the state encouraged groups representing large areas to request blanket permits. Seventeen agencies formed the Mendota-Crows Landing Agricultural Return Flow Group to acquire a NPDES permit and monitor salinity, flow and suspended solids at sites in Mud and Salt sloughs, Orestimba Creek, the Delta-Mendota Canal and other locations. As the largest entity in the group, CCID took primary management responsibility, and manager C.W. Bates served on a valley-wide advisory committee on water quality regulation. In the midst of these challenges he was also a consistent advocate for agriculture at public forums; in the case of a 1973 conference in Davis he was the only one of 150 participants directly affiliated with an irrigation district.[352]

The monitoring program found no significant problems except sediment loads, which were judged to be a minimal threat to water quality. The effort ended in 1977 when Congress removed agricultural return flow from the NPDES program. Having concluded that only greater care with agricultural management practices was needed to address the sediment problem the regional board in 1982 granted a waiver that removed irrigation return flows and storm runoff from agricultural lands from state regulatory requirements. In the mid-1980s attention turned to reducing selenium discharges to the river but salt remained a major problem that ultimately mandated the imposition of a Total Maximum Daily Load (TMDL) requirement. The Bureau of Reclamation was recognized as having primary responsibility for addressing salinity because the Central Valley Project had altered basin hydrology by cutting off low salinity river flows and substituting higher salinity water from the Delta.[353] By 1999 a revised water quality Basin Plan was in the works, and CCID found itself facing some of the same threats it had faced more than three decades earlier. General Manager Chris White, who had just succeeded Mike Porter in that post, warned that the proposed San Joaquin River salinity

---

[352] "Background Document on San Joaquin River Salinity," http://cvsalinity.org/index.php/docs/lower-san-joaquin-river-committee-documents/supporting-documents/2336-recommended-changes-to-the-expanded-notes-on-sjr-basin-description-historical-water-use-and-salinity-buildup-8-30-12/file.html, 10; CCID Annual Report for 1973, 14; CCID Annual Report for 1974, 14-15.
[353] Central Valley Regional Water Quality Control Board (hereafter cited as "CVRWQCB"), "A Review of Options for Controlling Discharges from Irrigated Lands - Irrigation Return Water - Storm Water Runoff," July 2001, 33.

standard "is so restrictive that our water supply quality often exceeds that level."[354] Regulators avoided a confrontation by creating collaborative processes for drainage and salt reduction like the Central Valley Salinity Coalition founded in 2008. Meanwhile the Grassland Bypass Project, with substantial financial support from the Bureau of Reclamation, was able to reduce the total average salt load of the San Joaquin River where it entered the Delta near Vernalis by 17 percent.[355]

By 2000 the waiver exempting discharges from irrigated lands from regulation was under fire from environmental advocates and, as a result of changes to state law, was scheduled to expire at the end of 2002 unless the regional board and the State Water Resources Control Board took steps to extend it. In December 2002 the Central Valley regional board adopted a two-year conditional waiver that required monitoring for pesticides, nutrients, sediments and other constituents that could impair beneficial uses of valley streams. As had been the case in the 1970s the board preferred to work through third-party organizations covering large geographic areas rather than deal directly with thousands of individual farmers. On the west side, the San Joaquin Valley Drainage Authority formed the Westside San Joaquin Watershed Coalition, and despite considerable uncertainty over the requirements and obligations associated with the program CCID joined the coalition and urged its consumers to sign up, pointing out that the alternative to coalition membership was to request an individual waiver and pay the high costs of an individual monitoring program. On behalf of its growers CCID also decided to pay the annual per acre fee assessed by the coalition to cover the costs of monitoring and other compliance requirements, and the district worked to promote the adoption of best management practices that would keep surface runoff and subsurface drainage out of waterways. Exceedances of some water quality parameters, including specific pesticides, general toxicity, sediment and salinity, were found at sites within CCID, which required follow-up monitoring, and if not promptly corrected would lead to the development of detailed management plans for the farms contributing to the problem. The Irrigated Lands Regulatory Program was significantly revised beginning in

[354] *CCID Observer*, Issue 3, 1999, 4.
[355] "Salinity Real-Time Management Program Framework, Draft," October 17, 2014, http://www.swrcb.ca.gov/centralvalley/water_issues/tmdl/central_valley_projects/vernalis_salt_boron/reg_bd_usbr_maa/2014_1017_westside_salinity_rtmp_rev.pdf, 9, 21-23.

2011 to require a higher level of monitoring and, for the first time, information from individual growers. It was also extended to the protection and monitoring of groundwater quality. CCID continued to pay the basic coalition assessment for the 97 percent of its water users who had joined the coalition but had to begin collecting additional assessments to pay for the expanded scope of the new program.[356]

In the years following CCID's formation the drainage problem rose in importance as it became an environmental as well as an agricultural hazard. For the district, it became a necessary preoccupation, and one that required active cooperation with an array of local interests as well as state and federal agencies. It was not, however, the only issue that called for regional alliances and innovative solutions.

---

[356] CVRWQCB, "A Review of Options," 33; *CCID Observer,* Issue 1, 2002, 5-6; *CCID Observer,* Issue 1, 2003, 2-3; *CCID Observer,* Issue 3, 2003, 3; *CCID Observer,* Issue 4, 2012, 3; *CCID* Observer, Issue 4, 2014, 2; CVRWQCB, "Resolution No. R5-2011-0032, Short-Term Renewal of the Coalition Group Conditional Waiver of Waste Discharge Requirements for Discharges from Irrigated Lands," June 9, 2011.

12

Water Management for a New Era

In 1954, the agricultural landscape served by CCID canals was dominated by alfalfa, grain and pasture with smaller but still significant acreages of beans, cotton and rice. In the years that followed, the crop mix became more diverse. Sugar beets became a prominent crop and so did tomatoes, while rice, grain and pasture gradually declined. Cotton became the leading crop, covering 44,000 acres at its peak in 1991. By the early years of the twenty-first century, alfalfa saw a resurgence that returned it to its traditional place as the leading crop, and corn planting expanded rapidly. Orchard acreage remained stable from the 1970s through the 1990s at around eight thousand acres but by 2005 the increasing popularity of almonds led to a steady increase in the land devoted to trees. On the other hand, the beet sugar industry had run its course in the valley, and the acreage in beans and rice had dropped. In a notable departure from the pattern of summer crops, grain acreage soared beginning in 2007. Oats remained the most widely planted grain crop but the increase in wheat, the region's original cash crop, was especially dramatic. While dozens of different crops were grown in the district, in 2012 the six leading crop categories—alfalfa, grain, cotton, corn, orchards and tomatoes—made up 88 percent of CCID's irrigated acreage.[357]

Insuring that those crops had water available when they needed it continued to be a concern, especially during the peak summer months. The 1956 and 1967 revisions of the Exchange Contract had reshaped the Delta-Mendota Canal delivery schedule to better match seasonal demand and increase scheduling flexibility but the district continued to negotiate with the Bureau of Reclamation for still greater leeway in adjusting the water supply to match evolving crop patterns. At the same time, increasing demands in the Delta-Mendota Canal service area made it harder for the Bureau to accommodate requests for modification of Exchange Contract deliveries.

---

[357] CCID, "Various Crops, Total Acreage Irrigated (Including double cropping)," c. 1979; CCID, "Crop Report Data," February 21, 2002; CCID, "Irrigated Crop Acreage in CCID (includes all cropping for the year)," 2015.

By the mid-1980s management of the Delta-Mendota Canal itself became an issue when the Bureau of Reclamation decided to transfer responsibility for day-to-day operation and maintenance to the canal's users, or even to a private contractor. The San Luis and Delta-Mendota Water Users Association, set up in 1977 to serve as a forum for the agencies supplied by the canal, seemed to be a logical choice to manage the facility but before it could do that it had to reorganize itself to become a contracting entity and resolve issues like financial liability. In the interim, CCID stepped in with an offer to operate the southernmost 30 miles of the canal from Check 13 near San Luis Dam to the Mendota Pool. In July 1987 the district took operational control of that section under an agreement that provided for full reimbursement of its expenditures, and it solved the liability problem by simply increasing the number of miles of canals covered by its existing insurance policy. One benefit of the operating agreement was that equipment acquired for use on the Delta-Mendota Canal could also be used on the district's other canals. As negotiations continued among the water users and with the Bureau of Reclamation, CCID discussed extending its operation of federal facilities all the way to the Delta and for a time had the support of the water users association. Finally, in 1990 the association was superseded by the new San Luis and Delta-Mendota Water Authority and in 1992 it took control of the entire Delta-Mendota Canal and later extended its management to the Central Valley Project's Delta facilities, San Luis Dam and the San Luis Drain.[358]

Operation and maintenance of the Delta-Mendota Canal was another example of CCID's willingness to take a leading role in addressing issues that crossed agency boundaries. That had been true in the long fight to control drainage, during which the district led the effort to insure construction of the San Luis Drain and then worked to negotiate cooperative solutions to regional water quality problems. In that regional context the district's longest and closest association was with the other Exchange Contractors. Linked by a common water supply and their Miller & Lux heritage, the four entities had

---

[358] CCID Board Minutes, 6: 157 (May 22, 1985); CCID Board Minutes, 6: 209 (January 21, 1986); CCID Board Minutes, 7: 65 (July 26, 1989); CCID Board Minutes, 7: 95 (November 8, 1989); CCID Annual Report for 1990, 4; Daniel G. Nelson, "How 32 Local Water Agencies Got Together to Assume Operations & Maintenance of Regional Federal Central Valley Project Facilities (The San Luis & Delta-Mendota Water Authority Experience)" in Mark Svendsen, Dennis Wichelns, and Susan S. Anderson, (ed), Water District Management and Governance, Third International Conference on Irrigation and Drainage (U.S. Committee on Irrigation and Drainage, 2005), 65-73; San Luis & Delta-Mendota Water Authority, "Learn More: About Us," http://www.sldmwa.org/learn-more/about-us/.

worked together for decades and in 1993 they created a new joint powers agency—the San Joaquin River Exchange Contractors Water Authority—to improve coordination and act on behalf of the member agencies. The creation of a stronger organizational structure was part of a broader response to the rapidly changing circumstances of water management on the west side.

One of the most important of those changes was the passage of the Central Valley Project Improvement Act in 1992. The act was a fundamental reauthorization of the project that transformed the maintenance and enhancement of fish and wildlife from a subordinate function to one of its primary purposes and set aside 800,000 acre-feet per year (600,000 acre-feet in critical years) for environmental uses. Grassland waterfowl habitat, both on private lands and on state and federal refuges, was one of the beneficiaries of the act's reallocation of project water, and delivery of that water had to be routed through canals belonging to the Exchange Contractors. The contractors in turn sought to use the conveyance of additional water to the grasslands as leverage in their negotiations for greater control over scheduling deliveries under the Exchange Contract. In a series of annual contracts, they agreed to carry water to the grasslands at a reduced cost in exchange for an enhanced ability to shift water from month to month during the May-August period and to exceed the 2,316 second foot delivery cap in the Exchange Contract to meet short-term peak demands. By 1998 a long-term conveyance agreement had been negotiated that did not give CCID everything that it wanted but did provide a higher cap on summer diversions. CCID's share of the peak delivery was 1,580 second-feet, which was substantially below the maximum demand of 2,000 second-feet. About half of the difference could be met by the district's wells, and canal spill reduction and recaptured drainage further narrowed the gap but the district still faced tight supplies—and farmers faced delayed deliveries—at times of peak demand on the canal system.[359]

Since additional flexibility in Exchange Contract deliveries was unlikely, the district had to make better use of its existing water supply. Increasing the efficiency and reliability of the canal system had always been one of the district's priorities. CCID had been replacing timber weirs and other canal

---

[359] CCID Board Minutes, 7: 490 (May 12, 1993); CCID Board Minutes, 8: 13-14 (July 14, 1993); CCID Board Minutes, 8: 166 (July 27, 1994); CCID Board Minutes, 8: 431 (July 24, 1996); CCID Board Minutes, 9: 98 (October 8, 1997); CCID Board Minutes, 9: 107 (November 12, 1997); CCID Board Minutes, 9: 193 (June 24, 1998).

structures with improved concrete ones on a regular basis since 1954 but it was still a system designed in the nineteenth century that now required more fundamental improvement. For example, flow could fluctuate at the north end of the Outside Canal by as much as 50 second-feet, caused by farmers starting and stopping individual diversions and by the notorious west side wind that played unpredictable tricks on the movement of water. To deal with the problem the district built a 100 acre-foot regulating reservoir next to the Outside Canal southwest of Gustine in 1966. When the flow in the canal temporarily exceeded demand, the excess was stored for release when needed to meet spikes in demand, and the reservoir also equalized flow through a small turnout in the Delta-Mendota Canal nearby.[360]

During the 1980s the district began exploring other water conservation opportunities on its canal system. In 1991 a consultant reported that the district was losing approximately 10 percent of its total water supply to spills, seepage and evaporation from the water surface of district canals. The next year the district developed a long-range plan for the phased improvement of its canal system to reduce losses by limiting operational spills at the ends of canals and by lining sections of canals that had the highest seepage. By 1996 the district's pumps at the north end of its system had been automated to reduce flow fluctuation and spills by running only when needed to supplement water coming down the canal. A more ambitious project was the automation of the lower Main Canal, completed in 1999. New weirs equipped with electrically-operated radial gates could be programmed to maintain a constant downstream flow, all monitored and adjusted from the main office. This so-called "downstream control" system in effect pulled only enough water through the canal to meet demand and would, when fully implemented, virtually eliminate spills. It was estimated that the project could save up to 7,500 acre-feet a year, and by allowing more consistent pump operation could increase groundwater yield by a similar amount. In Dos Palos, the Colony canal system was losing 6,000 acre-feet per year and variable water levels frustrated canal workers and growers. Beginning in 1998 the district installed two small regulating reservoirs, automated weirs and improved monitoring to

---

[360] CCID Board Minutes, 2: 264 (June 24, 1959); CCID Board Minutes, 3: 255 (September 22, 1965); CCID Annual Report for 1966, 12, CCID Annual Report for 1967, 13.

stabilize flow and reduce spills. Like the simultaneous work on the Main Canal, the Dos Palos project and others like it not only saved water but also improved service to farmers.[361]

The district saw another kind of opportunity in the expanding interest in small hydroelectric generation. Responding to energy shortages in the 1970s and federal legislation to promote small, non-utility projects, California aggressively promoted the development of renewable energy, and in 1981 CCID filed preliminary permit applications with the Federal Energy Regulatory Commission for potential power plant sites at the Wolfsen Bypass between the Delta-Mendota Canal and the Outside Canal west of Los Banos, and at the San Luis Bypass between the Outside and Main canals a little further north. For the district the attraction was not the revenue potential as much as it was the opportunity to double the capacity of the bypasses to improve the distribution of water from the Delta-Mendota Canal and make it easier to manage the subsidence area on the Outside Canal. The 1,000 kilowatt Wolfsen plant and the 600 kilowatt San Luis plant were built in 1985 by Sverdrup Hydro Projects under a contract that promised the district rental payments and an opportunity to eventually purchase the plants. While the enlarged bypasses provided immediate operational benefits to CCID, the plants did not produce the expected profits and passed through a series of operating companies after Sverdrup abandoned them in 1996.[362]

Even before the district began to upgrade its own 230 miles of canals it worked to improve the privately-owned community ditches that each served multiple farmers and carried an estimated 40 percent of the water delivered by CCID. In his first report to William C. Ralston in 1871, Robert Brereton warned against leaving the distribution system in the hands of the irrigators, but it was the common practice to do exactly that, and the canal company would have been hard-pressed to pay for and operate a more comprehensive system. The community ditches were, of course, no more than small canals but with only intermittent flow and usually haphazard maintenance by the landowners along their banks they often became weed-choked and inefficient.

---

[361] CCID Board Minutes, 7: 324 (December 11, 1991); *CCID Observer*, Issue 1, 1999 3; *CCID Observer*, Issue 2, 1999, 3-4; *CCID Observer*, Issue 3, 1999, 1-2.
[362] CCID Annual Report for 1982, 18-19; CCID Board Minutes, 6: 425 (February 24, 1988); CCID Annual Report for 1990, 3; CCID Board Minutes, 8: 209 (October 26, 1994); CCID Board Minutes, 8: 423 (June 12, 1996); CCID Board Minutes, 9: 45 (May 21, 1997).

The problem was readily apparent and CCID's 1955 annual report noted that the Board of Directors had "adopted a policy of doing everything within its power to assist consumers within the District in any and all consumer lateral problems including but not limited to the construction of control boxes and gates, weed spraying, dredging and other phases of water control within the consumer owned laterals."[363] To assist in the work the district made its three drag-line excavators available at cost and installed 8,000 gallon weed oil tanks at four locations to supply the district's own spray equipment and to sell oil to farmers doing their own ditch maintenance. By 1960 CCID was doing over three hundred consumer jobs per year.[364]

To make it easier for growers to afford upgrades like concrete lining, the Board of Directors first considered the formation of improvement districts, a system of district-sponsored landowner associations pioneered by the Turlock Irrigation District in the 1920s, but in 1957 the district took a different approach. A bill sponsored by Senator James Cobey of Merced, a former CCID attorney, offered a more flexible alternative by authorizing long-term contracts for maintenance or improvements, or both, initiated by a petition signed by two-thirds of the landowners on a ditch. For improvements like concrete lining a Permanent Maintenance Agreement offered a ten-year low-interest loan and on-going maintenance by CCID under the direction of a ditch committee. A companion program offered low-cost financing agreements for improvements like pipeline construction with a five-year repayment schedule. Lining and pipelines proved to be popular because they dramatically reduced maintenance costs, used less land than dirt ditches and made it easier to manage deliveries. Maintenance agreements were also used for drainage improvements, like the 1964 project that deepened a drain along the Main Canal near Los Banos to lower the water table on three thousand acres. By 1980 CCID had provided over $1.5 million in financing without suffering a single repayment delinquency.[365]

The most obvious impact of the improvements to distribution ditches was easier operation and reduced maintenance costs, but there was also a water conservation benefit that grew with the number of upgraded ditches. A

---

[363] CCID Annual Report for 1955, 10.
[364] CCID Annual Report for 1960, 12.
[365] CCID Board Minutes, 1: 206 (September 8, 1954); CCID Board Minutes, 1: 210 (September 22, 1954); CCID Annual Report for 1957, 13-14; CCID Annual Report for 1964, 13; CCID Annual Report for 1980, 18.

broader and more direct impact on conservation came with changes to the structure of water rates. Except for a short, controversial experiment in the early twentieth century, the canal company had sold water service by the acre, a practice that allowed consumers to use as much as they wanted. With a tax assessment on all acreage in the district, CCID provided water without cost until July 1 during its first year of canal operation and then charged by the acre-foot during the summer growing season. The result was an artificial peak in demand and stress on the canal system in late June as irrigators hurried to use all the free water they could. To avoid a repeat of that experience, the district allocated six inches of free water for use during June and July and charged the ordinary summer rate for water delivered in excess of that amount.[366]

Drought and rising irrigation demand increased the amount of supplemental water that CCID had to purchase or pump, and that in turn forced the district to restructure rates in 1960. It began to measure all deliveries, with no charge for the first acre-foot and $2.00 for each additional acre-foot. In 1963 the free water allotment was reduced to six acre-inches, and was eliminated altogether in 1974. The flat rate per acre-foot rose to $2.50 in 1974 and to $5.00 in 1980. A six-year drought that began in 1987 led to a renewed emphasis on conservation. A policy of tiered water rates was introduced in 1989 that priced the first three and a quarter acre-feet per acre at $5.50 per acre-foot and all additional water at $15.00 per acre-foot, reflecting the higher cost of providing more water, mostly from groundwater pumping. Over the ensuing years, the rate per acre-foot and the amount in each tier varied with water supply conditions and district revenue requirements. By the late 1990s the tiered rate was applied to the primary April through October irrigation season, with water in January-March and in November-December (when available) sold separately and generally at the same price as the base tier. For example, in 2002 there were five tiers for April-October deliveries with the first three acre-feet per acre priced at $6.00 per acre-foot, the next half an acre-foot at $15.00 with additional increases at half acre-foot increments to a top rate of $45.00 per acre-foot for water used in excess of four and a half acre-feet

---

[366] CCID Annual Report for 1955, 9.

per acre. CCID also routinely sold so-called "developed water," primarily from wells, to specified Class 2 lands outside of district boundaries on an if-and-when-available basis.[367]

Tiered rates by themselves were an incentive to conserve water, and when they produced an additional $635,000 in revenues in 1989 the CCID Board of Directors decided to use the money to fund new on-farm conservation programs. During the previous year, conservation had been proposed as one solution to post-Kesterson drainage problems; the less water growers applied the lower the total volume of drainage. The California Department of Water Resources provided a $225,000 grant to hire a water conservation coordinator for the eight local districts, including CCID, that drained into the grasslands, and the arrival of Peter Canessa to fill that position in early 1989 coincided with CCID's implementation of tiered rates. Canessa advised growers on practical ways to increase water efficiency but most of those ideas came with an upfront cost. The new CCID water conservation loan program offered low-interest five-year loans for on-farm improvements and extended the work begun with community ditch maintenance agreements and financing contracts.[368]

The loans helped pay for a variety of projects. One early example was the replacement of a dirt ditch serving 250 acres near Firebaugh with a concrete pipeline. The grower reported that "We used to turn the water on at the canal and go to the field three hours later to set pipe; now the water gets to the field in only twelve minutes. Our main motivation in doing this project was to avoid wasting the water that used to fill the ditch, and now, after installing the pipeline, we get to irrigate with that water."[369] Other farmers releveled fields for more uniform irrigation or installed tailwater recovery systems to recapture water from the lower end of their fields and pump it back for reuse. In 1999 the district enhanced its financial assistance program by offering grants for up to 25 percent of the cost of community ditch improvements, and in 2000 the grant program was expanded to include all ditch projects. The

---

[367] CCID Board Minutes, 2: 280 (September 9, 1959); CCID Annual Report for 1960, 11; CCID Annual Report for 1963, 16; CCID Annual Report for 1974, 13; CCID Annual Report for 1980, 13; CCID Board Minutes, 9: 125 (January 4, 1998); *CCID Observer*, Issue 1, 2002, 1.
[368] CCID Annual Report for 1990, 6; CCID Board Minutes, 6: 456-457 (July 13, 1988); CCID Board Minutes, 7: 14 (March 8, 1989).
[369] *CCID Observer*, Issue 2, 1990, 6.

following year cost-share grants were increased to 50 percent for ditch work, and other on-farm improvements became eligible for 25 percent grants. Growers appreciated the simplicity of the district's program, which required a review of plans to confirm acceptable system design and water savings but had little additional red-tape. By reinvesting loan repayments, the program was essentially self-funding.[370]

CCID's efforts to balance supply and demand through water conservation yielded unexpected benefits by creating opportunities to transfer water. The first evidence of that came during the critical dry year of 1977 when CCID farmers cut water use so much that the district had well water available for sale to the hard-hit Panoche Water District. In 1990, the fourth year of the six-year drought, CCID was again able to sell surplus developed water to nearby Central Valley Project districts to help keep trees and vines alive, and excess water was available again in 1991. While these were isolated instances, the extended drought brought statewide attention to water transfers between willing sellers and buyers who were running out of water. The Department of Water Resources created a drought water bank in 1991 that bought water in the Sacramento basin and sold it to agencies in the San Francisco Bay Area and southern California. Water transfer provisions were also part of the 1992 Central Valley Project Improvement Act. The act allowed farmers using CVP water, including those in CCID, to sell part of their project allocation to buyers in other districts or even other parts of the state as long as there were no detrimental impacts on groundwater or environmental resources. CCID soon found itself at the center of a controversy that tested the limits of that policy.[371]

The growing interest in water transfers and the occasional availability of extra CCID developed water prompted a general discussion of the issue by the Board of Directors in early 1992. A few months later, Areias Dairy Farms proposed a transfer to the Westlands Water District by pumping from three private wells into the CCID canal system. Similar transfers of private well water across district boundaries had been allowed in the past but a transfer to Westlands would exceed the district's ten-mile transfer limit. Although it had misgivings, the Board approved the 1992 pump water transfer and a limited

[370] *CCID Observer*, Issue 1, 1999, 5; *CCID Observer*, Issue 3, 1999, 5; *CCID Observer*, Issue 3, 2001, 5.
[371] CCID Board minutes, 5: 68 (May 7, 1977); CCID Board Minutes, 5: 89 (July 13, 1977); CCID Board Minutes, 7: 170 (June 27, 1990); CCID Board Minutes, 7: 290 (August 14, 1991); Water Education Foundation, *Layperson's Guide to Water Marketing and Transfers* (Sacramento: Water Education Foundation, 1996), 8-13.

transfer of the Areias surface water allocation. The following summer Assemblyman Rusty Areias told the directors that growing forage crops on his family's 2,500-acre farm was becoming unprofitable so they had made a fifteen-year deal with the Metropolitan Water District of Southern California to transfer their CCID surface water entitlement—estimated at 32,000 acre-feet—at $175 per acre-foot. The money would be used to make water conservation improvements on the Areias farm and switch to higher value crops using groundwater.[372]

The outcry was immediate. The executive director of the newly-created Exchange Contractors' organization, Dee Swearingen, summed up local reaction when he said "MWD has swaggered in with their cash and political power and told us it's either their way or the highway. They're going to suck this valley dry so Los Angeles can grow more suburbs and swimming pools and golf courses all the way out to Palm Springs."[373] A special CCID board meeting was held at Los Banos city hall to accommodate the large crowd opposed to sending water to southern California, and it reflected a fear that once begun, the loss of water could become irreversible and threaten the economy of the west side. A central issue was who actually owned the water; CCID insisted that it, not individual landowners, held the contractual right and that any transfers should be made by the district itself. Since the CVPIA gave water users the right to make, and profit from, transfers, CCID attorney Paul Minasian advised the board to establish a formal transfer policy to maintain control over the process. Following the district's new transfer rules, Redfern Ranches sought permission to fallow 1,400 acres in the drainage problem area near Firebaugh and transfer the water to land the family owned in the Westlands, San Luis and Panoche water districts. With CCID's cooperation and approval that 1995-1997 transfer became the first long-term transfer under the CVPIA. Meanwhile negotiations on the Areias transfer dragged on until the deal was quietly cancelled in 1996.[374]

Transfers, whether from surface water delivered under the Exchange Contract or from pumped water, could affect the district's groundwater

---

[372] CCID Board Minutes, 7: 344 (February 26, 1992); CCID Board Minutes, 7: 371 (May 13, 1992); CCID Board Minutes, 8: 21-22 (August 11, 1993; *Los Angeles Times,* July 3, 1994.
[373] *Los Angeles Times,* July 3, 1994.
[374] CCID Board Minutes, 8: 40-42 (September 16, 1993); CCID Board Minutes, 8: 231 (August 2, 1995); Water Education Foundation, *Layperson's Guide to Water Marketing and Transfers,* 9.

resources. Even though the shallow, water table aquifer—the focus of drainage concerns—is not directly connected to the deeper aquifer tapped by agricultural wells, the deep percolation of applied water recharges the underground water supply and permits the conjunctive use of surface water and groundwater. During the Areias controversy CCID lacked detailed knowledge of the aquifer underlying the district and could only speculate about the groundwater impacts of the proposed transfer. The district spent two years collecting and analyzing groundwater data so that it could evaluate future transfer requests and maintain a reliable supplemental water supply. CCID continued its annual review of groundwater conditions and used that information to set tier prices and determine whether groundwater transfers would be allowed from each of a dozen subareas. In addition, growers pumping water that they planned to take in another district were only allowed to pump for two consecutive years in order to protect the aquifer.[375]

In 1993 the newly organized San Joaquin River Exchange Contractors Water Authority negotiated the sale of 18,000 acre-feet to other Central Valley Project water users. There were no sales the following year but beginning in 1995 the Exchange Contractors transferred water to the Bureau of Reclamation for use on wildlife refuges as well as to other CVP agencies, and there were some smaller, grower-to-grower transfers. The transfer of water from the Exchange Contract entitlement was offset by conserved water, mostly recovered tailwater that would otherwise have escaped from ditches and drains. Groundwater substitution and temporary fallowing of agricultural land made smaller contributions to water transfers. By virtue of its acreage, CCID received almost two-thirds of the Exchange Contract entitlement and was entitled to participate in transfers up to the same proportion, with each of the four entities determining on an annual basis how much water they could safely contribute to the transfer pool. Transfers in 1995 totaled over 27,000 acre-feet, rising to nearly 112,000 acre-feet in 2009, with most of the water going to refuges, the Westland Water District and other federal contractors. A twenty-

[375] CCID Board Minutes, 9: 10-11 (February 12, 1997); CCID Board Minutes, 9: 30 (April 9, 1997).

five year extension of the program running until 2038 could allow transfers of up to 150,000 acre-feet per year.[376]

In a virtuous circle, transfers funded conservation programs and conservation made more water available for transfer. CCID completed its conversion of the lower Main Canal to downstream control in 2003 with construction of the 200 acre-foot Ingomar regulating reservoir and then turned its attention to the automation of weirs on the upper Main Canal between Mendota Dam and Los Banos and on the Outside Canal. Subsidence on a section of the Outside Canal near Firebaugh of as much as four feet since the early 1950s had reduced its flow from 750 second-feet to not more than 450 second-feet, and extensive earthwork was needed to restore the lost capacity. In all the district spent over $30 million on the canal improvement plan outlined in 1992, providing better service and saving an estimated 35,000 acre-feet per year. In 2011 CCID partnered with experts from Cal Poly San Luis Obispo to update its plan for district facilities, and the next year announced that it was moving forward with plans for new regulating reservoirs on the Poso Canal and on the East Ditch-Parsons system, aided by a $1 million grant from the Bureau of Reclamation.[377]

The reservoirs were not only expected to add to water conservation savings but would help the district adapt to the variable irrigation demands created by the installation of drip and micro-sprinkler systems funded in part by the district's matching grant and low-interest loan programs; systems that had been installed on close to a third of the district's acreage. CCID's quarterly newsletter advertised the benefits of those low-volume irrigation technologies. On one Dos Palos area farm, drip tape buried a foot below the soil surface reduced costs, improved cotton yields and saved 100 acre-feet of water per year on one 200-acre field. Installation of such a system could cost over $2,000 per acre, offset by up to $400 per acre in CCID matching grants and $1,000 per acre in low-interest loans. By fall 2017 the water conservation program had

---

[376] CCID Board Minutes, 8: 189-190 (September 26, 1994); *CCID Observer*, Issue 1, 1999, 6; CCID Board Minutes, 7: 484-485 (April 12, 1993); San Joaquin River Exchange Contractors Water Authority, "San Joaquin River Exchange Contractors Water Authority 25-Year Water Transfer Program Water Resources Analysis," prepared by Daniel B. Steiner, March 2012, 2-6.
[377] *CCID Observer*, Issue 3, 2003, 1,3; *CCID Observer*, Issue 4, 2004, 3; *CCID Observer*, Issue 3, 2005, 5; *CCID Observer*, Issue 3, 2006, 1-2; *CCID Observer*, Issue 4, 2011, 1-2; *CCID Observer*, Issue 2, 2012; 1.

made 547 loans since its inception totaling over \$17 million, and since 1999 635 matching grants had provided almost \$14.4 million in direct assistance.[378]

The loans and grants to water users were another example of the way CCID had expanded the functions it performed. Starting from the basic water delivery role that it inherited from Miller & Lux the district became a more customer-oriented water service agency. It was an intentional decision reaching back to the district's early days that was evident in the assistance offered to farmers for the maintenance of their community ditches and then in efforts to control drainage and help landowners navigate the increasing complexity of agricultural runoff regulations. Those initiatives complemented steps taken to create a more flexible and adaptable water supply and canal system. Efficiency, adaptability and regional alliances would all become more important as CCID and its customers faced fresh challenges in the twenty-first century.

---

[378] *CCID Observer,* Issue 2, 2009, 2-3; *CCID Observer,* Issue 1, 2013, 2; CCID, "Monthly Accounting of Low-Interest Water Conservation Loan Fund, as of September 30, 2017," October 23, 2017.

13

Return to the River

In 1939 when the Purchase and Exchange contracts paved the way for the construction of Friant Dam, the San Joaquin River had been at least partially controlled for decades, its water used to generate electricity and irrigate thousands of acres of crops and grass. But despite all of that it still had an important salmon run. The chinook (or king) salmon is the largest of the five species of Pacific salmon and the San Joaquin River was at the southern end of its historic range. On the upper river the spring run was the most important, swimming upstream against snow-melt floods high into the mountains where they could spend the summer in cold water before spawning in the fall. The fall run arrived when the rains brought the river back to life and spawned in gravel reaches closer to the edge of the valley. The juveniles from both runs rode the winter and spring freshets down the river to the ocean. Hydroelectric development cut off part of the spring run's summer habitat above the Kerckhoff powerhouse, but there was still enough space below that point to support runs that numbered in the tens of thousands of fish. Twenty-two miles below Mendota, Sack Dam—a sandbag dam that Miller & Lux installed each summer to divert water into the Arroyo Canal—blocked the fall run until it washed out. Mendota Dam had a simple fish ladder, and when the river was high enough some fish were able to leap over the flashboards. There were even reports of fall-run salmon swimming up sloughs and canals to re-enter the river above Mendota Dam.[379]

Salmon were not part of the plan for the ultimate operation of Friant Dam. Except during floods, water would be released into the San Joaquin River only for limited irrigation use immediately downstream from the dam, and a stretch of the river between the last irrigation diversion and the Mendota pool would be dry. The same would be true below Sack Dam, where a concrete structure

---

[379] Ronald M. Yoshiyama, Eric R. Gerstung, Frank W. Fisher and Peter B. Moyle, "Historical and Present Distribution of Chinook Salmon in the Central Valley Drainage of California," *Contributions to the Biology of Central Valley Salmonids*, 2001, 85-92.

replaced the seasonal dam in 1946. Construction of Friant did not immediately impact salmon numbers. There were 56,000 spring run spawners in 1945 and 30,000 the following year, but in 1948 the Bureau of Reclamation planned to release only enough water into the San Joaquin River to meet water rights requirements and send the rest into the Friant-Kern and Madera canals. The California Department of Fish & Game built a temporary fish collection fence in the river near Hills Ferry and trucked almost two thousand spring run salmon to the Outside Canal to continue their journey to the cold pools below Friant Dam. Unfortunately, low flows in the spring of 1949 stranded the offspring of those fish in the sand below Sack Dam. Following the failure of an effort to divert the 1949 spring run into the Merced River, Fish & Game engineered a pathway up Salt Slough and through a temporary fish ladder into the Arroyo Canal in 1950 but only a few fish made it through the warm, tule-choked slough where they were easy prey for poachers.[380]

Meanwhile federal and state fishery agencies pushed for the release of enough water to save the salmon run. In a 1944 report on the Central Valley Project the U.S. Fish & Wildlife Service estimated the existing mainstem San Joaquin River salmon population at 15,000 fish and recommended a minimum flow of 350 second-feet below Friant to sustain the run. They also suggested building a bypass channel around the Mendota pool to separate salmon from irrigation diversions. The Department of Fish & Game had similar concerns but state policy favored irrigation development and in 1951 California Attorney General Edmund G. Brown ruled that the federal government was not obligated to maintain a fishery below Friant Dam. Nevertheless, Fish & Game officials persisted in their efforts to save the San Joaquin run. In 1952 the department filed a formal protest in proceedings to issue the water rights necessary to operate Friant in an effort to add a minimum flow requirement.[381] The Water Rights Board did not issue its decision until 1959 and by that time the salmon were gone. The board dismissed Fish & Game's petition, noting that the damage had already been done: "Regrettable as these facts may be, the

[380] "Expert Report of Peter B. Moyle, PhD, "August 14, 2005, 15; George Warner, "Remember the San Joaquin," in Alan Lufkin, editor. *California's Salmon and Steelhead: The Struggle to Restore an Imperiled Resource*, (Berkeley: University of California Press, 1990), 61-69; G.L. Rogers, "A Review of General Conditions Extant Along the San Joaquin River c. 1936," March 1979.
[381] *Los Banos Enterprise*, July 13, 1945; U.S. Department of Interior, *Central Valley Basin*, 249-258, 413; Lufkin, *California's Salmon and Steelhead*, 18-19.

sense of urgency has been removed in that failure to take action at this time will not destroy any existing runs nor prevent a possible later re-establishment thereof."[382] Department of Fish & Game attorney Wilmer Morse prepared a petition for judicial review of the decision but at the last minute Governor Brown intervened and the petition was not filed.[383]

The salmon may have been gone but in an era of increasing environmental awareness and activism they had not been entirely forgotten. As the Bureau of Reclamation began to renew the original Friant-Kern Canal water delivery contracts in 1988 a coalition of environmental advocacy groups led by the Natural Resources Defense Council filed suit to restore salmon to the San Joaquin River. Four years later, the Central Valley Project Improvement Act set a general goal of doubling the natural population of anadromous fish (salmon and steelhead) in Central Valley rivers and specifically required the development of a plan to return salmon to the river below Friant Dam. The act, however, prohibited the release of water from Friant for fish without specific congressional authorization. Litigation and unsuccessful settlement negotiations dragged on until a federal district court ruled in 2004 that the Bureau of Reclamation was subject to a California law that required the operator of any dam to maintain fish below the dam in good condition, the same law that the Department of Fish & Game had tried to use a half century earlier. Friant was in violation of that requirement. Talks between environmental interests, the Bureau and Friant water users resumed, resulting in an agreement announced on September 13, 2006 to improve the river channel and reintroduce salmon by the end of 2012. The agreement also sought to minimize, as far as possible, the water supply impact on Friant contractors, in part by recapturing restoration flows.[384]

Protected by the Exchange Contract, the Central California Irrigation District did not anticipate any water supply impacts from the river restoration plan, but it was concerned about the effects that higher flows could have on land along the river. Miller & Lux had built levees along the western bank of

[382] State Water Rights Board, Decision D-935, June 2, 1959, 40-41
[383] California Department of Fish & Game, Petition for Writ of Mandate (not filed), June 30, 1959, see especially pages 77-82; Lufkin, *California's Salmon and Steelhead*, 17-20.
[384] Central Valley Project Improvement Act, Section 3406 (b)(1), (c)(1); NRDC, et.al. vs. Roger Patterson, etc. et.al., Order, August 27, 2004; Natural Resources Defense Council, "Agreement Signals Start to Historic San Joaquin River Restoration," September 13, 2006, https://www.nrdc.org/media/2006/060913.

the San Joaquin, and CCID's Poso and Riverside canals ran close to those levees. High water had always been a threat, and after the damaging 1955 flood work began on a system of flood control bypasses beginning upstream from Mendota Dam designed to reduce the strain on the main channel. Floods still filled the river in years like 1983 when the Kings River spilled through Fresno Slough and water was pumped from the flooded bed of Tulare Lake into the San Joaquin River through the James Bypass, and in 1997 when a peak flow of over 60,000 second-feet passed Friant. In those periods, CCID crews kept watch on the levees, and in 1983 the district held water in the canals to create back pressure on the levees. But in most years the river between Mendota and Sack Dam carried only the San Luis Canal Company's entitlement and was nearly dry below that point. In fact, the river channel north of the Sand Slough Control Structure was so clogged with vegetation that it was no longer used, even during the 1997 flood. When water levels did rise in the usually placid stream, seepage worked its way under or through the levees, pushing up the water table under adjoining farm lands, sometimes to the point of drowning crops. Of course, seepage had always been a threat, but the combination of high-value crops and the reduced capacity of the post-Friant river channel raised the stakes for proposed changes in the flow regime. In 2001 the San Joaquin River Resource Management Coalition was formed to give landowners and local organizations, including CCID, a voice in on-going flood control and river restoration planning.[385]

Federal legislation was required to implement and fund the settlement agreement, and that step was so important that Exhibit A of the Stipulation of Settlement provided draft legislative language. The proposed law would authorize federal appropriations of $250 million, and it was assumed that additional money would be available from the state and from the CVPIA Friant restoration fund. Although the Congressional Budget Office estimated a total federal cost of $500 million, CCID and other local interests believed that the cost would be more than twice that amount. The Exchange Contractors

---

[385] CCID Annual Report for 1955, 10; CCID Annual Report for 1990, 2; CCID Board Minutes, 6: 10 (September 14, 1983), CCID Board Minutes, 6: 21 (October 26, 1983), CCID Board Minutes, 6: 25 (November 23, 1983); San Joaquin River Flood Control Project Agency, "Upper San Joaquin River Regional Flood Management Plan, Regional Setting and Flood Hazard Assessment," June 19, 2013, 2-21-2-41; ECorp Consulting, Inc., *Tulare Lake Basin Hydrology*, 37-38; U.S. Geological Survey, "Floods in Northern California, January 1997", USGS Fact Sheet FS-073-99, April 1999, Table 2; *CCID Observer*, Issue 2, 2004, 1,7.

worked to get a place at the negotiating table to insure that third-party impacts were not ignored. Seepage was a major concern, as was the worry that inadequate appropriations in the future would delay fish protection measures like a Mendota bypass channel and put CCID operations at risk. By 2008 the bill had been renegotiated under the leadership of Senator Dianne Feinstein to meet the requirements of the new pay-as-you-go congressional spending policy, and the Exchange Contractors had won assurances that they would have the protection they needed. The San Joaquin River Restoration Act finally became law in early 2009, but although legislative action had been delayed the deadlines for the reintroduction of river flows and salmon remained fixed by the settlement agreement. The Bureau of Reclamation scrambled to make up for lost time, and with the added urgency of a compressed schedule CCID worked to negotiate agreements that would shield the district from liability for any unexpected consequences of the complex river restoration program.[386]

Experimental restoration flow releases began in October 2009 and were suspended the following month so CCID could do routine maintenance work at Mendota Dam. When releases resumed in February 2010 CCID used its network of groundwater monitoring wells—shallow wells drilled in the early 1980s to measure the depth of the water table—to track seepage, especially in the reach below Sack Dam that had historically been dry. The wells revealed that water, and salts, were moving upward in the soil profile near the river, with up to 15,000 acres impacted to some extent. The Bureau of Reclamation was notified and it scaled back flows, allowing the water table to return to more normal levels. It was now obvious that seepage was going to be a serious problem, and flood releases during the wet spring of 2011 gave CCID an opportunity to closely monitor eight sites from Mendota Dam to the northern end of the Riverside canal system. Based on the lessons learned in 2010 and 2011, the Bureau halted restoration releases below Sack Dam until a seepage management program could be implemented. By 2014 the estimated cost of seepage monitoring on 23,000 acres, mitigation projects and seepage easements totaled $185 million in added costs. That year CCID received a contract to build and operate over $6 million in seepage projects including

[386] NRDC vs. Kirk Rodgers, Stipulation of Settlement, September 13, 2006; *CCID Observer,* Issue 2, 2007, 7; *CCID Observer,* Issue 4, 2007, 1-2; *CCID Observer,* Issue 4, 2008, 3; *CCID Observer,* Issue 4, 2009, 1,3; *CCID Observer,* Issue 1, 2010, 2.

interceptor lines, drainage ditches, berms and land re-leveling in an effort to bring back the river without damaging surrounding farms. By early 2015 the Bureau of Reclamation was ready to try again to establish a continuous stream using the main channel of the San Joaquin River to the Sand Slough Control Structure and then into the flood control system's East Side Bypass to reconnect to the natural river further downstream, but drought conditions prevented the release of restoration flows until 2016.[387]

Another significant problem came to light in 2012 when restoration engineering studies revealed that Sack Dam and the adjacent CCID Poso Canal were suddenly dropping in elevation, the result of land subsidence centered east of the river in the Red Top area of Madera County. That region had recently been converted to irrigated crops and was entirely dependent on groundwater. Faced with reduced conveyance capacity in their canals if subsidence continued as well as a risk of flooding as river levees sank, CCID and the San Luis Canal Company took the lead in working with farmers on the other side of the river and local officials on a cooperative plan to reduce pumping of deep groundwater from beneath the Corcoran clay layer—the cause of local subsidence—and instead pump from the upper aquifer supplemented by surface water when it could be made available from the CVP and other sources. Meanwhile subsidence continued where it had first been identified in the southwestern part of the district, exemplified by the Russell Avenue bridge on the Outside Canal that was once high enough for a small boat to pass beneath it but was now partially submerged and in need of replacement.[388]

The first restoration salmon were fall-run fish trapped near the mouth of the Merced River in 2012 and transported to the San Joaquin River below Friant Dam, and in the spring their offspring were trapped and trucked

[387] *CCID Observer*, Issue 1, 2010, 2; *CCID Observer*, Issue 3, 2010, 1, 2; *CCID Observer*, Issue 2, 2011, 1, 5; San Joaquin River Restoration Program, "San Joaquin River Restoration Flows and Seepage Update," http://www.restoresjr.net/program_library/01-General_Outreach/Prog_Updates/20141202Update_web_ADA.pdf, December 2014; U.S. Bureau of Reclamation, "San Joaquin River Restoration Program to Work with Central California Irrigation District on Seepage Projects," August 28, 2014; San Joaquin River Restoration Program, *Program Update*, Fall 2016, 1.

[388] *CCID Observer*, Issue 3, 2012, 2; *CCID Observer*, Issue 2, 2013, 1-2; Patrick Healy, "Sinking Central California Farmland Reflects Massive Well Pumping of Groundwater for Irrigation," August 26, 2015 http://www.nbclosangeles.com/news/local/Sinking-Farmland-Reflects-Massive-Well-Pumpings-of-Groundwater-for--Irrigation-322909731.html.

downstream, a process repeated in the following years. In early 2014 an effort to revive the spring run started with the placement of 54,000 spring-run juveniles from the Feather River Hatchery in holding pens in the river below Friant where they became acclimated to the river before being transported to a release site just above the mouth of the Merced River. It was hoped that some of those fish would return to the San Joaquin as early as 2017 and become the basis of self-sustaining run but drought conditions and low river flows reduced the likelihood of early success.[389]

If restoration succeeded, salmon from the San Joaquin River would have to pass through the Delta on their way to and from the ocean, and in the twenty-first century the environmental health of the estuary became an ever more consequential concern for west side water users. The value of the Delta as an aquatic habitat was declining for a number of complex and contentious reasons including changes in the volume and timing of flows into and out of the estuary, the proliferation of non-native species, the loss of productive shallow water habitats, pollution and the effects of the Central Valley Project and State Water Project pumping plants. Beginning in the 1970s CVP and SWP operations in the Delta were subject to regulation by the State Water Resources Control Board, and as fish populations continued to decline those regulations became more restrictive. The federal and state endangered species acts added another set of rules. The Central Valley spring-run salmon was listed as a threatened species in 1999, joining the Sacramento River winter-run salmon. While salmon were the Central Valley's iconic fish, the Delta smelt, listed in 1993, was just the opposite. Only three inches long, nearly translucent and short-lived, its habitat in the brackish waters of the western Delta made it sensitive to a variety of stresses in the changing Delta and susceptible to loss at the export project pumps. Biological opinions issued under the federal Endangered Species Act to protect the Delta smelt and migrating salmon put additional limits on how much water the projects could pump and when they

---

[389] San Joaquin River Restoration Program, "Updated Field Activity Advisory, November 20, 2012, Trap and Transport and Streamside Spawning of Adult Fall Run Chinook Salmon"; U.S. Bureau of Reclamation, "Final Environmental Assessment Available for 2014 San Joaquin River Juvenile Salmon Trap and Transport Study," February 20, 2014; U.S. Bureau of Reclamation (hereafter cited as USBR), "Reclamation Releases Environmental Document for the 2015 San Joaquin River Juvenile Salmon Trap and Haul Study," February 8, 2015; USBR "San Joaquin River Restoration Program to Release Juvenile Spring-run Chinook Salmon into the San Joaquin River," February 18, 2014.

could pump it. The Delta had become an increasingly hazardous place for fish, and for water project operators.[390]

The Exchange Contractors had a first priority to Delta exports through the Delta-Mendota Canal for delivery of the substitute water supply that made operation of the CVP's Friant Division possible. Other Delta-Mendota water users, however, had their deliveries substantially reduced beginning in 1990, the fourth year of a six-year drought. As a result of the reallocation of water by the CVPIA and restrictions on the operation of upstream reservoirs and the Delta pumps to protect specific endangered species and environmental resources in general, reductions in deliveries became routine in all but the wettest years. In 2008 pumping restrictions to protect Delta smelt and operating limits on withdrawals from San Luis Reservoir led to a decision in June to restrict CCID summer deliveries to no more than the base amounts required by the Exchange Contract. The district quickly adjusted its tiered rates and rented wells, while growers took steps to conserve water to meet an anticipated shortfall of 10 percent during the critical summer growing season. As a third consecutive dry year unfolded the Bureau of Reclamation declared a critical year under the Exchange Contract in early 2009 but hydrologic conditions improved enough by March to return to a normal year schedule for CCID. Other CVP agricultural contractors south of the Delta did not fare as well. They had received half of their contracted supply in 2007, 40 percent in 2008 but got only 10 percent in 2009. Labeling the low allocation a "regulatory drought" hundreds of farmers and farmworkers staged a four-day "March for Water" from Mendota to San Luis Reservoir that attracted the support of Governor Schwarzenegger and other public officials, and the sympathetic endorsement of CCID.[391]

Rain and snow returned to California in 2010 and 2011 but conditions turned drier than normal again in 2012. Calendar year 2013 was among the driest in the state's history, and 2014 began the same way. After more than two

---

[390] The literature on the Delta is voluminous. For a concise introduction to environmental and regulatory issues see Jay Lund, et.al., *Envisioning Futures for the Sacramento-San Joaquin Delta* (San Francisco, Public Policy Institute of California, 2007), 1-98; Peter B. Moyle, William A. Bennett, William E. Fleenor, Jay R. Lund, "Habitat Variability and Complexity in the Upper San Francisco Estuary," *San Francisco Estuary and Watershed Science*, 8 (3), 2010, see especially 7-13; San Luis & Delta-Mendota Water Authority, "Bringing Flows into Focus," March 2014.

[391] Betsy A. Cody, Peter Folger, Cynthia Brougher, "California Drought: Hydrological and Regulatory Water Supply Issues," Congressional Research Service, December 7, 2009, 18, 23; *CCID Observer*, Issue 3, 2008, 1-3; *CCID Observer*, Issue 1, 2009, 1, 3; *CCID Observer*, Issue 2, 2009, 1, 7; *New York Times*, April 16, 2009.

years of drought, reservoir levels were perilously low. In mid-January CCID warned its growers to prepare for a critical year schedule, but was shocked when the first estimate of Central Valley Project deliveries gave the Exchange Contractors only 40 percent of a normal year supply rather than the 75 percent promised by the Exchange Contract. With little water likely to be available from the Delta-Mendota Canal the Exchange Contractors would for the first time since 1951 be forced to rely on the San Joaquin River, but the snowpack was meager and Friant storage was low. CCID responded by capping allocations to its growers and extending its tiered rates for the entire year. At the same time the district opened two supplemental water pools, one for groundwater to be purchased from farmers at $85 per acre-foot and another pool for growers who were willing to fallow land and sell the unused water to the district for $250 per acre-foot. As California's exceptional drought received national attention, President Barack Obama toured west side farms just south of CCID that would receive no CVP water at all that year; a stark contrast to the last presidential visit in 1962 that celebrated what was believed to be an abundant water future. The President promised federal relief funding, but he was unable to offer the water that the west side, and the rest of California, so desperately needed.[392]

In late January 2014 the Bureau of Reclamation and the Department of Water Resources informed the State Water Resources Control Board that without relief from Delta outflow requirements their Sacramento basin reservoirs might run out of water later in the year with potentially disastrous consequences, including the loss of salinity control in the Delta. The state board promptly approved a Temporary Urgency Change Petition allowing them to reduce Delta outflow, open the cross-channel gates at times when they would normally be closed to protect migrating salmon and export up to 1,500 second-feet for municipal and industrial health and safety needs. A modification on February 7 authorized higher export limits when storms allowed the projects to meet specified water quality control plan requirements

---

[392] Daniel L. Swain, et. al., "The Extraordinary California Drought of 2013/2014: Character, Context, and the Role of Climate Change," *Bulletin of the American Meteorological Society*, Special Supplement, 95, no. 9 (September 2014), S3-S7; Chris White to All CCID Landowners and Water users, January 16, 2014; CCID, "Important Updated Water Supply Information," February 3, 2014; CCID, "Supplemental Water Application Forms," February 7, 2014; *Fresno Bee*, February 14, 2014.

and additional natural flow was available in the Delta. In fact, it did finally begin raining. February precipitation in the Sacramento basin was 130 percent of normal; not enough to overcome the accumulated deficit of rain and snow but enough to lift Delta exports above the 1,500 second-foot threshold and improve reservoir levels.[393]

Despite that good news, it was soon apparent that the state board intended to interpret its health and safety export approval to ban the delivery of water from the Delta-Mendota Canal for agricultural use by the Exchange Contractors. That possibility threatened to reduce CCID's already low allocation. Project operators, the Exchange Contractors and federal and state legislators complained that the board's interpretation was unnecessary and unwise. A public rally was planned for Firebaugh on March 18 to keep up pressure to restore water deliveries. The day before the rally, CCID general manager Chris White got a call from the executive director of the state board informing him of the board's decision to modify its order to allow Delta exports to be used for irrigation. The board also changed Delta outflow requirements to allow the Central Valley Project and State Water Project to capture additional storm runoff. The crowd of more than a thousand people at the Firebaugh rodeo grounds greeted the news with a sense of relief mixed with outrage that the fight to defend their irrigation use had been necessary in the first place.[394]

As water conditions modestly improved, the Bureau of Reclamation finalized its critical year plan in May, allocating 529,000 acre-feet to the Exchange Contractors for April through October and bringing the total supply to about 65 percent of normal. That decision allowed CCID to increase its allotment to 2.35 acre-feet per acre of Bureau of Reclamation water plus half an acre-foot per acre of CCID pumped water. Releases from Friant Dam also began in mid-May, soon reaching 1,300 second-feet—about 1,000 second-feet higher than normal summer releases—and they continued at that level for the next four months. Seepage into the dry riverbed absorbed 40 percent of the

[393] CCID, "Exchange Contractor Water Supply Alert," March 2, 2014; Dianne Feinstein, Barbara Boxer, Jim Costa, John Garamendi to Tom Howard, March 5, 2014; *Modesto Bee*, March 19, 2014; *CCID Observer*, Issue 1, 2014, 1.
[394] State Water Resources Control Board, "March 18, 2014 Order Modifying an Order That Approved a Temporary Urgency Change in License and Permit Terms and Conditions Requiring Compliance with Delta Water Quality Objectives"; "Central Valley Project and State Water Project Drought Operations Plan and Operational Forecast, April 1, 2014 through November 15, 2014," April 8, 2014, 1-12.

flow at first, but losses were reduced when the system reached equilibrium. The river supplied less than half the water delivered to the Exchange Contractors, supplementing minimal Delta pumping and water stored in San Luis Reservoir. The Bureau of Reclamation was also able to provide 25,000 acre-feet in November, which the district made available on a first-come, first-served basis. With its users held to a strict allocation limit for the first time in over twenty years CCID facilitated farmer-to-farmer exchanges to stretch the available water supply and it used its canals to transport private groundwater to Class 2 lands that, as was always the case in critical years, received no water from the district. On the other side of the valley, Friant water users faced a zero allocation for the first time. In an effort to maintain regional cooperation the San Joaquin River Exchange Contractors Water Authority helped negotiate small transfers of borrowed water from San Luis reservoir to Friant and sold another 13,500 acre-feet made up in part of water that CCID bought from its growers for that purpose.[395]

The 2015 water year got off to a promising start with heavy December rains, especially in the Sacramento basin, but January was extremely dry, with many locations recording no rain at all in what is usually California's wettest month. It was also the warmest winter on record and by March the snowpack was only a fraction of normal and many slopes usually covered by snow were completely bare. In January CCID warned its growers that another critical year was inevitable and set a February and March allocation while reminding farmers that, "Each individual water user must weigh the information as we know it today, make their individual risk assessment and decide on when and how much to plant and irrigate."[396]

Not surprisingly the Bureau of Reclamation announced in February that it might not be able to provide the water required by the Exchange Contract. As runoff projections worsened, CCID announced in early April that it was substantially reducing its projected January-August allocation and at the same time it alerted its growers to a new threat. The State Water Resources Control

[395] CCID, "Important Updated Water Supply Information," April 10, 2014; CCID, "Important Updated Water Supply Information," May 16, 2014; U.S. Geological Survey, "San Joaquin River Release at Friant Dam" (Site No. 11250110, daily discharge report); Mark Grossi, Earth Log: 40% losses expected in Friant Dam water releases, http://www.fresnobee.com/2014/05/19/3933755/40-losses-expected-in-friant-dam.html?sp=/99/406/, May 19, 2014; CCID Observer, Issue 3, 2014, 1, 3; CCID Observer, Issue 2, 2014, 1.
[396] CCID, "Important Water Supply Information: Preparing for a Critical 2015 Water Year," January 15, 2015.

Board had ordered the Bureau of Reclamation submit a temperature management plan for Shasta that would maintain cold water in the reservoir for release in late summer to protect spawning of endangered winter-run Chinook salmon in the upper Sacramento River. If the Bureau had to keep more water in storage it would have to suspend Delta export pumping until late August and delivery to CCID could shrink to as little as 10 percent of normal. After receiving assurances that there would be enough cold water the state board approved an operation plan in mid-May that made water available south of the Delta, alleviating the immediate threat to CCID.[397]

Meanwhile the Bureau of Reclamation had been working with Friant water users and the Exchange Contractors to set up a complex water trade. Under such critical water supply conditions Friant would again have to release water down the San Joaquin River. Instead several Friant contractors agreed to release water banked in the state's share of San Luis Reservoir for delivery to the Exchange Contractors, and the Bureau made a deal with the Westlands Water District to, in effect, borrow water held in San Luis to support the Exchange Contractors' summer irrigation needs. In addition, the Exchange Contractors agreed to sell 10,000 acre-feet made available by their land fallowing program to Friant users at a price of $1,000 per acre-foot, and they voluntarily gave up the use of 5,000 acre-feet from Friant to be used for essential health and safety deliveries. As a result of those arrangements, the Exchange Contractors did not expect to need releases from Friant in 2015.[398]

Hope for the orderly management of one of California's driest years was short lived. Just two weeks after getting approval for its operations plan, the Bureau of Reclamation revealed that its Shasta temperature gauge was faulty and the lake was warmer than expected. Releases were immediately curtailed in a last ditch, and ultimately unsuccessful, effort to save that year's spawning season. With Delta-Mendota deliveries shut down, CCID scrambled to find alternative supplies. Water held by other agencies in San Luis was borrowed to continue deliveries through August, but the district lost its fall supply because

[397] *CCID Observer*, Issue 4, 2014, 1; CCID, "Public Meeting Notice," February 18, 2015; CCID, "Important Updated Water Supply Information," April 5, 2015; CCID, "Important Water Supply Information," April 16, 2015; Thomas Howard to Ron Milligan re: Approval of the June 25, 2015 Sacramento River Temperature Management Plan, July 7, 2015, 1-2.
[398] USBR, *Draft Finding of No Significant Impact, Exchange Agreement for Water in San Luis Reservoir and Millerton Lake Between Kern-Tulare Water District, Delano-Earlimart Irrigation District, and the San Joaquin River Exchange Contractors*, April 2015, 1-3; Steve Chedester to David G. Murillo, Ronald Milligan and Michael Jackson, May 22, 2015.

when Delta-Mendota pumping resumed its entitlement had to be sent to San Luis to pay back the borrowed water. An emergency pumping plant was installed in the Delta-Mendota Canal west of Newman to push water from San Luis Reservoir backwards up the canal to help agencies suffering from the cutback in Delta exports, including the northern corner of CCID. And despite protests from Friant contractors, water was released into the San Joaquin River again. The Friant users still got the water promised in their deal with the Exchange Contractors but water available above that amount flowed down the river to Mendota.[399]

Between Friant releases and water from San Luis and the Delta-Mendota Canal, the Bureau of Reclamation delivered 51 percent of CCID's normal entitlement under the Exchange Contract. Heavy groundwater pumping, bolstered by a surge in well-drilling, was able to prevent a significant reduction in irrigated acreage; by the end of the 2015 season wells were supplying up to 1,000 acre-feet per day to CCID canals.

The 2016 water year saw a return to average precipitation in northern California while conditions south of the Delta remained dry. With Shasta filling, CCID knew by mid-February that it would not be a critical year under the Exchange Contract but the district warned its users that regulatory constraints in the Delta could prevent the Bureau of Reclamation from delivering the full entitlement through the Delta-Mendota Canal, forcing releases from Friant for a third year. As a result, CCID irrigators were expected to lose the flexibility to shift water between months that they usually enjoyed, and the district staff worked to provide detailed information on water use and availability patterns to help farmers make planting decisions. As water conditions in the northern part of the state continued to improve, CCID announced in late April that it was able to reinstate April through October delivery flexibility and set adjusted tiered rates.[400]

While the district's farmers enjoyed a relatively normal summer, CCID managers and the Exchange Contractors struggled behind the scenes to insure that they would actually get the water they expected. Once again temperature management on the upper Sacramento River contributed to San Joaquin

[399] Thomas Howard to Ron Milligan, July 7, 2015, 2-5; USBR, *Final Environmental Assessment, San Luis & Delta-Mendota Water Authority 2015 Delta-Mendota Canal Reverse Flow Project*, May 2015, 1-4; *Fresno Bee*, July 13, 2015.
[400] CCID, "Important Water Supply Information Update," February 15, 2016; CCID, "Important Updated Water Supply Information," April 29, 2016.

Valley water supply problems. The National Marine Fisheries Service approved a temperature plan and Shasta release schedule at the end of March but when temperatures in the reservoir turned out to be warmer than expected in early May releases were cut back to protect the cold water pool until, after further study and negotiation, the original release schedule was reinstated in late June. By that time, a king tide event—extreme tides that can push salt water upstream into the Delta—forced the CVP and the State Water Project to increase Delta outflow to control salinity. Pumping into the Delta-Mendota Canal had already been restricted to protect environmental uses in the Delta, and now it slowed to a trickle.[401]

The Bureau of Reclamation relied on San Luis Reservoir to support its deliveries south of the Delta including water for Santa Clara Valley customers served by the San Felipe Unit. It was apparent by the spring of 2016 that the reduced flow through the Delta-Mendota Canal would require borrowing water from the State Water Project and from federal and state contractors. In May the State Water Resources Control Board approved a set of transfers and exchanges, but it did not approve a critical trade between the Bureau and the Kern-Tulare Water District for almost 50,000 acre-feet. The Bureau began borrowing water that federal contractors had stored in San Luis in June and by mid-July it was running out and needed to borrow more; however it could not make the transfers without further action by the state board. When it failed to get the permits it needed, the Bureau notified twenty-six water districts on July 21 that their water would be shutoff in three days. Intense negotiations with state board staff resulted in approval of the proposed transfers, including the one involving the Kern-Tulare Water District, and the shut-off notices were suspended. By August 1, San Luis storage was down to one-tenth of the reservoir's capacity and the Bureau was left with a repayment obligation of almost 400,000 acre-feet for the water it had borrowed to meet its delivery commitments in 2016.[402]

CCID and the other Exchange Contractors had been dependent on Shasta and the Delta since 1951 and from that arrangement they had received the

[401] *Bakersfield Californian*, August 13, 2016.

[402] *Bakersfield Californian*, August 13, 2016; SWRCB, Division of Water Rights, "Order Approving in Part a Petition for Temporary Changes in Place of Use of License and Permits of the California Department of Water Resources and United States Bureau of Reclamation," May 17, 2016; Thomas Howard to Nancy Quan and Pablo Arroyave re: Request for Additional Exchange of Water Pursuant to Division of Water Rights May 17, 2016 Order ..., July 21, 2016.

benefit of enviable water supply reliability. The drought years, and 2016 in particular, revealed that dependence on distant sources came at a price. Even with Shasta nearly full, concerns over its ability to meet the temperature criteria established to protect the last cohort of wild winter-run salmon put deliveries to far-away Mendota Dam in jeopardy. In the Delta, the problem of transferring water from north to south was as old as the Central Valley Project itself but regulatory efforts to stem the decline of native species increased the risk of interference with even the most senior CVP entitlements south of the Delta. After more than half a century, water supply uncertainty re-emerged as an issue confronting CCID. Miller & Lux usually treated competing water users as legal adversaries, but the district's response was to seek cooperative solutions, first by joining with the other Exchange Contractors, and then by working either through the Bureau of Reclamation or directly with other water agencies, both locally and across the valley. It was not an easy task because negotiations often had to be conducted under rapidly changing circumstances and on tight timeframes. Putting together trades and transfers also required CCID management to acquire new levels of expertise in CVP operations and develop a constantly evolving knowledge of interagency relationships.

In a reversal of fortune that confirmed the extreme variability of California rainfall, 2017 became one of the wettest years on record. San Luis refilled and Fresno Slough carried the overflow from the Kings River to Mendota Dam. Life along the canal returned to normal. It was a welcome respite for CCID after three years of shortage and uncertainty but the realities of twenty-first century water management on the west side remained. Subsidence continued unabated but after years of preparation and patient negotiation construction was about to begin on a pipeline from CCID's Poso Canal across the river to the hardest hit section of the Red Top subsidence area where water transfers would help Madera County farmers reduce pumping from the deep aquifer. Further up the river, the Bureau of Reclamation was ready to award the first construction contract for the Mendota Bypass facilities, the beginning of a $400 million project designed to keep the hoped-for salmon runs away from irrigation diversions. At the foot of the Diablo Range, CCID and several local partners had completed the first stage of a project to turn the Los Banos Creek Detention Dam and its small flood control reservoir into a 14,000 acre-foot per year water supply. All of those projects were examples of ways in which the district was adapting to changing circumstances. The problems might seem more complex and the solutions often more collaborative but CCID was just doing what it had done from the start, sustaining the irrigation-dependent community that is the legacy of the great canal.

www.ingramcontent.com/pod-product-compliance
Lightning Source LLC
LaVergne TN
LVHW051303080426
835509LV00020B/3131